Divided
Opportunities

Minorities, Poverty,
and Social Policy

ENVIRONMENT, DEVELOPMENT, AND PUBLIC POLICY

A series of volumes under the general editorship of
Lawrence Susskind, *Massachusetts Institute of Technology, Cambridge, Massachusetts*

PUBLIC POLICY AND SOCIAL SERVICES

Series Editor: Gary Marx, *Massachusetts Institute of Technology, Cambridge, Massachusetts*

Other subseries:

ENVIRONMENTAL POLICY AND PLANNING

Series Editor: Lawrence Susskind, *Massachusetts Institute of Technology, Cambridge, Massachusetts*

CITIES AND DEVELOPMENT

Series Editor: Lloyd Rodwin, *Massachusetts Institute of Technology, Cambridge, Massachusetts*

Divided Opportunities

Minorities, Poverty, and Social Policy

Edited by

GARY D. SANDEFUR

School of Social Work and
Institute for Research on Poverty
University of Wisconsin-Madison
Madison, Wisconsin

and

MARTA TIENDA

University of Chicago
Chicago, Illinois
and Institute for Research on Poverty
University of Wisconsin-Madison
Madison, Wisconsin

Plenum Press • New York and London

ISBN 0-306-42876-8

Contributors

LARRY BUMPASS, Department of Sociology, University of Wisconsin-Madison, Madison, Wisconsin

CHARLES HIRSCHMAN, Center for Studies in Demography and Ecology, and Department of Sociology, University of Washington, Seattle, Washington

LEIF JENSEN, Income and Well-Being Section, Economic Research Service, U.S. Department of Agriculture, Washington, D.C.

ROBERT D. MARE, Department of Sociology and Institute for Research on Poverty, University of Wisconsin-Madison, Madison, Wisconsin

SARA S. MCLANAHAN, Department of Sociology and Institute for Research on Poverty, University of Wisconsin-Madison, Madison, Wisconsin

LAWRENCE M. MEAD, Department of Politics, New York University, New York, New York

PETER H. ROSSI, Social and Demographic Research Institute, University of Massachusetts, Amherst, Massachusetts

GARY D. SANDEFUR, School of Social Work and Institute for Research on Poverty, University of Wisconsin-Madison, Madison, Wisconsin

JAMES P. SMITH, The RAND Corporation, Santa Monica, California

MARTA TIENDA, Department of Sociology, University of Chicago, Chicago, Illinois, and Institute for Research on Poverty, University of Wisconsin-Madison, Madison, Wisconsin

WILLIAM JULIUS WILSON, Department of Sociology, University of Chicago, Chicago, Illinois

CHRISTOPHER WINSHIP, Departments of Sociology, Statistics, and Economics, Northwestern University, Evanston, Illinois

Foreword

The outlook for reducing poverty in the late 1980s remains severe for many of the groups that make up American society. Even if the current economic recovery continues through the end of the decade, poverty for all persons will decline only to the levels of the mid-1970s. Poverty rates, as officially measured, for all minority children, white children living in single-parent families, minority elderly persons, and elderly white widows all exceed 20%. A national rate of 20% led President Johnson to declare war on poverty, which consisted of a broad range of social and labor-market interventions.

The chapters in this volume focus on the persistently high poverty rates of blacks, Hispanics, and Native Americans. They compare the changing economic status and family makeup of different minority groups over the past several decades, assess the antipoverty impacts of public transfers, examine educational differences, and analyze the problems of the homeless, the jobless, and families in poverty. The complex issue of whether social programs should treat different groups uniformly is addressed, and the past and possible future course of policy toward minority groups is discussed.

Two recurrent themes emerge. The first theme concerns differences both within and between the minority groups: Some individuals within each group are succeeding economically, others are not; some minority groups are faring better than others. Whether these different experiences are simply a matter of the ablest and most energetic getting ahead first, perhaps soon to be followed by the rest, or whether a permanent "underclass" is developing cannot yet be determined from available data. The material presented here brings the reader to the social science frontier, and also suggests avenues for further investigation.

The second theme concerns the effects of the economy. As a proximate cause of poverty, the labor market for men may have as much impact as the personal characteristics of unmarried women who have children. Related to this theme are the topics of job availability, the willingness of the poor to accept low-wage jobs, and male unemployment.

The authors have built on what we know and don't know about the causes and consequences of poverty. The reader will not find here the simple, ideological statements that characterized many academic and policy debates in the late 1960s and early 1970s. Those debates typically viewed the poor either as, on the one hand, victims of their own inadequacies, often mired in a culture of poverty, or, on the other hand, as victims of societal deficiencies such as inadequate schooling, lack of labor-market opportunities, and discrimination. The studies in this volume emphasize the diversity of the poverty population and reflect an awareness that the polar views of individual inadequacies and societal inequities each apply to only a small portion of the poverty population. The poverty problem of the elderly widow differs from that of the family whose head seeks full-time work but finds only sporadic employment; the poverty of the family head who works full time but at low wages differs from that of the family head who receives welfare and either cannot find a job or does not find it profitable to seek work.

The authors emphasize that a healthy economy is the best offense against poverty, but caution that growth alone cannot close the wide gap between the poverty rates of minorities and whites. They provide a firm, factual basis for formulating and evaluating antipoverty proposals for the 1990s. As such, this volume constitutes a major resource for both scholars and policy analysts.

Sheldon Danziger
Director
Institute for Research on Poverty

Madison, Wisconsin

Acknowledgments

With support from the Ford Foundation and the Rockefeller Foundation, a conference was convened in November, 1986, to consider the condition of minorities in the United States. Most of the chapters in this volume emanated from that meeting, which was sponsored by the Institute for Research on Poverty at the University of Wisconsin-Madison.

A number of people contributed to the success of the conference. Sheldon Danziger, Irwin Garfinkel, and Eugene Smolensky, all at the Institute for Research on Poverty, William Diaz at the Ford Foundation, and Bruce Williams at the Rockefeller Foundation provided helpful advice throughout the planning and execution stages. At the Institute, Joyce Collins expertly handled many of the arrangements; Catherine Cameron, Cathy Esser, Laura Friedrichs, and Nancy Rortvedt provided clerical assistance; and Elizabeth Evanson helped both in organizing the conference and in preparing this volume. The staff at Airlie House, Airlie, Virginia, ensured smooth proceedings.

Comments from the following discussants at the conference provided useful guidance during the process of revision: Walter Allen, Frank Furstenberg, Heidi Hartmann, John Henretta, Robert Hill, Edward Lazear, Jonathan Leonard, Sar Levitan, Douglas Massey, Milton Morris, Cesar Perales, Margaret Simms, Michael Sosin, Russell Thornton, and Daniel Weinberg.

We are grateful for the assistance and encouragement received from all the individuals and institutions named above, and for the ready cooperation given by the contributors of this volume.

G.D.S.
M.T.

Contents

III. Social Policy

1

Introduction

Social Policy and the Minority Experience

GARY D. SANDEFUR AND MARTA TIENDA

"The idea of the melting pot is as old as the Republic," wrote Nathan Glazer and Daniel P. Moynihan in 1963. Yet their classic study of New York City ultimately refuted that idea, concluding that racial and ethnic differentiation, not assimilation, prevailed.[1] Twenty-five years later their conclusion is supported by the evidence in this volume concerning differences in minority well-being as compared to majority whites. Moreover, the extent of socioeconomic inequality among as well as within minority groups appears to have increased rather than decreased over time: Poverty has risen among some members of particular groups while other members of those groups have prospered.

If it seems clear that the metaphor of the melting pot is outmoded, the reasons for the persistence of racial and ethnic differences are less evident. Drawing on decennial and annual Census Bureau data and the longitudinal studies newly available, this volume endeavors to bring into sharper focus the complex picture of changing minority status since 1960. It concentrates on blacks, Hispanics, and American Indians[2] because members of those groups, unlike those of Asian origin, are represented in greater numbers among the disadvantaged.

---

[1]Glazer & Moynihan, *Beyond the Melting Pot: The Negroes, Puerto Ricans, Jews, Italians, and Irish of New York City* (Cambridge: MIT Press, 1963). The quotation appears on page 288.
[2]Throughout this book, the title "American Indian" is used interchangeably with the title "Native American."

GARY D. SANDEFUR • School of Social Work and Institute for Research on Poverty, University of Wisconsin–Madison, Madison, Wisconsin.   MARTA TIENDA • Department of Sociology, University of Chicago, Chicago, Illinois and Institute for Research on Poverty, University of Wisconsin–Madison, Madison, Wisconsin.

Diversity in social and economic status is paralleled by the variety of social programs that followed the declaration of a national "war on poverty" more than 20 years ago. Some of these programs are available to all poor Americans, although minorities participate in them in disproportionate numbers; others are designed specifically for minority-group members. The contours of social policies and their effects on minority circumstances are also described in these chapters.

The studies that follow thus bring together existing information concerning the incidence, causes, and consequences of poverty among minority groups in the United States. They focus on a period that marked a sharp increase in social spending on the poor. As a part of the national intent to create a Great Society, public expenditures on antipoverty programs increased dramatically after 1964. In constant 1983 dollars, means-tested cash assistance to the needy rose from approximately $8 billion in 1965 to $31 billion in 1980, then declined to $28 billion in 1983. During the following 2 years, public expenditures for these cash assistance programs rose, although in 1985 they remained $1 billion below their 1980 level (Danziger & Weinberg, 1986). Net of inflation, expenditures on noncash benefits for the poor rose from $6 billion in 1965 to $93 billion in 1980 and to $106 billion in 1983 (U.S. Bureau of the Census, 1984).

The declines in poverty during the first part of this spending period were impressive. From 1965 to 1973, the share of Americans below the official poverty line fell from approximately 17% to 11% (Danziger & Weinberg, 1986). Thereafter, the national poverty rate fluctuated in accordance with the business cycle, rising during economic downswings and falling during periods of recovery. During the early 1980s, the share of poor persons rose, reaching 15% by 1983, the highest level since the War on Poverty was declared in 1964. It declined slowly after 1983, despite the end of the recession.

That poverty has persisted in the face of massive expenditures on antipoverty programs and has proven sensitive to changes in the business cycle raises questions about what type of social policy is needed to bring about further reductions in the proportion of persons with incomes below the poverty level when the rate of economic growth slows. Especially difficult for the design of social policies are the persisting differentials in poverty according to race and national origin. According to the 1980 census, blacks, Hispanics, and Native Americans together composed approximately 19% of the U.S. population, but almost 42% of all persons in poverty. This aggregate statistic conceals differing poverty rates among the groups, as well as other varying social and demographic characteristics.

Despite ample evidence that poverty is a more serious problem for minority populations than for white Americans, there is little comparative information indicating whether the circumstances that maintain economic disadvantage among blacks, Puerto Ricans, Mexicans, and Native Americans are similar or different, and in what ways. Because our understanding of minority poverty has not kept pace with our knowledge of poverty in general, it may be possible to increase the effectiveness of antipoverty measures by tailoring them to accommodate group-specific circumstances. For example, efforts to fight poverty among Puerto Ricans require additional information about its underlying causes prior to determining what antipoverty measures would be most effective.

The chapters contained here have as their objectives documentation of changes in relative economic status among minority groups over the past several decades, evaluation of the effectiveness of social policy in responding to the minority experience with poverty, and identification of the directions in which future research might prove fruitful, both in clarifying why poverty has evolved in the manner it has and determining what measures will be most effective in reducing poverty among racial and ethnic minorities in the future.

The volume is organized around three broad topics: relative economic status, family and intergenerational processes, and social policy. Within those topics a variety of issues are treated, ranging from empirical evidence on the problems of homelessness and joblessness to more theoretical questions involving family policy and the intergenerational transmission of disadvantage. To the extent that data permit, the authors approach their subject matter comparatively, seeking to learn whether individual and family responses to and consequences of poverty vary among the racial and ethnic groups and to identify what specific sets of circumstances distinguish group-specific outcomes.

As a general background, the following section provides historical and sociodemographic profiles of the major disadvantaged minority populations. Our intent is to document the diverse social and economic histories of blacks, Mexicans, Puerto Ricans, and Native Americans in order to highlight unique experiences—historical or contemporary—that can aid in explaining persisting socioeconomic differentials along racial and ethnic lines.

U.S. MINORITIES: A PROFILE OF DIVERSITY

The term "minority" often has imprecise referents, but is generally applied to groups that are numerically small and are identifiable on the basis of race or national origin.[3] In 1980, blacks composed 11.7%, Hispanics 6.4%, and Native Americans less than 1% of the total U.S. population. As many studies have documented (Borjas & Tienda, 1985; Bean & Tienda, 1988), it is necessary to

[3]Not all ethnic groups are minorities, but virtually all minority groups are ethnic, in the sense of being culturally distinguished from the mainstream white population. For further discussion of this issue, consult Nelson and Tienda (1985). This distinction among Hispanic groups corresponds roughly with Joan Vincent's (1974) and Herbert Gans' (1979) notion of symbolic ethnicity versus minority status.

disaggregate Hispanics according to national origin. Our interest in minority populations requires separating Mexicans and Puerto Ricans from the group we term *other Hispanics,* which include Cubans, Central or South Americans, and a large residual group that cannot be assigned a specific national origin.[4]

Blacks

The current economic standing of the black population has its origins in a history of slavery and subjugation, but especially in the intense racial discrimination that was openly tolerated until the enactment of the civil rights legislation of the 1960s. Although the Civil War legally emancipated blacks, their break with the plantation economy occurred very gradually, owing to limited alternative economic opportunities and intense discrimination in the South. Following World War I, this situation began to change as the growing demand for unskilled labor in the industrial centers of the North initiated an internal migration process of unprecedented proportions (Taeuber & Taeuber, 1965; Lieberson, 1980). The volume of black migration that ensued, especially after World War II, transformed the "black way of life," not only because it involved a shift from rural areas to urban centers, but also because it established the black presence in the industrial North. On the one hand, residential redistribution provided better employment opportunities than were available in the rural South; on the other hand, the residential segregation patterns in the large urban centers established new forms of isolation. The economic ramifications of this isolation have become more evident as employment opportunities in the urban ghettos have greatly diminished (Wilson, 1987).

Since 1945, the socioeconomic circumstances of blacks as a group have improved appreciably, especially in the wake of the civil rights movement, yet the vestiges of decades of unequal treatment persist. This is evident in the significantly higher infant mortality rates of blacks as compared to whites (Reid, 1982) and substantial income and employment differences favoring whites over blacks (Farley, 1985). Income (especially wage) differentials are partly attributed to lower educational attainment and to the poor quality of educational facilities in urban ghettos. Between 1940 and 1980, however, the median years of schooling completed by black adults aged 25 and over more than doubled, rising from less than 6 to 12 years, compared to 8.7 to 12.5 years for whites (Reid, 1982 [see also Chapter 7, this volume]). Thus, the past 40 years have

---

[4]The "residual" category consists of four broad groups: (a) Hispanics who are descendants of the original Spanish settlers; (b) Spaniards; (c) persons of mixed Hispanic origin (e.g., Puerto Rican and Cuban parentage); and (d) persons who did not report a specific national origin. See Bean and Tienda (1988, Chapter 2).

witnessed a substantial convergence in black–white educational levels. That employment outcomes, especially occupational status and earnings, have not converged to the same extent may attest to the persistence of labor market discrimination and residential isolation in restricting access to better-paying jobs (see Chapters 9 and 10, this volume), as well as to the ineffectiveness of equal opportunity programs in providing blacks with expanded job options.

The most controversial topics regarding the socioeconomic progress of blacks include the role of family disorganization in perpetuating economic disadvantages and the development of an "underclass," defined as individuals characterized by weak labor-market attachment, persisting poverty, and long-term dependence on welfare. The causal connections among poverty, family status, and reproductive behavior are complex; to say that family disorganization is a *primary* cause of the socioeconomic disadvantages experienced by blacks ignores a large body of evidence pointing to discrimination and to the employment consequences of industrial restructuring in states where blacks are highly concentrated (Wilson, 1987). When appraised against the formidable social barriers confronted by U.S. blacks in the past and at present, their socioeconomic progress since 1960 is remarkable; yet the persisting inequities, as documented in several of the chapters to follow, indicate major impediments to be overcome and pose a formidable policy challenge.

Mexicans

The Mexican-origin population, which represented roughly 60% of all Hispanics in 1980, has a much longer U.S. history than Puerto Ricans, Cubans, or Central and South Americans.[5] Mexican Americans are distinguished by their residential concentration in the Southwest and their extensive socioeconomic and demographic heterogeneity (Bean & Tienda, 1988). The antecedents of diversity are rooted in the history of U.S. westward expansion, geographic proximity to Mexico (which facilitates continued immigration), and the historical labor functions of Mexican workers in the agricultural, mining, and railroad industries. Along with changes in immigration policies and the resurgence of ethnicity that accompanied the more recent Chicano movement (Tienda, 1981), these factors were decisive in molding the contemporary socioeconomic position of the Mexican-origin population.

---

[5]There is some disagreement concerning the most appropriate date demarcating the Mexican presence in the United States. The most conventional marker is 1848, when the Treaty of Guadalupe Hidalgo was signed (see Chapter 8 by Gary Sandefur). Other writers prefer to emphasize that the Mexican presence in the United States predates the formation of the American nation. For the purposes of this historical vignette, the decision is not critical.

Especially important to an understanding of their contemporary socioeconomic status is the phenomenon of immigration, which gained momentum after the Mexican Revolution of 1910 and propelled thousands north of the Rio Grande in search of political refuge and jobs. The volume of immigration from Mexico to the United States in the twentieth century has resulted in extensive publicity and reform of immigration laws.[6] Also, the process of movement across the border has become self-sustaining owing to kinship ties and ethnic barrios, which provide contacts and resources for incoming workers (Tienda, 1980; Massey, 1983).

Despite the success of the Chicano movement initiated in the mid-1960s in calling attention to the social injustices endured by earlier generations of Mexican-origin workers, the imprint of previous social segregation and exclusion remains today, albeit somewhat altered. For example, although persons of Mexican origin are principally now an urban-based population, they continue to be disproportionately represented in agriculture—not as farmers, but as seasonal and permanent laborers. This is a clear vestige of their rural agricultural history. Moreover, in the nonfarm sector, the Mexican-origin population has become firmly established as a blue-collar work force, experiencing limited rates of social mobility beyond what is to be expected on the basis of changes in the structure of opportunities (Snipp & Tienda, 1984, 1985).[7]

Nevertheless, urban residence has provided access to a wider range of employment opportunities than was true in the past, and has brought improvements in the relative socioeconomic status of native-born generations. Cultural manifestations of changes associated with the urbanization experience include language shifts away from Spanish, the declining isolation of the barrio, and indicators pointing to a greater degree of assimilation into Anglo society (Massey, 1981). The continuing influx of immigrants from Mexico maintains nativity differentials in social and economic characteristics, but the importance of nativity in differentiating the Mexican-origin population depends, to a large extent, on the impact of immigration policies in regulating the flow of workers from Mexico to the United States, and on the success of these workers in securing employment.

---

[6]The 1976 amendments to the Immigration and Nationality Act, which extended the ceiling of 20,000 quota admissions to the Western Hemisphere countries, levied the heaviest toll on Mexicans because Mexican immigrants constituted from one-third to one-half of legal quota admissions during the early 1970s. Moreover, the 1986 Immigration Reform and Control Act, which targets illegal immigrants, also will affect the Mexican origin population disproportionately.

[7]This means that most of the intergenerational and intragenerational occupational mobility experienced by Mexicans results from changes in the occupational structure over time, most notably a decline of farm occupations, rather than improvements in the relative positioning of Mexicans under conditions of static occupational configurations.

Puerto Ricans

Puerto Ricans have a much shorter history than Mexicans in the United States, and they compose a smaller share of the Hispanic population (14% compared to 60%). Under existing law, island-born Puerto Ricans are U.S. citizens and thus enjoy virtually unrestricted access to the United States. Nonetheless, they have fared worse socially and economically than other Hispanic groups, and Chapter 2, by Tienda and Jensen, shows that their economic position deteriorated significantly during the 1970s and early 1980s.

Since the 1940s, the political and economic dominance of the U.S. government over the Commonwealth of Puerto Rico has gradually modified the ethnic and cultural identities of Puerto Ricans. Their accommodation to the English language and American customs has come at the expense of traditional cultural values (Nelson & Tienda, 1985). However, the image of an isomorphic Puerto Rican community spanning two locations is incorrect. Even though about 70% of the population residing on the U.S. mainland in 1980 was born on the island of Puerto Rico, there persist sharp differences in social and economic status tied to place of birth (Tienda, 1984; Bean & Tienda, 1988).

The comingling of Puerto Rican and North American identities was facilitated by an intense migration between the island and the mainland after World War II. Although there existed a small Puerto Rican community in New York before the war, the major exodus from the island to the continental United States began in the 1940s and accelerated after 1950. Average rates of migration from Puerto Rico to New York more than doubled during the 1950s, rising from an average annual flow of 18,700 persons from 1940 to 1950 to 41,200 during the 1950s (Nelson & Tienda, 1985). The sharp decrease in the average annual Puerto Rican influx between 1960 and 1970 was just as impressive, falling to less than 15,000 per year. Reduced labor market opportunities on the mainland—especially in the Northeast—are the primary explanation for the decline in Puerto Rican migration.

The persistent inability of many island migrants to secure steady employment on the mainland, coupled with the massive displacement of Puerto Rican workers from declining textile and garment industries in the Northeast during the 1970s, also were responsible for setting in motion a return migration process whose scale, duration, and consequences have not been assessed.[8] Of all Hispanic-origin groups, Puerto Ricans have the lowest labor-force participation

[8]Recent evidence indicates that part of the deterioration of the labor market position of Puerto Rican men and women during the 1970s was due to the changing (younger) age structure of the Puerto Rican population, and the recent entry of a large cohort of young people into the labor market (Charles Hirschman, personal communication, April, 1987).

rates, the highest unemployment levels, the highest incidence of poverty and of welfare utilization, and the lowest average levels of education (Tienda, 1984; Tienda & Jensen, Chapter 2). More importantly, the circular migration process appears to have disrupted families and contributed to the rapid increase in the number of families headed by women. The influence of migration on family disruption and labor market nonparticipation has not, however, been analyzed empirically.

Despite the different circumstances behind establishment of the Puerto Rican and Mexican communities in the United States, there are several parallels between them that are pertinent to an understanding of their poverty experiences (Massey, 1983). First, both migratory movements were fundamentally wage labor flows toward unskilled jobs. Second, both groups were destined for regional labor markets—the industrial Northeast in the case of Puerto Ricans, and the agricultural Southwest in the case of Mexicans. Third, like Mexicans in the Southwest, Puerto Ricans in the Northeast have been the victims of intense discrimination and prejudice, perhaps even greater than that experienced by Mexicans in Texas (U.S. Commission on Civil Rights, 1976). However, these parallels do not explain the deteriorating economic status of Puerto Ricans at a time when Mexicans experienced modest to moderate improvements in economic status. One logical explanation for their divergent economic experiences is that Mexicans were residentially concentrated in a region of the country that has experienced considerable economic growth and diversification while the traditional areas of Puerto Rican geographic concentration experienced severe economic decline (see Sassen-Koob, 1985). The extent to which industrial restructuring is responsible for the divergent labor-market experiences of Mexicans and Puerto Ricans is an important policy question requiring further research.

Native Americans

Indigenous to the North American continent, Native Americans have a history that long predates the formation of the United States as a nation. The American Indian population as a group composes less than 1% of the total U.S. population, but it represents many distinct communities formed around a wide range of traditions and customs. Of over 700 tribal entities that existed in the United States at the end of the 1970s, many still share elements common to American Indian culture: an emphasis on harmony with nature, sharing and cooperation rather than accumulation and competition, a respect for age, and a present rather than future orientation toward the world. Often these values conflict directly with those of the dominant Anglo culture (Hart, 1979).

Native Americans collectively have been victims of discrimination and persecution throughout the history of the development of the United States. The contemporary expression of subjugation and discrimination has changed considerably from the blatant destruction experienced a century ago, when westward expansion of white settlers nearly demolished the American Indian way of life. Thousands of American Indians, especially those residing on reservations, continue to experience abject poverty (Snipp, 1984).

Through familial and economic roles, both men and women have preserved the cultural traditions common to most tribes and those specific to each tribe. But economic need has compelled Native American conformity with Anglo expectations in order to secure employment in the dominant society. Owing to the minority status of American Indians who live outside of reservations, very few Native Americans live exclusively in either the Indian world or the "white man's world." In this sense, there is a parallel with the Puerto Rican situation, which involves straddling two worlds.

Despite substantial increases in educational attainment over the past few decades, many Native Americans remain unprepared to compete in a highly technical and bureaucratized world of work. Consequently, there persist income and employment differentials relative to comparably schooled whites (Sandefur & Sakamoto, 1988; Sandefur & Scott, 1983). This situation may improve as larger shares of Native Americans complete postsecondary schooling. However, to the extent that job possibilities on reservations remain limited while large shares of Native Americans reside on them, the prospects for economic parity with whites probably will not be realized. Moreover, within the American Indian population, sharp differences in relative economic status between reservation and nonreservation residents will remain.

COMPARATIVE SOCIAL AND DEMOGRAPHIC CHARACTERISTICS OF MINORITY FAMILIES

The diverse social histories of the four most disadvantaged U.S. minority groups have parallels in distinct demographic and social profiles, shown in Table 1. Cross-sectional differentials in family characteristics are as striking as the changes over time among and within groups.

Nativity

Owing to their particular histories, virtually all (96% to 99%) of black and American Indian family heads are native born, a characteristic which likens them to non-Hispanic whites. This contrasts with the Mexican, Puerto Rican, and other Hispanic populations, for whom immigration has been an important component of demographic growth and differentiation (Bean & Tienda, 1988). Between 1960 and 1980 the share of foreign-born family heads among other Hispanics more than doubled, reflecting the substantial volume of immigration from

Table 1. Selected Social and Demographic Characteristics of Minority and Nonminority Families: 1960, 1980, 1985[a]

	Black			Mexican			Puerto Rican[b]			Other Hispanic			American Indian[c]		Non-Hispanic white		
	1960	1980	1985	1960	1980	1985	1960	1980	1985	1960	1980	1985	1960	1980	1960	1980	1985
Nativity of head (%)																	
Native	99.0	96.6	—	56.6	64.4	—	6.3	19.1	—	75.7	38.8	—	96.2	96.8	92.0	95.2	—
Foreign	1.0	3.4	—	43.4	35.6	—	93.7	80.9	—	24.3	61.2	—	3.8	3.2	8.0	4.8	—
Type of headship (%)																	
Couples	75.1	57.0	51.2	83.4	78.8	75.7	79.6	60.8	52.1	85.6	75.3	74.8	82.8	80.1	89.0	86.3	84.8
Single females	20.6	37.0	43.7	12.3	16.4	18.6	15.8	34.8	43.9	10.8	19.8	20.0	14.2	16.1	8.4	10.6	12.0
Single males	4.2	6.0	5.1	4.4	4.9	5.8	4.6	4.4	4.0	3.6	4.9	5.2	2.9	3.8	2.7	3.2	3.2
Family type (%)																	
Extended	21.6	16.2	12.0	16.7	14.2	13.4	21.3	13.4	6.7	13.4	17.6	13.9	—	—	12.0	7.6	6.1
Nuclear	78.4	83.8	88.1	83.3	85.8	86.6	78.7	86.6	93.3	86.6	82.4	86.1	—	—	88.0	92.4	93.9
Family size (members)	4.3	3.7	3.5	4.9	4.1	4.1	4.3	3.7	3.6	4.3	3.5	3.4	4.9	3.8	3.5	3.2	3.1
Education of head (years)	7.4	10.5	11.1	6.1	8.8	9.0	7.2	9.5	9.8	8.4	11.1	11.2	7.3	8.2	10.3	12.2	12.6
Number of earners																	
0	9.9	17.7	21.1	6.0	9.7	12.8	10.7	28.9	35.3	8.1	11.3	16.3	18.2	11.2	7.9	12.6	17.8
1	39.2	33.8	35.1	48.5	35.1	34.8	45.3	34.8	34.7	47.9	32.0	31.1	43.3	28.2	46.8	31.8	30.6
2	38.6	36.0	32.9	32.6	39.5	38.8	33.7	28.4	20.6	34.4	41.6	41.2	38.5[d]	60.6[d]	34.8	41.3	39.3
3+	12.4	12.4	10.8	12.9	15.7	13.6	10.3	7.9	9.4	9.5	15.1	11.4	[d]	[d]	10.6	14.2	12.3

[a]The census definition of family is two or more persons related by blood, marriage, or adoption and residing together. Dashes indicate data not available.
[b]Native and foreign refer to mainland and island birth, respectively.
[c]Data not available for 1985 (sample size too small for analysis).
[d]Data available only for two or more earners.
SOURCES: 1960 and 1980 public-use microdata files from the decennial censuses; data tapes from the March 1985 Current Population Survey conducted by the U.S. Bureau of the Census (data are from 1959, 1979, and 1984).

Latin America during this period. Cubans and South Americans constituted most of the new entrants during the 1960s; Central Americans did so during the 1970s (Bean & Tienda, 1988).

As Leif Jensen demonstrates in Chapter 5, between 1960 and 1980 immigrant poverty rates increased while those of native-born families declined. Jensen attributes these diverging trends to the 1965 amendments to the Immigration and Nationality Act, which changed the criteria for admission from an emphasis on labor certification to one favoring family reunification. This legislation also changed the racial and ethnic mix of immigrants. Contrary to popular perceptions that greater poverty among immigrants has resulted from their changed racial/ethnic composition, Jensen concludes that white families who immigrated in recent years were a prime contributor to the overall rise in immigrant poverty after 1965. Persisting differentials in poverty risks according to birthplace suggest that immigration will continue to enlarge racial and ethnic stratification over the foreseeable future.

Family Headship

Poverty risks also vary according to family characteristics: type of headship, whether the family is extended or nuclear, its size, and the number of earners it contains. A comparison of changes in these characteristics is therefore central to understanding changes in relative economic well-being. Higher poverty rates are associated with female headship and with fewer earners; if particular groups are characterized by greater female headship, fewer earners, or more family members, their poverty rates will be raised accordingly.

Although couples remained the modal headship type for all groups between 1960 and 1985, the growth of single-head living arrangements proceeded at quite different rates depending on race and national origin. Families headed by single men were rare, accounting for 3% to 6% of all units in any given year. The predominant changes in headship arrangements involved growing shares of units headed by single women and declining shares of units headed by couples. Throughout the period, female headship was more pervasive among minority as compared to nonminority families. In spite of a 43% increase in the share of non-Hispanic white female-headed families between 1960 and 1985, single women headed only 12% of these families at the end of the period. By contrast, approximately two of every five black and Puerto Rican families were female-headed as of 1985. In 1960, Puerto Ricans had been more similar to Mexicans and other Hispanics than to blacks with respect to headship structure.

The significance of family structure for the economic and social well-being of minority families is addressed by James Smith (Chapter 6) and Robert Mare and Christopher Winship (Chapter 7), the latter including a comment by Sara McLanahan and Larry Bumpass. Smith documents a growing divergence over time in the economic status of intact and female-headed families. Both of these trends, he claims, result directly from the growth of father-absent families. The poverty implications of changes in family composition, therefore, depend not only on the rate of growth of female headship, but also on the mechanisms through which female headship operates to transmit economic disadvantage.

On this point, Chapter 7 shows that Native American, Puerto Rican, and Mexican American youth had the lowest school enrollment rates of all minority groups, even though high school completion had become the norm by 1980. The calculations of McLanahan and Bumpass show that children in families headed by mothers are much less likely to be in high school than children in two-parent families. Because a high proportion of youth today are enrolled in school, dropouts face even more disadvantages relative to their peers.

Extended versus Nuclear Families

Families headed by single women are more likely to be extended than are those headed by couples (Tienda & Angel, 1982; Tienda & Glass, 1985). Despite the growth of single-headed families among all groups, the shares of extended families decreased during the 1960s, 1970s, and early 1980s for all groups except other Hispanics. Extended families of other-Hispanic origin increased by 31% during the 1970s, but decreased to the 1960 level by 1985. That extended coresidence facilitates the process by which immigrants adjust to a new environment (Tienda, 1980) may explain the rise in extended family structure among other Hispanics during the 1970s, but concrete evidence on this question is lacking. Another way in which extended family structure influences relative economic well-being is by expanding the number of earners per family. In other words, extended family structures may increase the flexibility of families in coping with economic hardships, including those associated with the loss of a spouse and secondary earner (Tienda & Glass, 1985). The higher incidence of extended structure among minority as compared to nonminority families partly reflects this circumstance (Tienda & Angel, 1982).

These relationships are examined in Chapter 2, by Marta Tienda and Leif Jensen. They note that among married-couple families, the relative contribution of earnings of the head declined during the 1960s and 1970s, while the average earnings of other family members (particularly spouses, but also other family members including extended relatives) increased. More important, the earnings of secondary workers served to keep a substantial number of families out of poverty. Among single-parent families, the percentage of total labor income contributed by the head also increased, although Puerto Ricans were an exception. From this evidence, Tienda and Jensen conclude that the generally decreasing absolute poverty rates among minorities prevented an increase in earnings poverty during the slow-growth period beginning in the mid-1970s.

Number of Workers in the Family

Changes during these years in the spread of work among family members varied according to race and national origin. With the sole exception of Native Americans, the share of families with no earners (and hence likely to be in poverty) rose among minority as well as nonminority members between 1960 and 1985; the lowest increase was 4.8 percentage points (Mexicans); the highest was a startling 24.6 percentage points (Puerto Ricans). Changes in the number of workers per family between 1960 and 1985 point to a process of economic bifurcation wherein the share of families with multiple earners and with no earners increased simultaneously among several groups.

These varied patterns of change in the intrafamilial distribution of work raise questions about how the time trend of income inequality has been affected by the different income-packaging strategies pursued by minority and nonminority families. That is, a decrease in family work effort usually signals a decrease in economic well-being of the family members, unless nonlabor income is used to offset lost earnings. Chapter 2 discusses these issues in some detail.

Educational and Employment Differences

To close our discussion of sociodemographic differentiation, we call attention to the educational characteristics of minority and nonminority family heads. Despite notable improvements in the educational attainments of minority members heading families throughout the last quarter century—as described by Mare and Winship (Chapter 7)—marked differentials remained in 1985, and they mirrored those existing in 1960. Native American and Mexican-origin family heads were the most educationally disadvantaged in the later period, averaging 8 to 9 years of graded schooling, whereas non-Hispanic white family heads completed just over 12 years of education on average. If educational attainment ensured labor-market success, we would expect improvement in the relative economic well-being of those groups whose average schooling levels converged with those of non-Hispanic whites.

However, as Charles Hirschman (Chapter 3) illustrates, this has by no means described the experience of black and Hispanic youth. His data show that despite educational convergence among minority and nonminority populations since the 1950s, racial and ethnic unemployment differentials have gradually increased. That cyclical downturns in the economy were more severe for minority men brings into focus the importance of structural causes of poverty that are systematically correlated with race and national origin. Hirschman concludes that the U.S. economy is increasingly less able to provide employment opportunities for young men, especially young black men, and that macroeconomic policy may be a partial solution for the increasing levels of joblessness and idleness among minority youth.

Homelessness

Further evidence of increasing material deprivation among some segments of the population is found in the growth in the number of persons and families who are homeless. In Chapter 4, Peter Rossi profiles the homeless population as revealed in a survey in Chicago, including details on the racial and ethnic composition of this group. He identifies major causes of homelessness that have direct implications for social policy: the diminishing stock of urban housing available to the extremely deprived; the changes in household composition which have increased the demand for separate dwelling units; the lack of welfare benefits for groups at high risk of becoming poor, namely chronically unemployed men of working age; a weakening social responsibility toward the homeless because of the (alleged) prevalence of alcoholism, mental illness, and deviant behavior among them; and the decline of low-skilled jobs in the inner city. These circumstances are reminiscent of the growth of the urban underclass, as William Julius Wilson (Chapter 9) points out.

SOCIAL POLICY AND MINORITIES

Three chapters in this book deal specifically with social policy: those by Gary Sandefur (Chapter 8), William Julius Wilson (Chapter 9), and Lawrence Mead (Chapter 10). Other chapters provide observations on the successes and failures of current policies and some suggestions for changes in the future. There is a good deal of consensus among the authors as to what constitutes major problems faced by the minority poor: female family headship, educational underachievement, and the unavailability of jobs paying above-poverty wages for workers with limited skills.

There is also consensus on the view that existing social policy is not adequate for fighting poverty among minority-group members. Although the research reported here and elsewhere indicates that the current cash transfer system significantly reduces poverty among members of racial and ethnic minority groups, the evidence provided by Tienda and Jensen indicates that the cash transfer system does not affect all groups in the same way. The main reason for this is that the most generous transfers emanate from social insurance programs, primarily social security and unemployment insurance, and minority-group members benefit less from participation in these programs (see Chapter 8).

The adequacy of programs in which many minority-group members participate—means-tested public assistance programs, such as Aid to Families with Dependent Children (AFDC) and food stamps—is challenged by several authors on two major grounds. First, as Sandefur points out, benefits provided by these programs have not kept pace with inflation, so the material conditions of recipients of means-tested programs deteriorated more than did those of social security recipients. Second, Mead raises a quite different concern: that means-tested programs do not expect the employable to work. He further suggests that requiring work is essential for two reasons: (a) the poor are morally obligated to help themselves, and (b) such obligation is necessary to justify new and improved efforts to aid the poor.

Sandefur and Wilson also review the impact of a set of programs that are not directly antipoverty in nature, but have been a key part of the federal government's effort to assist members of minority groups. Both authors characterize these programs as "group specific," and trace the origin of many of them to the civil rights legislation and War on Poverty of the mid-1960s. The evidence on the impact of these programs is not extensive and perhaps insufficient to allow a fair assessment of their effectiveness. The wages of nonwhites have converged with those of whites (Smith and Welch, 1986; Hirschman, Chapter 3, this volume), and there is good reason to believe, but little compelling evidence, that this is due to affirmative action and other equal opportunity programs. There is indication of convergence in high school completion and college attendance among most minority groups and nonminority whites, at least through 1980, but there is no way to know the extent to which school desegregation, compensatory education, and other programs account for this convergence. The direct evidence on compensatory education cited by Sandefur and discussed at more length by Glazer (1986) indicates that there are no clear effects of these programs on educational performance. Finally, the health conditions of American Indians have improved dramatically—much more than those of blacks—which suggests but does not conclusively demonstrate that geographical targeting such as that practiced by the Indian Health Service may be an effective way to improve health status.

It is also clear, as Wilson (Chapter 9) points out, that group-specific programs have not addressed the problems of the most disadvantaged minority populations. To do so, Wilson believes, requires that we:

> . . . recognize the dynamic interplay between economic organization and the behavior and life chances of individuals and groups and develop a program that is designed both to enhance human capital traits of poor minorities and open up the opportunity structure in the broader society and economy to facilitate social mobility. (p. 249)

Mead (Chapter 10) agrees that the work activities of the poor are important, but sees the "work discipline" of the poor as the key factor that needs to be changed. In Mead's view, there are jobs available, and we must insist that the employable poor take these jobs.

Future Policy Initiatives

Wilson and Mead are in agreement that the leading social policy initiative being considered for altering the antipoverty effort is "workfare." The pros and cons of this strategy are discussed in some detail in their exchange. It is worthwhile, however, to consider how workfare would affect each of the minority groups. Because it is directed primarily at AFDC participants and to a lesser extent at food stamp recipients, workfare clearly would involve a greater proportion of nonwhites than of whites who receive transfers.

Unfortunately, the current preoccupation with workfare ignores children, who should probably be our central concern. This is even more true for minority groups than for whites. For example, according to the 1983 Current Population Survey, 36% of poor whites are under the age of 18 and 14% are under the age of 6. On the other hand, 45% of poor blacks are under the age of 18 and 17% are under the age of 6; 51% of poor Hispanics are under the age of 18 and 20% are under the age of 6 (U.S. Bureau of the Census, 1984). A focus on the parents of these children as opposed to the children themselves may lead us to make serious errors in the formulation of new antipoverty efforts (see Preston, 1984). Given the inconclusive evidence regarding the second-generation effects of welfare and the overrepresentation of children among the poor, especially among minority groups, we should be preoccupied with ways to guarantee these children a minimum standard of living before turning to the possible welfare dependence of their parents.

One way to improve the standard of living of children would be through making the current income tax personal exemption a refundable tax credit (Smolensky, Danziger, & Gottschalk, 1987), which means that families would qualify for this credit whether they incurred a tax liability or not. Unlike the social insurance system, this exemption would benefit minority groups as much as or more than white Americans. That policy could be supplemented with special health insurance for children, similar to Medicare, which could be funded from a portion of the tax credit that would not be refunded to parents. It is difficult to understand why a national health insurance program for children is less desirable and acceptable than a national health insurance program for the aged. One indicator of the need for such a program is the high level of black infant mortality.

The major problem for the parents of poor minority children appears to be the inability to find and keep jobs that enable them to support their families. Workfare is designed to force parents to work, but it focuses only on those who received public assistance for more than short periods of time, and thus does nothing for individuals who move on and off public assistance or low-wage earners who never utilize public assistance. What would help all unemployed or low-wage earners are programs that create jobs and policies that reward people for working. Creating jobs appears to be very difficult (Gramlich, 1986), but CETA did create public service jobs and working in these jobs increased the earnings capacity of participants, especially women and the very disadvantaged (Bassi & Ashenfelter, 1986). An expansion of the Earned Income Tax Credit appears to be an effective way to reward people for working at low-wage jobs (Smolensky, Danziger, & Gottschalk, 1987).

Another area in which social policy discussions should be concentrated is homelessness. As Rossi (Chapter 4) indicates, blacks and American Indians are overrepresented among the homeless, at least in the metropolitan area of Chicago. This may be due to their overrepresentation among the long-term poor. Whatever the cause, solutions to the problems of the homeless will be disproportionately beneficial to members of minority groups.

Finally, the apparent success of the Indian Health Service in improving the health of reservation Indians suggests that geographical targeting of health care may be an effective way to improve the health status of minority group members. The highest infant mortality rates are in the central cities of major metropolitan areas. Those who are concerned with health policy might do well to consider the nature of barriers to health care in these areas and develop specific strategies for overcoming these barriers that parallel the efforts of the Indian Health Service on reservations.

REFERENCES

Bassi, L. J., & O. Ashenfelter. (1986). The effect of direct job creation and training programs on low-skilled workers. In S. H. Danziger and D. H. Weinberg, Eds., *Fighting poverty: What works and what doesn't.* Cambridge, MA: Harvard University Press.

Bean, F. D., & M. Tienda. (1988). *The Hispanic population of the United States.* New York: Russell Sage.

Borjas, G., & M. Tienda, Eds. (1985). *Hispanics in the U.S. economy.* Orlando, FL: Academic Press.

Danziger, S. H., & D. H. Weinberg, Eds. (1986). *Fighting poverty: What works and what doesn't.* Cambridge, MA: Harvard University Press.

Farley, R. (1985). Three steps forward and two back? Recent changes in the social and economic status of blacks. In R. D. Alba, Ed., *Ethnicity and race in the U.S.A.: Toward the twenty-first century.* Boston: Routledge and Kegan Paul.

Gans, H. J. 1979. Symbolic ethnicity: The future of ethnic groups and cultures in America. *Ethnic and Racial Studies, 2,* 1–19.

Glazer, N. (1986). Education and training programs and poverty. In S. H. Danziger and D. H. Weinberg, Eds., *Fighting poverty: What works and what doesn't.* Cambridge, MA: Harvard University Press.

Gramlich, E. M. (1986). The main themes. In S. H. Danziger and D. H. Weinberg, Eds., *Fighting poverty: What works and what doesn't.* Cambridge, MA: Harvard University Press.

Hart, D. (1979). Enlarging the American dream. In Toni Constantino, Ed., *Women of color forum: A collection of readings*. Madison, WI: Wisconsin Department of Public Instruction.

Lieberson, S. (1980). *A piece of the pie: Black and white immigrants since 1880*. Berkeley: University of California Press.

Massey, D. S. (1981). Dimensions of the new immigration to the United States and the prospects for assimilation. *Annual Review of Sociology, 7*, 57–85.

Massey, D. S. (1983). *The demographic and economic position of Hispanics in the United States: The decade of the 1970s*. Washington, DC: National Commission for Employment Policy.

Nelson, C. & M. Tienda (1985). The structuring of Hispanic ethnicity: Historical and contemporary perspectives. *Ethnic and Racial Studies, 8*, 49–74.

Preston, S. H. (1984). Children and the elderly: Divergent paths for America's dependents. *Demography, 21*, 435–457.

Reid, J. (1982). Black America in the 1980s. *Population Bulletin, 37*(4). Population Reference Bureau.

Sandefur, G. D., & A. Sakamoto. (1988). American Indian household structure and income. *Demography, 25* 71–80.

Sandefur, G. D., & W. J. Scott. (1983). Minority group status and the wages of white, black, and Indian males. *Social Science Research, 12*, 44–68.

Sassen-Koob, S. (1985). Changing composition and labor market location of Hispanic immigrants in New York City, 1960–1980. In G. J. Borjas and M. Tienda, Eds., *Hispanics in the U.S. economy*. Orlando, FL: Academic Press.

Smith, J. P., & F. R. Welch. (1986). Closing the gap: Forty years of economic progress for blacks. Report of the Rand Corporation, Santa Monica, CA.

Smolensky, E., S. Danziger, & P. Gottschalk. (1987). *The declining significance of age in the United States: Trends in the well-being of children and the elderly since 1939*. Institute for Research on Poverty, Discussion Paper no. 839-87, University of Wisconsin-Madison.

Snipp, M. (1984, October) *American Indian population*. Paper presented at Population Laboratory Conference, Census Analysis Workshop: "Minority Population, Data and Trends," Madison, WI.

Snipp, M., & M. Tienda. (1984). Chicano occupational mobility. *Social Science Quarterly, 65*, 364–380.

Snipp, M., and M. Tienda. (1985). Chicano career mobility. *Studies in Social Stratification and Mobility, 4*, 177–194.

Taeuber, K. E., & A. F. Taeuber. (1965). *Negroes in cities*. Chicago: Aldine.

Tienda, M. (1980). Familism and structural assimilation of Mexican immigrants in the United States. *International Migration Review, 14*, 383–408.

Tienda, M. (1981). The Mexican American population. In A. Hawley and S. Mills Mazie, Eds., *Nonmetropolitan America in transition*. Chapel Hill, NC: University of North Carolina Press.

Tienda, M. (1984). The Puerto Rican worker: Current labor market status and future prospects. In *Puerto Ricans in the mid-eighties: An American challenge*. Washington, DC: National Puerto Rican Coalition.

Tienda, M., & R. Angel. (1982). Headship and household composition among blacks, Hispanics and other whites. *Social Forces, 61*, 508–531.

Tienda, M., & J. Glass (1985). Household structure and labor force participation of black, Hispanic and white mothers. *Demography, 22*, 381–394.

U.S. Bureau of the Census. (1983). *General population characteristics*. Washington, DC: U.S. Government Printing Office.

U.S. Bureau of the Census. (1984). *Estimates of poverty including the value of noncash benefits: 1983*. Technical Paper 52. Washington, DC: U.S. Government Printing Office.

U.S. Commission on Civil Rights. (1976). *Puerto Ricans in the continental United States: An uncertain future*. Washington, DC: GPO.

Vincent, J. (1974). The structuring of ethnicity. *Human Organization, 33,* 375–379.

Wilson, W. J. (1987, February). The ghetto underclass and the social transformation of the inner city. Plenary lecture prepared for the Annual Meeting of the American Association for the Advancement of Science, Chicago, IL.

I

The Economic Status of Minority Groups

2

Poverty and Minorities

A Quarter-Century Profile of Color and Socioeconomic Disadvantage

MARTA TIENDA AND LEIF JENSEN

If the significance of race and national origin was predominantly symbolic rather than economic, the concept of a minority group would be restricted to numerical and cultural considerations. That blacks, Hispanics, and Native Americans continue to be disproportionately represented among the ranks of the disadvantaged two decades after enactment of the Great Society programs attests to the resilience of ascription as a basis for deciding who gets ahead, by how much, and how fast. The existence of higher rates of minority compared to nonminority poverty is not a denial of the accomplishments of the War on Poverty, for, as the following sections show, the incidence of poverty has been reduced appreciably for all racial and ethnic groups over the past quarter century. Yet the differential responsiveness of minority poverty to social interventions defies easy explanation. More important, it raises theoretical and practical questions about how race and national origin operate as stratifying mechanisms, and whether their importance in assigning social standing has been altered in recent years.

In the following sections, we examine the economic content of race and national origin by tracing the poverty experiences of black, Mexican, Puerto Rican, other Hispanic, and Native American families over the past 25 years. Through a broad overview of changes in the relative economic status of these groups, we seek to identify the sociocultural dimensions of inequality which have been most and least resistant to change. Our specific objectives are (a) to document the economic status of five racial/ethnic groups during the past quarter

MARTA TIENDA • Department of Sociology, University of Chicago, Chicago, Illinois, and Institute for Research on Poverty, University of Wisconsin–Madison, Madison, Wisconsin. LEIF JENSEN • Income and Well-Being Section, Economic Research Service, U.S. Department of Agriculture, Washington, D.C.

century, both in absolute and relative terms, and in comparison to nonminority whites, (b) to assess the effectiveness of various income-packaging strategies in reducing the extent of minority poverty, and (c) to evaluate the impact of changing demographic composition—especially headship type and labor force behavior—in explaining changes in the relative and absolute economic status of minority groups.

The importance of tracing changes in the relative economic status of minorities from 1960 to 1985 resides in three sets of circumstances which have implications for social policy. First, the 1960s marked a major turning point in social policy with the enactment of civil rights legislation and the declaration of the War on Poverty. As a result of these changes in social policy, we should observe substantial improvements in the economic well-being of minority populations, who were their main beneficiaries.

Second, the 1960–1985 period witnessed four recessions—two of them major. Although individual well-being tends to fluctuate in accordance with the business cycle, socioeconomic inequities between minority and nonminority groups could nonetheless converge over the long term. However, this would not occur if the regressive impacts of downturns in the economy were more severe for racial and ethnic groups than for non-Hispanic whites. A gradual improvement in the relative economic status of minorities (compared to nonminorities) would suggest that the social and economic consequences of recessions do not fall disproportionately on minority populations, although limited improvements or widening gaps between minority and nonminority populations would provide evidence to the contrary.

Finally, a quarter-century time frame for evaluating changes in the relative economic status of minorities also provides a long-term perspective for evaluating past trends, for making forecasts about prospects for change in the near future, and for drawing policy recommendations to accelerate or redirect the course of change in accordance with the social goals set forth at the beginning of the period. It is with these broad objectives that we begin our account of changes in the relative socioeconomic standing of minorities.

The first section documents the relative economic well-being of minority and nonminority families, tracing the evolution of family incomes between 1959 and 1984 and comparing changes in absolute and relative poverty over the same period. The second section documents changes in the composition of family income over the past quarter century to determine whether and how the sources of family incomes have evolved over time, and to evaluate the significance of these changes in reducing poverty. The following section examines the effects of changes in headship arrangements and in the labor force status of heads in accounting for the observed changes in various measures of poverty and economic well-being. The concluding section summarizes optimistic and pessimistic scenarios about the prospects of reducing the significance of race and national origin in determining poverty risks. All empirical analyses of economic well-being use families as units of observation, defined as a head and all members related by blood, marriage, or adoption.[1] We identify our minority groups according to the race and ethnicity of the head. The technical appendix provides further discussion of methodological details.

RELATIVE ECONOMIC STATUS, 1960–1985: THE MINORITY EXPERIENCE IN COMPARATIVE PERSPECTIVE

Our objective in this section is to document the relative economic standing of minority and nonminority families based on money income. We accomplish this by comparing median family incomes and two measures of poverty—absolute and relative—for black, Mexican, Puerto Rican, other Hispanic, Native American, and non-Hispanic white families. In light of the vast social expenditures on antipoverty programs since 1965, we expect large improvements in the economic status of minorities relative to non-Hispanic whites. Our discussion focuses on *differential* rates of improvement in economic well-being over time (to identify uneven impacts of recessionary periods on minority and nonminority families) and among groups (to identify the significance of race and ethnicity as a barrier to economic mobility).

Definitions

Although seemingly straightforward, the concept of economic status is complicated because a fixed level of money income means different statuses, depending on the number of individuals who generate and consume it, and on the relative prices of goods and services (Danziger & Gottschalk, 1983). Current money income refers to the sum of money wages and salaries, net income from self-employment, social security income and cash transfers from other government programs, property income, and other forms of cash income, such as alimony and private pensions (Danziger, 1984). Census income data does not subtract taxes owed, nor does it include capital gains, imputed rents, and in-kind benefits provided by public and private sources (e.g., fringe benefits).

Whereas the money-income concept is an imperfect measure of relative

[1]The U.S. Census Bureau distinguishes between families and households, noting that the former requires relationship by blood, marriage, or adoption among all persons sharing a residence, whereas the latter does not. As such, households can and do include roomers/boarders and their spouses, as well as resident employees. Because the unrelated members are unlikely to pool their resources with the primary family, we have confined our analyses to family income rather than household income. However, auxiliary analyses showed relatively little difference between family and household income because extended living arrangements largely involve related individuals.

economic well-being, its appeal resides in it being reasonably comparable over time and easily adjusted for inflation and minor deviations in reporting procedure.[2] All money-income tabulations reported in the following tables are expressed in constant 1985 dollars to adjust for rising prices over time, but several tables include nominal incomes to convey the actual income gaps among minority groups in each period.

Family Income Differentials

A simple question guides our foray into the changing economic status of minority families: Is there any evidence of narrowing income differentials along racial and ethnic lines, and if so, are these uniform among groups? Table 1, which reports three measures of economic well-being based on money incomes, provides a basis for assessing trends in racial and ethnic income inequality since 1960. Two broad generalizations derive from these tabulations.[3] First, between 1959 and 1979 real family incomes rose gradually for all groups except Puerto Ricans. However, owing to uneven rates of growth in family incomes according to race and national origin, the convergence in minority and nonminority incomes was not uniform. Second, real family incomes *declined* between 1979 and 1984 for all groups, but the impact of recession appears to have been relatively harsher for minorities. Specifically, white median family income fell 5%, whereas the declines in black and Puerto Rican family incomes were 14% and 19%, respectively, and those of Mexicans and other Hispanics approximately 9%.

The median and mean family incomes of blacks and Native Americans, and to a lesser extent other Hispanics, converged with those of non-Hispanic whites between 1959 and 1979, but diverged again during the early 1980s. However, the family incomes of Mexicans and Puerto Ricans evolved in different ways. The Mexican-white family income ratios declined during the 1960s and increased during the 1970s, resulting in a stable income gap over the 20-year

---

[2]Although the Census Bureau used roughly similar definitions of income between 1960 and 1980, except that the amount of detail on income sources increased over time, one change in reporting procedure could affect our presentation of results. Family incomes were truncated at $50,000 in 1970, as compared to $75,000 in 1980. Because this truncation affected the comparisons of mean more than median incomes, we conducted a series of sensitivity tests with alternative, more comparable top-coding of incomes in both years. Our tests revealed that the comparisons of mean incomes with comparable top codes were virtually identical for minority populations, with discrepancies ranging from 1% to 3%, and only slightly different for non-Hispanic whites, with the discrepancy between mean incomes adjusted and unadjusted for the variable top codes falling in the range of 5% to 6% in both years. On this basis, we opted not to adjust our top codes in generating means for time-trend comparisons. We used comparable procedures in 1985.

[3]In groups with highly skewed distributions, such as blacks and whites, the means show greater parity than the medians, but for the most part, the generalizations based on the means and medians (top and middle panels of Table 1) are similar.

Table 1. Evolution of Minority and Nonminority Family Incomes, 1959–1984 (Means and Medians in Constant 1985 Dollars)

	Blacks	Mexicans	Puerto Ricans	Other Hispanics	American Indians	Non-Hispanic whites
Median family income						
1959	$9,696	$13,634	$12,345	$15,004	$10,577	$19,812
1969	16,252	18,586	16,181	23,178	18,279	27,934
1979	17,714	20,821	14,988	23,684	23,687	30,057
1984	15,202	18,912	12,282	21,651	NA[a]	28,564
Mean family income						
1959	$13,360	$17,020	$15,660	$19,326	$12,854	$24,713
1969	20,502	21,988	19,389	27,176	21,020	33,353
1979	22,639	24,497	19,407	28,649	26,206	35,090
1984	20,252	22,780	17,553	27,023	NA[a]	33,958
Mean family income per capita						
1959	$3,879	$4,169	$4,214	$5,567	$3,405	$7,867
1969	5,966	5,612	5,472	8,064	6,029	10,966
1979	6,892	6,755	5,895	8,921	7,995	12,128
1984	6,522	6,410	5,259	8,751	NA[a]	12,054
Minority/white per capita ratio						
1959	0.49	0.53	0.54	0.71	0.43	NA[b]
1969	0.54	0.51	0.50	0.74	0.55	NA[b]
1979	0.57	0.56	0.49	0.74	0.66	NA[b]
1984	0.54	0.53	0.44	0.72	NA[a]	NA[b]

[a]Data not available.
[b]Not applicable.
SOURCE: Computations from 1960, 1970, and 1980 Public Use Microdata Files of the U.S. Census; March, 1985 Current Population Survey.

period. Thereafter, the Mexican-white median family income ratio fell slightly (from .69 to .66). By contrast, the Puerto Rican-white median income ratio deteriorated throughout the period, dropping from approximately .62 in 1959 to .50 in 1979, and falling even more precipitously during the early 1980s to .43. Native Americans experienced the greatest convergence in median family incomes relative to whites, with median income ratios rising from .53 to .79 during the 1960s and 1970s. Unfortunately, data limitations—namely, insufficient observations in the Current Population Survey (CPS)—prevented us from examining whether the deterioration in median family incomes observed for other minority groups also obtained for American Indians.

Divergent rates of family income growth according to race and ethnicity repositioned the minority populations in the income hierarchy. In 1959, blacks and Native Americans occupied the lowest position based on their mean and median family incomes, which were approximately half the size of those received by non-Hispanic white families. By 1969, Puerto Ricans ranked lowest in the income hierarchy based on their mean and median family incomes. So severe was the deterioration of Puerto Rican family incomes after 1959 that by 1979 their economic standing relative to whites was similar to that of blacks 20 years earlier, prior to the implementation of the Great Society programs aimed at reducing racial and ethnic economic and social inequities. The recession of the early 1980s appears to have worsened their disadvantaged status.

At the other end of the spectrum, but equally impressive, is the dramatic convergence of Native American family incomes with those of whites. By 1979, median family incomes of American Indians were 80 percent of those received by whites. Native Americans experienced substantial income mobility over the period. However, we caution against interpreting the change for this group as a real improvement in economic status, because of the noncomparability of this population across censuses, especially between 1970 and 1980 (see Appendix, p. 52).[4]

The observed increases in family incomes until 1979 also must be tempered by the information in the third panel of Table 1, which shows that, owing to racial and ethnic differences in average family size, the well-being and consumption implications of mean and median incomes reported in the first and second panels differ for each group. Compared to non-Hispanic whites, Native Americans had the lowest average per capita incomes in 1959, only 43% of the level of whites. Owing both to different rates of growth in family sizes and incomes, by 1979 Native American per capita incomes were only 66% the size of white per capita incomes, whereas those of other Hispanics were almost 10% higher.

---

[4]There is a significant difference in the economic well-being of Indians in those areas where few changes in self-identification have taken place compared to those areas where changes in self-identification have been sizable.

Although other Hispanics enjoyed the highest average per capita incomes throughout the period, theirs still lagged behind those of whites by approximately 25% to 30%.

The substantial decrease in the average size of Puerto Rican families between 1960 and 1980 (from 4.3 to 3.7 persons) permitted their per capita family incomes to increase in real terms until 1979, albeit at a slower rate than those of other minorities or whites. Hence, their per capita incomes as a ratio of those received by non-Hispanic whites declined over the 20-year period, from .53 in 1959 to .44 by 1984. Had Puerto Rican fertility not declined during the 1960s and 1970s, their family per capita income would have been even lower, and the gap in relation to non-Hispanic whites even wider.

Absolute and Relative Poverty

A different perspective on changes in racial and ethnic income inequality is afforded by comparing minority family incomes with those of non-Hispanic whites in terms of relative and absolute poverty rates. As a measure of social welfare, the absolute poverty rate gauges the share of the population whose material standard of living is below the socially designated minimum. Operationally, this index reflects an income shortfall between family income and fixed minimum income cutoffs adjusted for household size, farm status, age and sex of the head of the household, and the number of children under 18. In 1984, the poverty level was $10,609 for a family of four on an annual basis, far below the national median family income for that year. Using the absolute metric, the elimination of poverty simply requires income transfers sufficient to ensure that all families receive the minimum level.[5]

Relative poverty thresholds focus on the degree of inequality at the lower end of the income distribution, rather than on the average amount of inequality (as in Table 1). This social indicator gauges the tolerable limits of inequality relative to the material conditions of the total population. Reduction of relative poverty requires changes in the shape of the income distribution—a more formidable task than providing families a designated income minimum. Although there is no single definition of relative poverty, the most common practice is to define the poor as those with less than half of the nation's median income (Schiller, 1986). This is slightly above the ratio of absolute poverty to the national median money income, which stood at .44 in 1965 (Danziger, 1984). Therefore, we also report a more restrictive definition of relative poverty, using one-fourth the national median for whites as the cutpoint.

Table 2 presents two measures of relative poverty and one of absolute

[5]There are many advantages and disadvantages of the absolute poverty income cutoffs. See Schiller (1986) for a recent summary.

poverty based on money incomes of families (see Appendix, p. 52, for technical details). The modest changes in relative poverty over the 25-year period attest to the rigidity of the income distribution and the difficulty of changing its shape. The sharp rise in nominal family incomes during the inflationary 1970s and the more modest increases in real family incomes shifted the income distribution toward the right over time, but did not alter the structure of income inequality. Overall, relative poverty was more pervasive among minority compared to non-minority families throughout the period, with Puerto Ricans and blacks standing apart as the two most disadvantaged groups, other Hispanics and whites as the most advantaged groups, and Mexicans and Native Americans intermediate between these extremes. Some shifts that did occur illustrate the changing importance of race and national origin in stratifying the U.S. minority population.

Slightly lower shares of black family incomes fell below half the national white median in 1979 compared to 1959, but the pattern of change was not linear. The decline of relative poverty from 44% to 42% between 1959 and 1979 resulted from a 4 percentage-point decline during the 1960s, in the wake of the civil rights movement, and a subsequent increase during the 1970s, following a period of slow economic growth and a serious recession. The recession during the early 1980s was even harsher on black families than that during the mid-1970s; consequently, by 1984 the share of black families with incomes below one-half the white median reached 46%, exceeding the 1959 level. Thus, in relative terms blacks have lost ground vis-à-vis whites.

Mexicans and Puerto Ricans illustrate a different pattern, as their relative poverty rates increased throughout the 25-year period, gradually for the former and quite dramatically for the latter. Native Americans were the only group to experience substantial declines in relative poverty between 1959 and 1979, but we cannot determine whether this continued into the 1980s. Whereas the relative poverty rate of Puerto Rican families virtually doubled between 1959 and 1984, rising from 28% to 54%, that for American Indians declined appreciably, falling from 48% to 34% in 20 years. The relative poverty of other Hispanics and non-Hispanic whites decreased during the 1970s, then rose to its 1959 level by 1979, producing a trivial net change over the period. Moreover, although relative poverty increased for these groups during the 1980 recession, the increases were less pronounced than those observed for other groups.

Table 2 also shows the percentage of families with incomes below one-quarter the median white family income in each of the years considered. Decreasing shares of minority families with incomes below one-fourth of the national median indicate relative improvements in the extent of inequality, whereas increasing shares indicate the opposite. Based on this metric, there was very little improvement in the relative economic standing of minority families, with the sole exception of Native Americans. Declines in the shares of families with incomes below one-fourth of the national white median obscure the fact that the

Table 2. Changes in Relative and Absolute Poverty for Minority and Nonminority Families, 1959–1984 (Medians in 1985 dollars)

	Blacks	Mexicans	Puerto Ricans	Other Hispanics	American Indians	Non-Hispanic whites
Percentage of families with incomes below one-half white median[a]						
1959 ($2,716)	44.4	30.8	28.1	28.0	48.2	16.9
1969 ($4,815)	40.3	32.1	38.1	23.0	38.6	16.3
1979 ($10,259)	42.0	33.7	49.1	28.8	33.6	18.0
1984 ($14,282)	46.5	36.6	54.3	29.1	NA[b]	18.7
Percentage of families with incomes below one-quarter white median[a]						
1959 ($1,358)	22.9	12.9	10.6	12.1	26.8	7.1
1969 ($2,407)	18.7	12.8	14.7	9.0	18.9	6.2
1979 ($5,129)	19.7	13.7	25.5	12.3	14.1	5.5
1984 ($7,141)	22.7	13.1	32.8	12.1	NA	5.9
Absolute poverty (%)						
1959	47.8	37.7	35.8	31.7	54.2	14.6
1969	29.8	28.3	28.8	20.7	29.5	8.1
1979	26.3	21.7	34.9	16.1	20.5	6.5
1984	30.6	24.0	41.4	17.8	NA	7.7
1959–1979 percentage change	−45.0	−42.4	−2.5	−49.2	−62.2	−55.5
1979–1984 percentage change	16.3	10.6	18.6	10.6	NA	18.5

[a]In nominal dollars.
[b]Data not available.
SOURCE: Computations from 1960, 1970, and 1980 Public Use Microdata Files of the U.S. Census; March 1985 Current Population Survey.

ratio of the two relative poverty measures (the percentage below one-fourth divided by the percentage below one-half) changed relatively little for Mexicans and other Hispanics (hovering between .36 to .43) throughout the period, and fell substantially for American Indians (from .56 to .42 in 20 years). For blacks, the ratio fell gradually until 1979 (from .52 to .47) and then rose slightly (to .49). By contrast, the ratio of the two relative poverty measures increased appreciably for Puerto Ricans, from .38 to .60, and virtually all of the increase occurred after 1969. Therefore Puerto Ricans have become considerably more concentrated at the lowest quartile of the income distribution, whereas other minority groups with incomes less than one-half of the white median have become more concentrated in the third quartile.

This story of changes in the relative economic status of minority and non-minority families is paralleled by that based on absolute poverty thresholds (bottom panel of Table 2). According to this index of economic well-being, American Indians and blacks were the most disadvantaged of the minority groups at the start of the period, when approximately half of these families had incomes below the absolute poverty line. For the Hispanic-origin groups, roughly one-third of all families were classified as poor in 1959 based on the absolute poverty index, whereas less than 15% of non-Hispanic white families were poor in that year.

Although absolute poverty rates declined for all groups during the 1960s and 1970s, the differential rates of change altered the poverty profile according to race and national origin. Only American Indians experienced faster declines in absolute poverty than non-Hispanic whites. Mexican poverty rates fell by 42%, other Hispanic by 49%, between 1959 and 1979. Puerto Rican poverty rates dropped 6 percentage points during the 1960s and rose 5 percentage points during the 1970s, producing a negligible net change in absolute poverty from 1959 to 1979. Although absolute poverty increased for all groups during the first half of the 1980s, it also did so differentially according to race and Hispanic national origin. Puerto Ricans and non-Hispanic whites experienced the sharpest rise in poverty—nearly 19%—but, for Puerto Rican families, this meant an increase of 6 percentage points in the share of families with poverty incomes, whereas, for whites, the comparable increase was just over one percentage point.

In summary, the varied patterns of change in relative and absolute poverty for minority and nonminority families show persisting inequities along racial and ethnic lines. Our results show both divergence and convergence in the trends. All measures show a significant deterioration in the economic status of Puerto Ricans as well as a remarkable improvement in the economic well-being of Native Americans. However, the measured improvement for American Indians must be interpreted with some caution, as this group was measured least comparably over time (see Appendix, p. 52). Blacks, Mexicans, and other Hispanics all improved their relative and absolute economic well-being during the 1960s and 1970s, but experienced substantial setbacks during the early 1980s. For Mexicans and other Hispanics, the slower rates of decline in relative and absolute poverty as compared to those of American Indians partly reflects the influence of immigration as a component of population growth. To the extent that new immigrants are disproportionately represented among the ranks of the poor (Jensen, 1987), gains in economic well-being among the native-born populations may have been offset by recent immigrants—making for limited average change over time. This explanation does not, however, account for the substantial rise in Puerto Rican poverty since 1970.

TRENDS AND DIFFERENTIALS IN FAMILY INCOME PACKAGING, 1959–1984

The trends and differentials in economic well-being summarized in the previous section are even more complex when evaluated against changes in headship arrangements and family composition. To the extent that race and ethnic differentials in headship and family size have become more diverse over time, as indicated in Chapter 1, the sources of family income should reflect these changes. For example, a decline in the share of families headed by couples usually involves an increased reliance on transfer income and/or modifications in family labor supply patterns. Changes in the prevalence of multiple-earner families according to race and national origin also will be reflected in the income-packaging strategies devised to cope with changes in employment opportunities.

Increased reliance on labor income from members other than the head as opposed to reliance on means-tested transfers focuses on a central policy debate concerning the proclivity of economically disadvantaged families—minority and nonminority alike—to become long-term welfare dependents. Accordingly, in this section we examine whether and how the sources of family income have evolved over time and analyze the implications of these changes. We begin by documenting changes in the composition of family income between 1959 and 1984 according to race and national origin for all families (Table 3) and then assess the relative influence of labor income (Table 4) and transfer income (Table 5) in reducing poverty. By comparing these tabulations, we make some general statements about the effectiveness of family labor resources versus the "institutional safety net" (i.e., cash transfers) as antipoverty measures.

Table 3 decomposes mean family income into four major sources: labor income, social insurance income, public assistance income, and other income.[6] In each year shown, labor income, which includes wage, salary, and self-em-

---

[6]In the 1960 Census, income sources were less precisely differentiated; therefore, for this year, we report only two categories of family income.

Table 3. Income-Packaging Strategies of Minority and Nonminority Families, 1959–1984 (In Constant 1985 Dollars)

Year: Source	Blacks		Mexicans		Puerto Ricans		Other Hispanics		American Indians[a]		Non-Hispanic whites	
	Dollars	Percentage	Dollars	Percentage	Dollars	Percentage	Dollars	Percentage	Dollars	Percentage	Dollars	Percentage
1959												
Wages and salary	$11,980	89.7	$15,815	92.9	$14,371	91.8	$17,549	90.8	$10,819	84.2	$22,258	90.1
Other income[b]	1,380	10.3	1,205	7.1	1,289	8.2	1,777	9.2	2,035	15.8	2,455	9.9
Mean, constant $	13,360	100.0	17,020	100.0	15,660	100.0	19,326	100.0	12,854	100.0	24,713	100.0
Mean, nominal $	3,662		4,666		4,293		5,298		3,523		6,774	
1969												
Wages and salary	$18,458	90.0	$20,419	92.9	$17,021	87.8	$25,214	92.8	$18,807	89.5	$29,888	89.6
Social insurance	763	3.7	551	2.5	321	1.7	543	2.0	618	2.9	979	2.9
Public assistance	724	3.5	476	2.2	1,666	8.6	379	1.4	573	2.7	118	0.4
Other income	557	2.7	542	2.5	381	2.0	1,040	3.8	1,022	4.9	2,368	7.1
Mean, constant $	20,502	99.9	21,988	100.1	19,389	100.1	27,176	100.0	21,020	100.0	33,353	100.0
Mean, nominal $	7,067		7,579		6,684		9,368		7,247		11,497	
1979												
Wages and salary	$19,219	84.9	$21,912	89.4	$16,009	82.5	$25,334	88.4	$22,932	87.5	$29,534	84.2
Social insurance	1,095	4.8	670	2.7	501	2.6	816	2.8	838	3.2	1,569	4.5
Public assistance	969	4.3	581	2.4	1,747	9.0	607	2.1	624	2.4	219	0.6
Other income	1,356	6.0	1,334	5.4	1,150	5.9	1,892	6.6	1,812	6.9	3,768	10.7
Mean, constant $	22,639	100.0	24,497	99.9	19,407	100.0	28,649	99.9	26,206	100.0	35,090	100.0
Mean, nominal $	15,453		16,722		13,247		19,556		17,888		23,952	
1984												
Wages and salary	$16,680	82.4	$20,073	88.1	$14,120	80.4	$23,344	86.4	NA[c]	NA	$27,296	80.4
Social insurance	1,183	5.8	852	3.7	591	3.4	974	3.6	NA	NA	1,840	5.4
Public assistance	670	3.3	338	1.5	1,601	9.1	349	1.3	NA	NA	96	0.3
Other income	1,720	8.5	1,516	6.7	1,240	7.1	2,356	8.7	NA	NA	4,726	13.9
Mean, constant $	20,253	100.0	22,779	100.0	17,552	100.0	27,023	100.0	NA		33,958	100.0
Mean, nominal $	19,782		22,249		17,144		26,395		NA		33,168	

[a] Head only.
[b] Includes social insurance and public assistance income.
[c] Data not available. There were too few American Indians in the CPS to permit reliable tabulations.
SOURCE: Computations from 1960, 1970 and 1980 Public Use Microdata Files of the U.S. Census; March 1985 Current Population Survey.

ployment income, was the major source for all groups. During the 1960s, labor income as a share of total family income increased slightly for other Hispanics and Native Americans, whereas Puerto Ricans registered a 4 percentage-point drop. However, during the 1970s—a period of slow economic growth laced with a severe recession—labor income as a share of total family income decreased for all groups, from 2 percentage points for Native Americans to 5 percentage points for blacks, Puerto Ricans, and non-Hispanic whites. Generally, these declines reflect structural changes in the economy leading to job dislocation, long-term unemployment, and decreasing shares of high-paying unskilled and semiskilled jobs. However, changes in the age structure of minority populations that made them eligible for an array of social insurance income sources also explain why nonlabor incomes increased over the period.

The early 1980s continued the trend of falling labor income shares, registered declines being most extreme for non-Hispanic whites and Puerto Ricans. Consequently, by 1984 wages and salaries composed approximately four-fifths of family income for these two groups, but notably more for Mexicans, other Hispanics, and Native Americans (1980 figure). The major distinction between Puerto Ricans and non-Hispanic whites is that for the latter, a decreased reliance on labor income was accompanied by an increasing reliance on other income sources (rents, dividends, interest, alimony, etc.), whereas for Puerto Ricans much of the decrease in labor income came at the expense of higher shares of public assistance income.[7] This finding is consistent with our data showing a sharp rise in poverty for this group.

Tabulations of nonlabor income reveal that public assistance comprised a slightly higher share of total family income in 1979 as compared to those of 1969 for all groups except Native Americans. For no group did the average family income share from public assistance increase by more than 1 percentage point during the 1970s, and during the early 1980s, average levels of public assistance fell for all groups except Puerto Ricans. These declines resulted largely from administrative policies to reduce federal expenditures on social programs, particularly means-tested transfers. Puerto Rican families relied more on public assistance income than did any other group in each year for which this breakdown is possible, but their average share never reached 10% of the total. Thus, with the possible exception of Puerto Ricans, these data show that transfer income has not

---

[7]This point becomes even sharper when the income shares are examined for families with incomes below 150% of poverty. Auxiliary tabulations (available from the authors) revealed that the decrease in labor income as a share of total family income was much more pronounced for the poor compared to the nonpoor. The extent of the decline in wage and salary income ranged from 14% for poor Mexican families to 53% for poor Puerto Rican families. Black and white families fall between these extremes, registering declines of wages and salaries as a share of total family income on the order of 34% and 25%, respectively.

become a major source of income growth for either minority or nonminority families.[8]

Changes in family income-packaging strategies have involved a greater reliance on social insurance by all groups during the 1970s and early 1980s, but especially by blacks and non-Hispanic whites. In no instance did the average share of family income from social insurance exceed 4% in 1969, 5% in 1979, and 6% in 1984. This gradual upward trend results both from the aging of the population as well as from increased reliance on unemployment insurance when cyclical downturns and industrial restructuring produce widespread joblessness.

Other-income sources, which include rents, dividends, and non-means-tested transfers (e.g., alimony payments and child support), comprised anywhere from 5% to 11% of 1979 average family income and 7% to 14% of 1984 average family income. Owing to differences in the distribution of wealth by race and national origin, income from interest, dividends, and rent probably is more important for nonminority than for minority families, but our data do not allow us to pursue this question further. More important for our present concern is that race and ethnic differentials in other income contribute to maintaining economic inequities between minority and nonminority families.

The predominance of wages and salaries as a source of family income throughout the period raises questions about whether increased reliance on secondary earners was responsible for the stable shares of labor incomes over time, particularly in light of the high unemployment rates and slow economic growth rates characterizing the 1970s and early 1980s. It is conceivable that the changing labor strategies of minority families—notably, their increasing reliance on the labor incomes of secondary workers—have been instrumental in bringing about a convergence in the economic status of minority and nonminority families, with the exception of Puerto Ricans.

Table 4 presents the relative share of labor income generated by the heads, spouses, and other adults for families headed by couples and for single-head families from 1959 to 1984. Among families headed by couples, heads were the primary earners in both minority and nonminority units, but the heads' share of family labor income declined for all groups between 1959 and 1979, then increased slightly, whereas the income shares from family members other than the

---

[8]Auxiliary tabulations for the subset of poor families reveal that public assistance as a share of total family income was modestly higher in 1980 as compared to 1970 for all groups except Puerto Ricans, who registered a 9 percentage-point increase in transfer income as a share of total family income. For the other groups, the average family-income share from public assistance rose by 3 to 6 percentage points during the 1970s. However, owing to federal conservatism toward social programs during the 1980s, the reliance of poor families on means-tested income decreased, with the sole exception of Puerto Ricans. By 1984, public assistance as an average share of total Puerto Rican family income surpassed the average income share composed of wages and salaries. This shift coincides with previous data showing continued impoverization of Puerto Rican families.

Table 4. Familial Work Strategies and Economic Well-Being of Minority and Nonminority Families, 1960–1984

Sources of wages and salary income	Blacks				Mexicans				Puerto Ricans				Other Hispanics				American Indians[a]			Non-Hispanic whites			
	1959	1969	1979	1984	1959	1969	1979	1984	1959	1969	1979	1984	1959	1969	1979	1984	1959	1969	1979	1959	1969	1979	1984
Couples																							
Earning shares																							
Head	70.4	64.1	54.2	57.0	73.3	65.3	66.9	67.7	72.7	71.0	63.7	66.1	77.3	74.1	64.1	65.0	77.2	75.1	70.1	76.1	70.8	65.3	68.5
Spouse	16.0	20.6	27.1	34.5	3.3	11.0	17.4	22.2	14.3	10.7	17.3	25.3	10.7	14.2	20.6	28.4	14.3	18.1	23.1	11.1	14.6	18.5	25.1
Other adults	13.6	15.1	18.7	8.5	13.4	23.6	15.7	10.1	13.1	18.3	19.0	8.6	12.0	11.8	15.4	6.5	8.5	6.8	6.8	11.9	14.7	16.4	6.4
	100.0	100.1	100.0	100.0	100.0	99.9	100.1	100.0	100.1	100.0	100.0	100.0	100.0	100.1	100.1	99.9	100.0	100.0	100.0	99.9	100.1	100.2	100.0
Earnings poverty																							
All workers	46.3	26.4	25.4	25.9	37.4	34.3	23.5	26.6	36.0	31.9	25.9	24.9	31.8	19.3	17.9	19.0	57.6	29.9	24.2	18.8	14.1	17.8	22.7
Head and spouse	50.4	30.1	29.2	29.0	44.2	40.8	28.7	33.0	41.9	39.5	28.3	27.0	35.2	22.1	21.1	20.5	60.9	33.4	26.6	21.3	15.5	19.6	24.7
Head only	58.2	39.2	41.0	44.6	48.6	46.5	36.6	44.0	52.7	46.4	36.1	39.9	40.4	27.5	29.9	36.0	66.7	40.2	36.8	25.5	20.1	25.4	32.7
Single heads																							
Earning shares																							
Head	46.0	50.0	54.1	—[b]	39.5	39.8	48.6	—[b]	41.1	44.4	29.5	—[b]	43.0	45.8	53.6	—[b]	46.3	67.0	66.4	46.5	52.5	55.8	—[b]
Other adults	54.0	50.0	45.9	—[b]	60.5	60.2	51.4	—[b]	58.9	55.6	70.5	—[b]	57.0	54.2	46.4	—[b]	53.7	33.0	33.6	53.5	47.5	44.2	—[b]
	100.0	100.0	100.0		100.0	100.0	100.0		100.0	100.0	100.0		100.0	100.0	100.0		100.0	100.0	100.0	100.0	100.0	100.0	
Earnings poverty																							
All workers	69.7	58.7	54.9	59.8	53.1	54.5	50.1	59.8	50.9	50.5	71.5	77.9	62.8	53.8	44.3	52.2	78.6	69.6	55.7	42.4	34.7	37.3	37.5
Head only	83.6	72.2	67.1	69.4	81.9	75.1	67.6	69.4	72.0	73.2	77.7	83.4	77.4	65.3	58.3	65.3	89.3	79.1	67.4	63.4	51.9	53.5	51.5

[a]Data not available for 1984. There were too few American Indians in the CPS to permit reliable tabulations.
[b]See Footnote 8 (p. 36).
SOURCE: Computations from 1960, 1970, and 1980 Public Use Microdata Files of the U.S. Census; March 1985 Current Population Survey.

spouse decreased markedly. The sharp decrease in the labor income shares of family members between 1979 and 1984 is partly an artifact of differences in the definition of families given in the census and in the Current Population Survey, and partly from the differences in the procedures used to derive these income shares in both periods.[9] Consequently, we do not dwell on the changes between 1979 and 1984 except to note a consistent and uniform pattern for all groups, namely the increasing labor income shares contributed by spouses throughout the early 1980s. This pattern is consistent with national trends showing increased labor-force participation by women, particularly married women, throughout this period.

In 1959, black family heads made the lowest average contribution to family labor income—approximately 70%. Moreover, during the 1960s and 1970s, the average share of family labor income contributed by black family heads fell by 16 percentage points, whereas the average contribution by black spouses to family labor income nearly doubled, rising from 16% in 1959 to 27% in 1979 and 34% by 1984. Overall, these changes point to important changes in the intrafamilial division of labor within black families, wherein spouses and other adults have assumed increasing responsibility for income maintenance.

Among American Indian families, heads' earnings as a share of total labor income declined 7 percentage points between 1959 and 1979, whereas the average share of labor income contributed by Native American spouses rose from 14% to 23%. All other minority groups fell between the extremes represented by the black and the American Indian families in terms of the declining shares of heads' labor income and rising shares of labor income contributed by other family members, especially spouses.

Tabulations on earnings shares for families headed by single persons (lower panel, Table 4) differ from the pattern observed among couple families in that the heads' average share of total family-labor income did not fall over time. With the exception of Puerto Ricans, heads' earnings as an average share of family labor income increased between 1959 and 1979 by 17% among blacks (up from 46 to 54 percentage points) and by nearly 43% for Native Americans (up from 46 to 66 percentage points). Earnings of American Indian single heads represented roughly two-thirds of family labor income in 1979. Between these extremes fell the

---

[9]Because the censuses provide a value for total family-labor income, we derived the labor income of other members as a residual. Hence, any measurement errors are captured in the shares of other family members. By contrast, the CPS reported separate labor incomes for all persons, and we computed the total family-labor income by summing the shares for heads, spouses, and other adults. Using this method, response errors are distributed across the three categories rather than concentrated in the other-adults category. These differences in the procedures for reporting and deriving labor income shares in the CPS and PUS samples produced especially large discrepancies for the subset of families with single heads. Therefore, we do not report these figures. As earnings poverty figures were less sensitive to these differences in reporting and deriving earnings shares, we present the 1984 tabulations for the subset of families with single heads.

increases in heads' average labor-income shares for Mexican and other Hispanic families, wherein the shares contributed by heads rose, respectively, 23% to 25%, on average. Among black and other Hispanic families with single heads, the labor income contributions of heads and other adults were approximately equal.

Puerto Ricans differ from all other minority groups in that the heads' average share of labor income among units with single heads dropped 11 percentage points, or approximately 28%, between 1959 and 1979. The Puerto Rican anomaly is consistent with the story of a deteriorating labor-market position of Puerto Rican women during this period (Tienda, 1984; Bean & Tienda, 1988, Chapter 9). Thus, other adults provided nearly three-fourths of all family labor income in Puerto Rican families headed by single persons by 1979, compared to approximately 60% 20 years earlier.

To appreciate the importance of secondary earners as a hedge against poverty, we have computed absolute poverty rates with and without the earnings of secondary workers, assuming all nonlabor income sources were zero. This index is denoted earnings poverty. The first row of the earnings poverty panel indicates what share of families (headed by couples or by single persons) would have been poor based strictly on the earnings of all family members, assuming no additional sources of income were available. Following a similar logic, the second row of the earnings poverty panel for families headed by couples indicates the share of families that would have been poor if only the head and spouse worked. When compared to the previous line, it indicates the reduction in poverty rates resulting from the labor income of the spouse. Finally, the third row reveals what share of families would have been poor if only the head worked. Taken together, these various comparisons indicate the extent to which increases in family labor supply keep families out of poverty. From a policy standpoint, these tabulations illustrate the importance of employment and training programs and policies as a strategy for combating poverty.

As would be expected, the poverty rates are consistently higher under the most restrictive assumption that only heads work and secondary earners, including spouses or other adults, do not. Also, and consistent with the trends reported in Table 2, earnings poverty rates fell throughout the 1960s and 1970s, but rose during the early 1980s, although not uniformly among groups. To illustrate, in 1979, 41% of black families headed by couples would have been poor if only the head worked, but earnings poverty was reduced by 39% through the labor income contributions of spouses and other family members. By 1984, the earnings poverty reduction due to secondary workers increased to 42%, even though the absolute-earnings poverty levels were higher. This serves to underscore the importance of the family system as a hedge against poverty, particularly during periods of economic stagnation.

Secondary earners in Mexican and other Hispanic families headed by couples reduced earnings poverty by 36% and 40%, respectively, in 1979, and by

39% and 47% in 1984. Among intact Puerto Rican families, secondary workers lowered earnings poverty by 28% in 1979 and by 37% in 1984. For American Indians and non-Hispanic whites the decreases in earnings poverty resulting from the labor incomes of secondary workers were 34% and 30%, respectively, in 1979.

The earnings-poverty-reducing effects of secondary workers among families headed by single heads not only were uniformly lower, but also the absolute-earnings poverty levels were considerably higher than those observed among couples. Earnings poverty rates for single-head families ranged from 37% (whites) to 78% (Puerto Ricans) in 1984, versus 23% (whites and other Hispanics) to 25% (Puerto Ricans) for families headed by couples. This large differential reflects the difficulties faced by spouse-absent families in committing workers to the labor force, particularly when there are young children in the household. Consequently, many are forced to rely on non-labor-income sources to provide basic needs.

Nevertheless, multiple-earner income strategies were effective in reducing earnings poverty of spouse-absent families, thus lowering their need for means-tested income transfers. In 1979, the percentage declines in earnings poverty of single-head families resulting from the labor incomes of secondary earners ranged from a high of 30% among non-Hispanic white families (representing a decrease in earnings poverty of 16 percentage points) to a low of only 8% for Puerto Ricans (representing a decrease in earnings poverty of 6 percentage points). For black families with single heads, the labor incomes of secondary workers decreased earnings poverty by 18%, for Mexicans 26%, and for other Hispanics 24% in 1979.

The 1984 data show that multiple-worker earnings strategies were less effective in reducing poverty for single-head families than they were in 1979, a pattern contrary to that observed for couple-headed families. Specifically, secondary workers reduced earnings poverty between 6% (Puerto Rican) and 27% (non-Hispanic whites) in 1984. The poverty-reducing effects of multiple-worker earnings strategies were greater among families with two heads compared to those with single heads, thus underscoring the greater flexibility of intact units in coping with economic decline. Also, the lower effectiveness of multiple-worker strategies in reducing the earnings poverty of minority compared to nonminority families indicates that the impacts of the recession were harsher for the former.

To summarize, the role of secondary earners in reducing poverty risks depends both on the labor market position of each minority and on the availability of other adults to generate income. As blacks and Puerto Ricans continue to face high levels of labor market discrimination and remain concentrated in areas experiencing economic decline, the poverty-reducing effects of multiple-earner income strategies will remain less effective when compared to those of non-Hispanic whites. That the levels of earnings poverty were appreciably greater among minority families as compared to those of non-Hispanic whites points to labor market constraints rather than individual recalcitrance as a major cause of poverty and economic disadvantage among racial and ethnic minorities. This is not to deny the existence of welfare dependency as a response to persisting poverty, but rather to emphasize that economic inequality could have been higher still in the absence of family efforts to increase the spread of work among their members.

Families headed by couples relied less on public assistance income as compared to those headed by single persons owing to the greater constraints faced by single heads in allocating time between market and domestic responsibilities (Tienda & Angel, 1982; Tienda & Glass, 1985) and rules that do not permit intact families to receive AFDC benefits in many states. As shown in Table 5, changes in families' reliance on transfer income varied not only by headship, but also by race and national origin. For example, during the 1970s reliance on transfer income declined among Mexican and other Hispanic couple-headed families, but increased appreciably for other minority groups, especially Puerto Ricans. The 1980s reversed the trend of increasing welfare reliance, as lower shares of all groups except Puerto Ricans received public assistance income. For Mexicans and other Hispanics, the 1980s continued the trend established during the 1970s, further reducing reliance on public assistance.

A greater reliance on social insurance income—a non-means-tested income source—largely accounted for the increase in the receipt of nonlabor income by both minority and nonminority families in 1979. As noted above, this results both because of increasing numbers becoming eligible for old age assistance and because more individuals receive unemployment compensation when the economy is sluggish. The shares of black, other Hispanic, and non-Hispanic white couple-headed families receiving social insurance income rose approximately 4 percentage points during the 1970s, but declined among families headed by Mexican and Puerto Rican couples. However, without exception, all groups registered higher shares of social insurance income in 1984 compared to 1979. As social insurance includes workers' compensation and unemployment insurance benefits, this increase probably reflects the effects of the 1982 recession in raising unemployment rates and prolonging their duration. The patterns of change for families receiving *both* public assistance and social insurance income transfers were roughly similar to those for families receiving only public assistance income, but of smaller magnitude.

An inspection of the various income poverty rates reveals that means-tested income transfers generally were less effective than non-means-tested income transfers in reducing income poverty.[10] For instance, in 1979, public assistance

---

[10]Recall also that public assistance transfers as a share of total family income never exceeded 9%, and for most groups averaged 2% to 5% of all families.

Table 5. Income Transfers and the Economic Well-Being of Minority and Nonminority Families, 1969–1984

	Blacks			Mexicans			Puerto Ricans			Other Hispanics			American Indians[a]		Non-Hispanic whites		
	1969	1979	1984	1969	1979	1984	1969	1979	1984	1969	1979	1984	1969	1979	1969	1979	1984
Couples																	
Share of families receiving:																	
Public assistance	4.3	5.1	4.4	5.0	4.7	4.4	5.4	9.4	11.6	5.1	4.0	2.1	10.2	11.4	1.3	1.9	1.2
Social insurance	11.3	15.1	21.6	14.8	7.2	11.8	11.9	6.2	10.4	6.2	10.3	14.8	7.7	7.2	13.8	18.1	22.8
Both	2.9	3.3	1.1	4.7	2.4	.6	2.9	1.9	.6	1.2	1.4	.2	3.1	3.1	0.8	1.4	.2
None	81.5	76.6	72.9	75.5	85.7	83.2	79.9	82.5	77.3	87.4	84.2	82.9	79.0	78.4	84.1	78.6	75.1
	100.0	100.1	100.0	100.0	100.0	100.0	100.1	100.0	100.0	99.9	99.9	100.0	100.0	100.1	100.0	100.0	100.0
Income poverty																	
Total	20.7	13.8	13.9	24.8	16.4	20.0	26.9	18.0	15.0	15.2	10.6	9.9	23.4	15.2	6.3	4.5	5.5
Without public assistance	21.9	15.2	14.4	27.1	17.9	20.3	28.1	20.8	18.0	16.6	11.7	9.9	24.9	16.8	6.6	5.0	5.7
Without social insurance	24.2	19.8	20.9	31.1	19.4	23.4	29.9	20.3	19.3	16.9	13.9	13.4	26.2	18.8	10.2	9.8	12.2
Single heads																	
Share of families receiving:																	
Public assistance	25.5	28.1	32.0	17.2	23.9	21.1	15.1	52.4	59.0	27.4	21.0	23.2	17.2	13.3	6.3	10.7	10.8
Social insurance	13.7	12.0	16.6	21.5	9.0	21.1	22.7	5.6	7.1	10.1	9.6	16.8	27.2	26.9	27.7	22.0	29.6
Both	4.3	4.3	3.6	7.7	3.4	2.1	4.7	1.9	3.2	2.5	2.4	2.3	8.9	7.7	2.4	2.4	1.3
None	56.5	55.6	47.8	53.6	63.8	55.7	57.5	40.2	30.8	59.9	67.0	57.8	46.7	52.1	63.7	64.8	58.2
	100.0	100.0	100.0	100.0	100.1	100.0	100.0	100.0	100.0	99.9	100.0	100.0	100.0	100.0	100.1	99.9	100.0
Income poverty																	
Total	48.9	43.0	48.1	42.9	41.6	36.7	36.1	61.1	70.2	43.0	32.8	41.2	57.6	42.0	20.9	19.0	19.9
Without public assistance	53.4	48.3	50.4	49.4	45.3	38.1	41.5	68.2	72.6	48.7	37.3	43.3	61.9	47.4	22.1	22.4	20.6
Without social insurance	52.4	48.3	53.0	47.2	44.8	42.2	42.5	63.6	73.2	47.1	35.7	44.5	63.0	46.0	26.5	25.3	26.8

[a]Data not available for 1984. There were too few American Indians in the CPS to permit reliable tabulations.

SOURCE: Computations from 1970 and 1980 Public Use Microdata Files of the U.S. Census; March 1985 Current Population Survey.

NOTE: Public assistance includes AFDC, SSI (Old Age Assistance, Aid to the Permanently and Totally Disabled, and Aid to the Blind before 1976) and general assistance. Social insurance includes social security, railroad retirement, unemployment insurance, workers' compensation, government employees' pensions, and veterans' pensions and compensation.

reduced the income poverty of black families headed by couples by 1.4 percentage points, whereas social insurance reduced black income poverty by 6 percentage points. In 1984, public assistance income was even less effective, and social insurance more effective, in reducing black income poverty. For Mexicans, social insurance income reduced income poverty by 3 percentage points both in 1979 and in 1984, considerably less than public assistance income. Only for Puerto Ricans was the poverty-reducing effect of means- and non-means-tested income sources roughly similar in 1979, with the greater effect corresponding to public assistance income transfers. By 1984, the poverty-reducing effects of social insurance rose for most intact families. This outcome coincides with an increase in the share of all families receiving some form of cash transfer payment.

Among families with single heads, the 1970s witnessed an increase in the shares of Mexican, other Hispanic, American Indian, and white families that did not receive any form of transfer income. The share of black single-head families not receiving any form of transfer income remained stable during the 1970s and fell during the early 1980s. In contrast, the share of Puerto Rican families with single heads that received no cash transfers of any kind decreased precipitously—from 57% in 1969 to 40% in 1979 and to 31% in 1984. The effectiveness of transfer income in reducing income poverty is evident in the lower posttransfer as compared to pretransfer rates. Our tabulations indicate that in 1979 income poverty would have been 3 to 7 percentage points higher for minority families in the absence of cash income transfers. Changes in work effort, as shown in Table 4, also served to reduce levels of earnings poverty—the largest component of absolute income poverty.

Welfare recipiency increased most dramatically among Puerto Rican families with single heads, up from 15% in 1969 to 59% in 1984, or a 293% increase in 15 years! Even though the reliance of these families on social insurance income fell 69% during this period, the decline was considerably less than the change in receipt of public assistance income. Increased welfare dependency is accompanied by equally striking rates of income poverty exhibited by Puerto Rican families with single heads. Whereas income poverty declined during the 1970s for all minority and nonminority families with single heads, Puerto Rican income poverty rates rose 69% between 1969 and 1979, and an additional 15% by 1984.

Lower posttransfer-income poverty levels speak to the importance of all types of cash transfers as poverty-reducing mechanisms, but they are only partial solutions. Multiple-worker income-packaging strategies appear to bring about more substantial reductions in poverty as compared to cash transfers of any sort. From the standpoint of both their effectiveness and their public acceptability, policies that improve the employability of individuals probably will be more successful in reducing racial and ethnic differentials in poverty. Unfortunately, the viability of strategies designed to reduce income and poverty inequities will be hindered to the extent that race and national origin continue to restrict the employment and income prospects of minority workers—particularly prime-aged men and youth. The goal of providing equal employment opportunities poses the most formidable policy challenge for future strategies to fight poverty.

Acknowledging the differential importance of the "public safety net" versus the private or "family safety net" as a hedge against poverty does not explain the precipitous increase in poverty among Puerto Ricans, nor the equally impressive declines in poverty registered by Native Americans. Although such an explanation is necessarily complex, we attempt in the final section of this chapter to examine the relative importance of two factors known to be associated with intertemporal variation in poverty—changes in family composition (especially a rise in the incidence of families with single heads) and changes in family labor-force behavior. Our focus on these two components reflects the growing empirical evidence that changes in labor status and changes in headship (specifically the rise in female-headed families) are two of the most important determinants of poverty—more so than either age of the head, family size, or location (see Danziger & Gottschalk, 1983). This heuristic exercise is not intended to explain changes in poverty rates, but to summarize the importance of changing demographic composition in producing the convergences and divergences in relative economic well-being.

DEMOGRAPHIC CHANGE AND RELATIVE ECONOMIC WELL-BEING, 1959–1984

Despite the impressive declines in pre- and posttransfer income poverty among minority and nonminority families during the 1960s and 1970s, racial and ethnic differentials persisted through 1979, and among Puerto Ricans absolute and earnings poverty rose sharply. The early 1980s brought generalized increases in income poverty—increases that were greater for minority than for nonminority families. Rising Puerto Rican poverty during the 1970s has been attributed to the rapid disintegration of families, whereas the rise in poverty during the 1980s has been linked to the deteriorating labor-market status of minority workers. Accordingly, in this section we provide empirical evidence on the effects of changing headship structure and in labor force status of heads in accounting for the observed changes in earnings poverty, absolute poverty, and mean family incomes between 1959 and 1984.

For this decomposition analysis, we divided each minority population into six mutually exclusive demographic subgroups (see Appendix Table A) to capture both headship structure and labor force behavior. In Table 6 we address two counterfactuals. First, what would have been the mean income, earnings pover-

Table 6. Decomposing the Effects of Changes in Employment Status and Headship on the Mean Incomes, Earnings Poverty Rates and Absolute Poverty Rates of Minority and Nonminority Families

	Blacks	Mexicans	Puerto Ricans	Other Hispanics	American Indians[a]	Non-Hispanic whites
Actual (1984)						
Mean income[b]	$20,252	$22,780	$17,553	$27,023	$26,057	$33,959
Earnings poverty	42.5	31.9	50.3	27.4	30.5	25.0
Absolute poverty	30.6	24.0	41.4	17.8	20.5	7.7
Expected 1984, assuming 1959 demographic composition[c]						
Mean income[b]	$23,107	$22,034	$23,239	$27,201	$23,824	$34,645
Earnings poverty	34.0	31.6	25.2	24.2	37.6	20.7
Absolute poverty	24.0	25.1	19.4	16.2	24.6	7.5
Expected 1984, assuming 1984 white demographic composition[c]						
Mean income[b]	$25,196	$24,016	$24,542	$27,891	$27,515	—[d]
Earnings poverty	30.7	30.0	26.9	26.4	26.7	—[d]
Absolute poverty	19.1	21.8	18.7	15.3	17.8	—[d]
Percentage difference due to change in demographic composition: 1959–1984[c]						
Mean income[b]	−12.4	3.4	−24.5	−0.6	8.6	−2.0
Earnings poverty	25.0	1.0	99.6	13.2	−18.9	20.8
Absolute poverty	28.0	−4.4	113.4	9.9	−16.7	2.7
Percentage difference due to minority demographic composition[c]						
Mean income[b]	−19.6	−5.1	−28.5	−3.1	−5.3	—[d]
Earnings poverty	38.4	6.3	87.0	3.8	14.2	—[d]
Absolute poverty	60.2	10.1	121.4	16.3	15.2	—[d]

[a]1979 for Indians, as 1984 data were unavailable.

[b]Incomes in constant 1985 dollars.

[c]Demographic composition refers to a combination of headship structure and employment status of the heads. See p. 46 for explanation.

[d]Same as actual 1985 white composition.

SOURCE: Computed from Appendix Table A.

ty, and absolute poverty rates of minority and nonminority families in the absence of changes in headship structure and labor supply patterns between 1959 and 1984? Second, what would these three measures of economic well-being have been in 1984 if the demographic composition of minority families had converged to that of non-Hispanic white families? A shift toward a greater prevalence of single-head families would be associated with increases in poverty, whereas increases in the proportions of families with two or more earners would produce the opposite effect. As these consequences are mutually offsetting, our decomposition analysis assesses the net impact resulting from both types of compositional change.

Beginning with blacks, our results show that changes in headship structure and labor force status were associated with a decline in the mean income of black families on the order of 12%. Stated differently, had the headship structure and employment patterns observed in 1959 remained constant over time,[11] the mean family income of black families would have been 12% higher, or $23,100 versus $20,200, on an average annual basis. Changes in demographic composition resulted in an earnings poverty rate 25% higher, and an absolute poverty rate 28% higher, than would have obtained had the demographic composition (and category-specific poverty rates) remained constant.

The next panel of Table 6 computes the predicted income levels along with earnings and absolute poverty rates, assuming that the 1984 headship structure and labor force status of black families was identical to that of nonminority families. This exercise shows that headship and employment differences between black and white families were responsible for 20% of the $13,700 average black family income deficit ($33,959 − $20,252 = $13,707). Moreover, with the 1984 headship structure and employment characteristics of white family heads, earnings poverty rates of black families would have been 38% lower, and their absolute poverty rates 60% lower, than those actually observed.

A comparison of the headship and labor force composition of the black population between 1959 and 1984 (see Appendix Table A) locates the sources of change which resulted in lower income and higher poverty rates in 1984 for blacks. First, the proportion of couple-headed families with both spouses employed increased slightly between 1959 and 1979 (up 7.6%), but this share fell again during the 1980s. Second, the share of single-head families in which the head was not employed more than doubled (up 110%), whereas the increase in the number of families with employed single heads was relatively smaller (up 82%). Thus, the faster growth of single-head families, especially those with heads who were not in the labor force, coupled with decreases in the share of couple-headed families where either the head or both spouses were employed, more than offset the poverty-reducing effects of secondary-worker income-packaging strategies documented in Table 4.

The results from the decomposition exercise for Puerto Ricans are similar to those for blacks except that the magnitude of the compositional changes on mean family incomes and earnings and absolute poverty rates are much greater. For example, the changes in the demographic composition of Puerto Rican families

[11]These calculations also assume invariant category-specific poverty rates.

between 1959 and 1984 resulted in a decrease of mean family income of approximately 25%, or twice the rate experienced by blacks. Comparable changes in headship structure and labor force status also produced increased earnings- and absolute-poverty rates of 100% to 113% compared to what would have been observed had these characteristics not evolved in the manner they did since 1959. Alternatively, with the headship structure and labor force characteristics of white families as of 1984, observed mean family incomes would have been 28% above those observed in 1984, whereas earnings- and absolute-poverty rates would have been, respectively, 87% and 121% below the actual rates observed in 1984.

These impressive differences in Puerto Rican mean family income and poverty rates relative to those of non-Hispanic white families can be traced to the dramatic increase in the proportion of single-head families with no head employed (which rose from 10% to 35% between 1959 and 1984, or by 248%), and to the increase in the proportion of couple-headed families with neither spouse employed between 1959 and 1984. During this period, the proportion of Puerto Rican couples with both heads employed fluctuated modestly, but registered a net decline of 14% by 1984, whereas the proportion of couples with neither head employed rose by one-third (from 9 to 12 percentage points). Aggregate earnings poverty and absolute poverty rates decreased for both black and Puerto Rican families during the 1959–1979 period and increased thereafter, and our computations suggest that the rate of decline in earnings poverty and absolute poverty was inhibited substantially by interdecade changes in the labor force status of the heads. Moreover, the deteriorating labor-market status of minority workers was primarily responsible for the increased poverty rates during the early 1980s. However academic in its execution, our analysis has clear policy implications in underscoring the urgency of increasing the employability of Puerto Rican and black family heads.

The patterns and impact of changes in demographic composition on Mexicans and American Indians were quite different from those observed among blacks and Puerto Ricans both in their magnitude and direction. For example, the changing demographic composition of these groups resulted in an increase in mean income. Alternatively stated, had the 1959 demographic composition remained constant over time, the mean income levels of Mexicans and American Indians would have been, respectively, 3.4% and 8.6% below the levels actually observed in 1984 and 1979, respectively. For Mexicans, demographic changes resulted in a decrease in earnings and absolute poverty on the order of 1% and 4%, respectively, and for Native Americans, 19% and 17%, respectively.

Increases in the proportion of families with both spouses employed or with at least one spouse employed largely accounted for the improvement in the relative economic well-being of Mexicans during the 1959–1984 period. Although the share of families with two heads employed declined after 1980, the share with a working spouse increased to offset the income losses associated with the former change. In contrast to changes observed for blacks and Puerto Ricans, the proportion of Mexican families with single heads who were unemployed rose modestly, and this increase occurred after 1980.

For Native Americans, improvements in relative economic well-being stemming from changes in demographic composition also can be traced to the increased shares of families with two employed heads, and larger shares with at least one spouse employed. Also, Native American single-head families with employed heads approximately doubled between 1960 and 1980, whereas the proportion with no head employed decreased. These patterns are the opposite of those observed among black and Puerto Rican families, and partly explain the divergent demographic influences acting upon income and poverty levels during the 1960s, 1970s, and early 1980s.

Our hypothetical exercise comparing the demographic composition of Mexicans and Native Americans with that of non-Hispanic white families shows that differences in headship structure and employment status were responsible for a small share of the persisting income and poverty gaps observed in 1984 and 1979, respectively. Specifically, with headship structure and labor force characteristics of non-Hispanic white families in 1984, mean income differences of Mexican families would have been 5% below those actually observed, whereas earnings- and absolute-poverty rates would have been, respectively, 6% and 10% below the actual 1984 rates. For Native Americans a similar pattern obtained, except that the magnitude of the convergence in poverty and income levels would have been greater had their demographic composition been identical to that of non-Hispanic white families in 1979.

In summary, it appears that intertemporal changes in headship structure and employment statuses of heads were associated with a large share of the observed decreases in the economic well-being of black, Puerto Rican, and to a much lesser extent, other Hispanic and non-Hispanic white families. The increase in earnings poverty due to changing headship structure and employment statuses of heads largely involved a growth of single-head families and decreases in the proportions of families with employed heads. Although the shares of families with employed spouses also rose for these groups, in the main these increases were insufficient to offset the losses incurred by higher rates of unemployment among heads. By contrast, for Mexican and American Indian families, changes in demographic composition favored the reduction of earnings poverty and absolute poverty over time, although the persisting differences in headship arrangements and labor force statuses contributed to the poverty gaps between these minority families and non-Hispanic whites.

Although instructive about the importance of demographic change in maintaining minority and nonminority poverty differentials, this exercise does not explain the reasons for the growth of single-head families and changes in employment statuses of heads, which are subjects of papers in their own right.

Nevertheless, our analyses do call attention to the differential impacts of slow economic growth on minority and nonminority families.

SUMMARY AND CONCLUSIONS

Our documentation of intertemporal changes in the relative and absolute economic status of minorities provides baseline information for additional investigations. However, our results are policy-relevant inasmuch as they illustrate the resilience of poverty differentials between minority and nonminority families and document the relative effectiveness of income transfers versus labor force participation as income maintenance strategies. What follows is a review of our key findings, with a focus on their policy relevance.

In terms of real income upgrading, the period 1959 to 1979 was one of significant improvement (Table 1), but the early 1980s reversed this trend. Increases in real family incomes were especially marked during the 1960s, when all of the groups we considered (blacks, Mexicans, Puerto Ricans, other Hispanics, American Indians, and non-Hispanic whites) registered sizable growth. Relative to non-Hispanic white families, black, other Hispanic, and (especially) American Indian families made significant advances during the 1960s and 1970s. Mexicans showed neither net improvement nor deterioration in their relative economic status, whereas Puerto Ricans had fallen much further behind whites in terms of median and mean family income by 1979. The slow economic growth that characterized the early 1980s took its toll on the 20-year trend, lowering real family incomes, although differentially by race and national origin. Our evidence suggests that the adverse consequences of the 1982 recession were stronger for minority than for nonminority families.

The considerable deterioration in the economic position of Puerto Rican families and improvement in the economic status of American Indian families are results that emerge from all our analyses. Some caution is advised regarding the American Indian results, owing to interdecade changes in measurement (see Appendix, p. 52), but the results for Puerto Ricans are not contaminated by changes in operational definitions over time. As such, we feel a sense of urgency in identifying the causes of this disadvantage and redressing its consequences. First in this agenda is the need to explain the deteriorating labor market position of Puerto Ricans, as increasing levels of joblessness are major causes of the growth of female-headed families and their increased impoverishment. Comparing the Puerto Rican and black experiences should prove especially fruitful, as these two minority populations have become more similar over time, yet their modes of incorporation into U.S. society differ markedly.

In terms of relative poverty, three patterns emerged (Table 2). Relative poverty among American Indians steadily declined from 1959 to 1979. Relative poverty for blacks, other Hispanics, and non-Hispanic whites declined during the 1960s, then increased slightly during the 1970s and 1980s. Finally, relative poverty among Mexicans and Puerto Ricans steadily increased. Moreover, Puerto Ricans were the only group to show a steadily increasing concentration in the lowest income quartile, that is, they were increasingly represented among the very poor. These changes, we believe, reflect economywide shifts in the nature and availability of work, which manifested themselves in the changing composition of family income, in the spread of work among family members, and in the increased reliance on transfer income, especially after 1979.

Of utmost concern were the consequences of these trends on the economic well-being of minority families. As a percentage of all family income, that stemming from labor force participation (earnings) was the greatest, slightly increasing during the 1960s and decreasing during the 1970s (Table 3). During the early 1980s, family income shares derived from earnings decreased further. We found only a very slight increase in the share of family income derived from public assistance. Among minorities, welfare simply is not a major source of family income (never exceeding 9%), especially in comparison to earnings (always exceeding 83%). There *was* an increase in the share of family income derived from social insurance over time, especially after 1980. We speculated that this increase reflected the greater numbers of elderly persons eligible for social security and other non-means-tested benefits and increased numbers of families collecting unemployment insurance benefits during the recession of the early 1980s. However, we were unable to verify these explanations with the available data.

Among couples, the relative contribution of total labor income by heads declined throughout this period, whereas that for other family members (notably the spouse) increased (Table 4). This increased spread of work probably contributed to the generally decreasing absolute poverty rates observed among minorities, but it certainly prevented earnings poverty from worsening during the climate of slow economic growth of the 1970s and early 1980s. Interestingly, among single-head families, the percentage of total labor income contributed by the head increased (though Puerto Ricans stood as an exception), indicating the willingness of single heads to work even in the face of greater constraints in allocating time to home and market production.

Spouse's earnings serve to keep a substantial number of families out of poverty (Table 4). The earnings of individuals other than the head or spouse also contribute in this way, but to a lesser extent, since most families are not extended, and many do not have adult children at home to serve as secondary earners during periods of economic need. Single heads clearly have a more difficult time committing workers to the labor force; still, secondary-earner strategies substantially reduced their poverty rates. That Puerto Rican families had less success with this strategy reflects their deteriorating labor-market position. This evidence points to the role of structural factors, namely, the restructuring of the New York labor market away from jobs traditionally held by Puerto Ricans in producing this outcome (see Tienda & Fielding, 1987, for preliminary supporting evidence). This circumstance requires programs designed to retrain displaced workers, rendering their skills more compatible with those required by the current job configurations of the labor markets where unemployment and poverty are most pervasive (New York and Chicago).

Except for Puerto Rican and Mexican couples, reliance on transfer income *per se* increased over the 1970s, mostly due to increased use of social insurance income (Table 5). Single-head families (except blacks and Puerto Ricans) decreased their utilization of transfer income during this period, but increased it during the 1980s. Although transfer income clearly has had some ameliorating effects on absolute poverty, it was not nearly as effective as increased family labor supply in reducing poverty. We reiterate a point made earlier: policies and programs designed to increase the employability of minority group members would appear to be a more effective way to combat poverty than increasing transfers, but employability does not ensure a job and hence an income. Therefore antidiscrimination policies must remain in full force—possibly even intensified—if the goal of eliminating persisting racial and ethnic differences will be realized in the future.

Finally, we documented the effect of changing demographic composition of minority groups on their average incomes and poverty rates (Table 6). Our decomposition analysis is an academic exercise in at least two ways: it is not possible to reverse the observed changes, nor is it possible to legislate direct remedies for changes in headship structure. Nevertheless, it is instructive to document how changes in heads' employment status have influenced poverty, for this, not headship status *per se,* is what ultimately determines who will be poor. Moreover, academic or not, our decomposition analysis focuses on two of the most important (and controversial) correlates of poverty inasmuch as employment status and headship structure are key elements of persisting poverty syndromes.

On balance, our comparative approach sheds some new light on the significance of race and ethnicity in the profile of persisting disadvantage, as well as the differing responsiveness of minority poverty to income transfers. Our tabulations provide ample evidence that Puerto Rican families have become more similar to blacks both in terms of their headship structure and employment patterns. That poverty rates soared for Puerto Rican families while they declined for black families largely can be traced to the greater success of black women in the labor market. Whereas participation rates for black women increased during the 1960s and 1970s, the rates for Puerto Rican women dropped during the 1960s and recovered during the 1970s, registering negligible change over the two-decade period (Bean & Tienda, 1988). Thus, further queries about the sources of Puerto Rican disadvantage must begin by answering why the labor market position of

Puerto Rican women has not kept pace with that of other minority women. To ignore this critical problem will practically ensure the emergence of a syndrome of persisting poverty among Puerto Ricans.

Our emphasis on the poverty experience of Puerto Ricans—a sobering lesson in "losing ground"—is not intended to deflect attention from the persisting inequities among other minority groups. Rather, we call attention to this group because it sharpens questions for future research and policy agendas. In the former arena, it is critical to ascertain the causal links between rising poverty rates, declining labor-force participation, and the sharp increase in families headed by women. These relationships have been examined in countless other studies, but the origins of variation in headship and employment patterns differ markedly according to race and national origin. Taking note of these differences as well as similarities in the pattern of relationships should enable future researchers to decode the complex causal structures.

In the area of policy, the need for employment and training policy cannot be overstated. Our data showed that secondary-earner income effects were far more effective hedges against poverty than were means-tested income transfers, yet some groups—notably blacks and Puerto Ricans—witnessed appreciable increases in the share of families with no earners. Are these families trapped in cycles of persisting poverty? Why have their numbers increased rather than decreased? And why have our welfare and employment policies failed them more than others of like or different ethnicity? We suspect that persisting labor-market discrimination and the persisting disability of race may hold partial answers, but it is doubtful that the origins of persisting poverty among black and Puerto Rican families are identical. Further comparative analysis probably will move us further in the direction of understanding better the underclass phenomenon, as well as bring into focus the appropriate cures for its various manifestations.

APPENDIX

In this analysis, we chose to study five minority groups in addition to non-Hispanic whites: non-Hispanic blacks, Mexicans, Puerto Ricans, other Hispanics, and American Indians. Obtaining valid and reliable measures of race and ethnicity is compounded by the use of various data sets because of comparability issues. For 1960, 1970, and 1980, our task was considerably simplified by using Public Use Microdata Samples (PUMS). This is because consistency with previous censuses is an important criterion for the Census Bureau in deciding what questions to ask on the census form and how to phrase them. Another important advantage in using the PUMS data derives from the large size, which reduces statistical error among relatively small groups such as Puerto Ricans or American Indians. In view of the important changes in socioeconomic well-being during the early 1980s, it was critical to examine data from the mid-1980s. Therefore, we also analyzed data from the Census Bureau's March, 1985, Current Population Survey (CPS). Some of the differences among all four of these data sets bear on the measurement of race and ethnicity. Accordingly, we briefly describe our definitions of the six race/ethnic groups for each year. This is followed by a discussion of the operational procedures used to determine absolute poverty thresholds.

Definitions of Race/Ethnicity

In this study we assumed that the race and/or ethnicity of the family head adequately represents the race/ethnicity of the entire family. To be sure, some error is possible when families are of mixed race/ethnicity, or when family members differ in the degree to which they admit or conceal ethnic markers. However, as it is the race/ethnicity of the head that generally determincs, for example, labor market insertion, residential location, and the life chances of other family members, we used it to typify the family's race/ethnicity.

To define our groups we used a self-reported race variable (which in the censuses includes white, black, and American Indian, among others, and in the CPS includes whites, blacks, and others) and one or more ethnic self-identification items. The somewhat cumbersome term "race/ethnicity" is necessary since Hispanic persons in general, and Hispanic subgroups in particular, differ less by distinct physical characteristics than by cultural ones (such as language or ancestral origin).

Hispanics

Individuals who identified themselves as Hispanic were so classified, regardless of their self-reported race. We disaggregated Hispanics into three groups: Mexicans, Puerto Ricans, and other Hispanics. Using the 1970 and 1980 PUMS and the 1985 CPS, this disaggregation is straightforward, as respondents who indicated they were of Spanish origin also were asked to indicate if they were Mexican, Puerto Rican, or of another origin. This Hispanic ethnicity item was not available in the 1960 census, so a more involved procedure was required to identify the Hispanic-origin subgroups. First, a head was defined as Hispanic if he or she met one or more of the following criteria: (a) he or she had a Spanish surname (five Southwest states only), (b) he or she was born (or at least one parent was born) in a Latin American country, (c) he or she reported Spanish as mother tongue, or (d) he or she identified self as being of Puerto Rican stock. The last was used to identify Puerto Ricans, whereas nativity of self (or parents) was used to identify Mexicans. Individuals identified as Hispanic but not Mexican or Puerto Rican were classified as other Hispanic.

Whites and Blacks

In all 4 years, white household heads were defined as those who were not Hispanic (see above) and who responded "White" on the color or race item. Similarly, black household heads were those who were not Hispanic and who responded "Negro" (1960 and 1970) or "Black" (1980) on the race item.

American Indians

American Indians were not identified on the 1985 CPS. In 1960, 1970, and 1980, American Indians include individuals who responded either "American Indian" or reported the name of a specific tribe in response to the race item. Owing to changes in coding, this category was somewhat more inclusive in 1980. That is, only in 1980 were Aleuts and Eskimos included in that category, but in 1960 and 1970 Aleuts and Eskimos were excluded from that category, and hence from our analysis. This could cause some upward bias in income and downward bias in poverty rates for Indians in 1980 to the extent that Eskimos and Aleuts reside in Alaska, a state with a substantially higher mean income and cost of living. Owing largely to rising ethnic pride among American Indians, people were much more likely to claim that they were Indian in 1980 than in 1970 or 1960. We have not adjusted for these differences in the self-identification of American Indians across censuses, and indicate the need for caution in interpreting the temporal patterns reported in the text.

Absolute Poverty

Families were defined as being poor if their annual money income in the year before the census was below a set of income thresholds used to designate a minimally adequate standard of living (Danziger & Gottschalk, 1983). In other words, a family is poor if the ratio of its total income to the poverty line appropriate for that type of family is less than one. These poverty ratios are included in the 1970 and 1980 PUMS and 1985 CPS records. Rather than use these, however, we chose the absolute poverty lines specified by Ross, Danziger, and Smolensky (1987). These authors used the poverty lines developed by Mollie Orshansky of the Social Security Administration for use with 1959 income data. In all, Orshansky specified 124 poverty thresholds that differ according to household characteristics and hence need. To make these thresholds comparable to 1969, 1979, and 1985 data we simply adjusted them using the consumer price index. The poverty lines used by the Census Bureau for the 1970 and 1980 PUMS and the 1985 CPS are a slightly modified version of the lines we employ here. Creating our own poverty thresholds affords greater flexibility to consider alternative definitions of poverty and maximizes intertemporal comparability.

Table A. Components of Change in Relative Economic Well-Being, 1959–1984 (In Constant 1985 dollars)

	Labor force status[a]					Mean income[b]				
	1960	1970	1980	1985	Percentage change 1960–1985	1959	1969	1979	1984	Percentage change 1959–1984
Blacks										
Couples										
Both employed	24.9	28.1	26.8	24.1	−3.2	$18,427	$30,856	$35,806	$35,632	+93.4
Head employed	36.3	26.6	14.9	10.7	−70.5	13,835	21,515	24,435	23,717	+71.4
Spouse employed	4.2	4.1	5.3	6.7	+59.5	12,414	18,050	25,278	24,683	+98.8
Neither employed	9.8	8.6	10.0	9.8	0.0	8,667	10,981	14,868	14,261	+64.5
Single heads										
Head employed	12.8	16.5	22.3	23.3	+82.0	11,788	17,248	19,648	17,050	+44.6
Head not employed	12.1	16.0	20.6	25.4	+109.9	7,268	9,983	10,385	8,336	+14.7
Total	100.1	99.9	99.9	100.0		$13,335	20,536	22,590	20,252	+51.9
Mexicans										
Couples										
Both employed	15.1	17.1	29.1	27.9	+84.8	$23,468	$30,747	$32,980	32,014	+36.4
Head employed	56.9	43.6	36.1	30.3	−46.7	17,732	22,554	24,266	22,816	+28.7
Spouse employed	1.7	3.7	3.5	5.7	+235.3	17,300	21,619	24,689	24,479	+41.5
Neither employed	9.6	16.3	10.1	11.8	+22.9	11,805	14,940	16,840	14,093	+19.4
Single heads										
Head employed	7.1	8.3	11.8	13.4	+88.7	14,323	17,964	20,305	20,436	+42.7
Head not employed	9.5	11.0	9.5	11.0	+15.8	9,528	12,227	11,718	10,498	+10.2
Total	99.9	100.0	100.1	100.1		$16,996	21,163	24,405	22,780	+34.0

(continued)

Table A. (continued)

	Labor force status[a]					Mean income[b]				
	1960	1970	1980	1985	Percentage change 1960–1985	1959	1969	1979	1984	Percentage change 1959–1984
Puerto Ricans										
Couples										
Both employed	20.6	18.3	20.6	17.7	−14.1	$20,544	$27,618	$33,271	34,842	+69.6
Head employed	47.2	45.9	27.3	17.8	−62.3	16,264	20,756	22,585	25,558	+57.1
Spouse employed	3.0	1.4	3.1	5.0	+66.6	15,020	20,184	22,426	21,963	+46.2
Neither employed	8.7	13.6	9.8	11.6	+33.3	10,380	14,572	12,894	11,470	+10.5
Single heads										
Head employed	10.5	10.7	12.3	13.5	+28.6	14,412	16,756	17,633	16,246	+12.7
Head not employed	9.9	10.1	26.9	34.4	+247.5	8,573	13,059	7,846	6,424	−25.1
Total	99.9	100.0	100.0	100.0		$15,639	19,953	19,260	17,553	+12.2
Other Hispanics										
Couples										
Both employed	18.5	25.7	33.0	34.1	+84.3	$26,059	$32,640	$37,743	$37,352	+43.3
Head employed	55.5	44.2	28.4	23.4	−57.8	19,817	24,654	30,633	28,840	+45.5
Spouse employed	2.4	2.2	4.1	6.8	+183.3	18,909	25,271	26,781	27,950	+47.8
Neither employed	9.3	8.2	9.8	10.5	+12.9	11,733	13,839	17,129	15,265	+30.1
Single heads										
Head employed	6.9	9.7	15.0	14.4	+108.7	14,952	20,580	21,698	20,203	+35.1

Head not employed	7.6	9.9	9.7	10.8	+42.1	11,808	9,959	11,984	10,527	−10.8
Total	100.2	99.9	100.0	100.0		$19,203	23,982	28,354	27,023	+40.7
American Indians										
Couples										
Both employed	12.6	22.2	29.5	—[c]	+134.1	$21,384	$30,602	$36,278	—[c]	+69.6
Head employed	42.7	38.1	28.6	—	−33.0	14,389	23,324	27,996	—	+94.6
Spouse employed	3.9	5.2	7.1	—	+82.0	15,976	23,482	25,955	—	+62.5
Neither employed	23.7	16.7	14.9	—	−37.1	8,723	12,146	16,842	—	+93.1
Single heads										
Head employed	4.7	6.8	9.8	—	+108.5	12,140	17,251	18,995	—	+56.5
Head not employed	12.5	11.1	10.1	—	−19.2	6,849	8,978	11,218	—	+63.8
Total	100.1	100.1	100.0			$12,944	21,077	26,057		+101.3
Non-Hispanic whites										
Couples										
Both employed	22.7	28.7	35.3	37.7	+66.1	$29,775	$40,594	$42,574	42,820	+43.8
Head employed	53.8	44.8	31.7	24.6	−54.3	25,820	35,279	37,571	36,401	+41.0
Spouse employed	2.4	3.1	4.4	6.0	+104.2	19,527	27,506	30,495	30,288	+55.1
Neither employed	10.1	11.1	15.0	16.5	+63.4	13,518	19,587	22,187	22,252	+64.6
Single heads										
Head Employed	6.0	7.0	8.1	9.5	+58.3	20,790	25,990	25,591	25,274	+21.6
Head not employed	5.0	5.2	5.6	5.7	+14.0	13,389	18,108	19,231	17,024	+27.1
Total	100.0	99.9	100.1	100.0		$24,401	33,269	34,726	33,959	+39.2

(continued)

Table A. (continued)

	Earnings poverty[b]					Absolute poverty[b]				
	1959	1969	1979	1984	Percentage change 1959–1984	1959	1969	1979	1984	Percentage change 1959–1984
Blacks										
Couples										
Both employed	28.8	9.2	5.9	4.6	−84.0	26.9	8.5	4.4	3.5	−87.0
Head employed	47.4	24.0	23.3	26.7	−43.6	44.6	20.9	17.5	21.6	−51.6
Spouse employed	61.4	47.7	30.7	23.2	−62.2	50.7	31.2	14.1	10.8	−78.7
Neither employed	80.3	79.4	77.7	79.3	−1.2	70.1	54.8	33.1	33.2	−52.6
Single heads										
Head employed	55.2	38.1	31.0	31.5	−42.9	51.9	31.7	24.5	24.8	−52.2
Head not employed	85.0	79.9	80.8	85.8	0.0	77.4	66.6	63.0	69.4	−10.3
Total	52.1	36.9	38.1	42.5	−18.4	47.8	29.8	26.3	30.6	−36.0
Mexicans										
Couples										
Both employed	18.5	10.6	8.1	8.6	−53.5	16.9	9.7	6.7	6.9	−59.2
Head employed	36.7	27.0	22.5	23.7	−13.0	34.7	23.8	19.3	21.9	−36.9
Spouse employed	40.3	44.4	32.0	29.2	−11.1	28.6	28.9	14.8	22.6	−21.0
Neither employed	71.2	76.3	68.2	75.6	+4.4	58.8	42.4	34.3	44.7	−24.0
Single heads										
Head employed	44.9	33.0	30.3	23.8	−47.0	40.2	24.0	25.5	18.3	−54.5
Head not employed	76.7	70.7	74.6	77.7	+1.3	66.8	57.1	61.5	59.0	−11.7
Total	41.7	38.2	29.2	31.9	−23.5	37.7	28.3	21.7	24.0	−36.3

Puerto Ricans										
Couples										
Both employed	13.9	13.7	6.8	2.0	−85.6	12.3	12.2	5.4	2.0	−83.7
Head employed	37.9	29.4	21.7	7.7	−79.7	35.4	26.6	18.6	6.1	−82.8
Spouse employed	32.8	25.0	28.5	33.9	+3.4	25.9	20.0	16.8	23.6	−2.3
Neither employed	79.2	65.3	76.9	82.6	+4.3	70.2	48.5	43.4	45.0	−35.9
Single heads										
Head employed	28.6	33.1	28.2	33.1	+15.7	25.6	26.0	23.2	27.7	+8.2
Head not employed	74.7	69.0	91.3	95.9	+28.4	70.0	46.9	78.5	86.8	+2.4
Total	39.0	35.8	43.8	50.3	+29.0	35.8	28.8	34.9	41.4	+15.6
Other Hispanics										
Couples										
Both employed	12.4	5.9	5.2	6.6	−46.8	11.3	5.3	4.2	3.9	−65.5
Head employed	30.9	17.3	15.2	13.8	−55.3	28.8	15.3	12.0	11.1	−61.4
Spouse employed	33.0	23.5	13.7	17.9	−45.8	21.4	14.4	7.6	4.9	−77.1
Neither employed	75.9	70.9	70.7	72.0	−5.1	58.6	45.7	29.5	29.6	−49.5
Single heads										
Head employed	47.0	25.2	24.2	32.5	−30.8	42.7	19.6	17.5	24.9	−41.7
Head not employed	77.2	82.0	75.3	78.4	+1.6	62.9	66.0	56.3	62.8	0.0
Total	36.3	26.1	24.5	27.4	−24.5	31.7	20.7	16.1	17.8	−43.8
American Indians										
Couples										
Both employed	26.3	9.2	6.4	—c	−75.7	21.9	7.6	4.8	—c	−78.1
Head employed	53.6	22.9	18.8	—	−64.9	48.0	20.8	14.6	—	−69.6
Spouse employed	51.2	29.7	25.8	—	−49.6	39.5	18.8	15.3	—	−61.3
Neither employed	82.6	73.5	69.2	—	−16.2	71.7	52.0	36.5	—	−49.1

(continued)

Table A. (continued)

	Earnings poverty[b]					Absolute poverty[b]				
	1959	1969	1979	1984	Percentage change 1959–1984	1959	1969	1979	1984	Percentage change 1959–1984
American Indians (cont.)										
Single heads										
Head employed	52.9	43.9	31.9	—	−39.7	49.0	37.1	24.4	—	−50.2
Head not employed	88.2	85.3	78.7	—	−10.8	81.6	70.1	59.1	—	−27.6
Total	61.2	37.0	30.5	—	−50.2	54.2	29.5	20.5	—	−62.2
Non-Hispanic whites										
Couples										
Both employed	5.6	2.0	2.4	4.0	−28.6	4.4	1.5	1.7	2.6	−40.9
Head employed	13.5	6.7	8.1	11.8	−12.6	10.9	4.9	4.4	6.0	−45.0
Spouse employed	30.0	19.0	20.3	20.0	−33.3	14.7	8.1	3.8	5.9	−59.9
Neither employed	73.9	73.3	73.7	82.8	+12.0	40.6	23.7	11.6	11.5	−71.1
Single heads										
Head employed	23.6	16.5	19.7	18.1	−23.3	16.8	11.7	12.5	10.7	−36.3
Head not employed	64.7	59.3	63.1	69.8	+7.9	45.2	33.2	28.5	35.2	−22.1
Total	21.4	16.6	20.4	25.0	+16.8	14.6	8.1	6.5	7.7	−47.3

[a]Demographic characteristics refer to the year of the census or CPS.
[b]Income and poverty rates are based on figures reported for the year prior to the census.
[c]Data not available.
SOURCE: Computatations from 1960, 1970, and 1980 PUMS files of the U.S. Census; March 1985 Current Population Survey.

ACKNOWLEDGMENTS

This research was supported by grants from the Ford Foundation and the Rockefeller Corporation. Computational support was furnished by the Center for Demography and Ecology. We gratefully acknowledge technical assistance from Gary Heisserer, Susan Walsh, Karen Booth, Diane Duesterhoeft, Alberto Martini, and Sarah Rudolph.

REFERENCES

Bean, F. D., & M. Tienda. (1988). *The Hispanic population of the United States.* New York: Russell Sage.

Danziger, S. (1984). Poverty. *Encyclopedia of social work,* 18th Edition.

Danziger, S., and P. Gottschalk. (1983). The measurement of poverty: Implications for antipoverty policy. *American Behavioral Scientist, 26*(6), 739–756.

Jensen, L. (1987, May). *Patterns of immigration and public assistance utilization, 1970–1980.* Paper presented at the annual meetings of the Population Association of America, Chicago, IL. (Forthcoming in *International Migration Review,* 1988.)

Ross, C., S. Danziger, & E. Smolensky. (1987). The level and trend of poverty in the United States, 1939–1979. *Demography, 24*(4), 587–600.

Schiller, B. R. (1986). *The economics of poverty and discrimination.* Englewood Cliffs, NJ: Prentice-Hall.

Tienda, M. (1984). The Puerto Rican worker: Current labor market status and future prospects. In *Puerto Ricans in the mid-Eighties: An American challenge* (pp. 63–91). Washington, DC: National Puerto Rican Coalition.

Tienda, M., & R. Angel. (1982). Headship and household composition among blacks, Hispanics and other whites. *Social Forces, 61*(2), 508–531.

Tienda, M., & E. L. Fielding. (1987). *Migration, preferential worker status, and employment: Divergent patterns of Hispanic market insertion in the United States.* Institute for Research on Poverty, Discussion Paper no. 837-87, University of Wisconsin-Madison.

Tienda, M., & J. Glass. (1985). Household structure and labor force participation of black, Hispanic and white mothers. *Demography, 22*(3), 381–394.

3

Minorities in the Labor Market
Cyclical Patterns and Secular Trends in Joblessness

CHARLES HIRSCHMAN

Forty years ago, with the fear of the Great Depression still etched in popular consciousness, Congress passed the Full Employment Act of 1946. The Act was, however, more of a statement of hope than a program of state policy. Eight recessions later, the United States has still not formulated an effective policy to deal with the human costs of the business cycle. The most visible signs of ineffective labor market policies are periodic bouts of high unemployment, which reached double-digit levels in the latest 1982–1983 recession. Even during periods of normal economic growth, unemployment remains persistently high—it was 7% in 1985, even after 3 years of a so-called economic recovery. The current unemployment rate is above the level typically experienced during most earlier economic recessions. Less visible are the growing numbers of discouraged workers and the problems of poverty and human misery that often accompany joblessness (Plotnick & Skidmore, 1975, pp. 118–121).

The employment problem—"crisis" may be a more appropriate term—is most severe for minority groups, especially the black and Puerto Rican communities (Freeman & Holzer, 1986; Lichter 1988; Rees 1986). Based upon 1979–1980 data, the estimated worklife of blacks was nearly 7 years shorter than that of whites (Smith, 1986). The rising tide of minority unemployment and nonparticipation in the labor force reached record levels in the 1980s. For young men, the inability to find productive and remunerative employment in the mainstream economy is particularly devastating (Ross & Hill, 1967). The opportunities for hustling and other forms of illicit activity have become relatively attractive in the

CHARLES HIRSCHMAN • Center for Studies in Demography and Ecology, and Department of Sociology, University of Washington, Seattle, Washington.

absence of legitimate means of getting ahead. Without hope for a steady income, many minority men find it economically impossible to form stable family unions. The result is a disproportionate number of poor households of women and children. Although none of these problems are new (Liebow, 1967; Wilson & Aponte, 1985), the extent and significance have grown enormously in the last decade. As joblessness has long-term as well as short-term consequences, the human costs may be even greater than they currently appear to be.

In this chapter, I provide a preliminary survey of trends in minority unemployment and labor force nonparticipation since the mid-1950s. (The Appendix describes the definition and measurement of labor force activity.) My primary focus is on men, particularly young men. The employment problems faced by women are certainly no less than those of men. In fact, women face considerably more obstacles in entering highly paid, typically male-dominated, occupations. But to provide an adequate account of the trend in both male and female employment would require a much more complex, and considerably longer, analysis. The first objective is simply to document the facts—with an emphasis on the fluctuations in minority employment in the 1970s and 1980s.

Explanation of these facts is a considerably more complex task. Here I only begin to address the questions with an analysis of the relationships between educational attainment, school enrollment, and joblessness. Although schooling is a key determinant of employment and unemployment, differences in educational background do not explain ethnic differences in unemployment.

CURRENT POPULATION SURVEYS: USES AND LIMITATIONS

This study, along with most other analyses of labor force trends, relies upon time-series data from the Current Population Survey (CPS). Since the late 1940s, the CPS, conducted monthly by the U.S. Bureau of the Census, has been the primary source of employment and unemployment statistics (U.S. Bureau of the Census, 1976). Although CPS data are exceptional in their content and quality, there are serious limitations of population coverage. By design the CPS sample is limited to the household population. This means that a small but important segment of the youthful population (those living in military bases, college dormitories, and other group quarters) are excluded from the CPS sample. The off-base military population is counted in the CPS, but almost all tabulations (including those reported here) are limited to the civilian labor force.

Another problem, one which plagues census data and presumably all household surveys, is the serious underenumeration of young minority men. Demographic analyses of census underenumeration have estimated that 12% to 18% of young black men are missed (Siegel, 1974; Passel & Robinson, 1984). Similar conditions are likely to mean that Puerto Rican and other minority men are also relatively underenumerated, although conclusive evidence is not available. With the differential in underenumeration, reported racial and ethnic inequality in unemployment is probably an underestimate of the actual difference. Other evaluation studies show that the unemployed and labor force nonparticipants are more likely to be underenumerated (Citro & Cohen, 1985, p. 234).

On the other hand, exclusion of the military removes a group that is employed, and may offset a part of the bias that is due to underenumeration. During the mid-1970s, inclusion of the armed forces personnel would have reduced white male teenage unemployment by 1 percentage point and nonwhite male teenage unemployment by 2.5 to 4 points (Ehrenberg, 1980). On balance, however, CPS data probably underestimate the level of unemployment and the black-white differential in unemployment.

TRENDS IN UNEMPLOYMENT

Open employment, the most visible sign of labor underutilization, is reported in Table 1 (and graphically in Figure 1) for men by race and Hispanic origin. Data for white and black men are available for each year from 1954 to 1985, whereas the figures for the Hispanic population were not tabulated until 1973 (and not until 1975 for Mexican, Puerto Rican, and Cuban workers). For all groups, there are two major patterns in the time series—the cyclical ups and downs of the business cycle and the general upward drift in unemployment rates for the entire period. During the span of years represented here, 1954, 1958, 1961, 1971–1972, 1975–1976, 1980, and 1982–1983 were recessionary periods. The 1960s were an exceptional decade of persistent low unemployment.

There are dramatic differences in the unemployment levels of white and minority men. Although there is a common cyclical pattern for all groups, the amplitude is much sharper for minority men. Up through the early 1970s, the white unemployment rate fluctuated between 2% and 6%, but the corresponding figures were from 5% to 11–12% for black men. The 1974–1975 recession broke the existing ground rules. White rates jumped to 7% in 1975 and then to almost 9% in 1982–1983. For black men, unemployment hit almost 15% in 1975 and then topped 20% in 1982–1983—a level that approaches the Depression era of joblessness. In 1985, when the standard economic indicators were reflecting prosperity and progress, white male unemployment remained above 6%, and more than 15% of the black male labor force was seeking a job. Although this is a period of apparent economic recovery, these figures are above the recession years of the 1950s and 1960s.

The conventional observation that the black unemployment rate is twice the white rate was an accurate description through the middle 1970s. But over the last decade, the ratio has crept up to 2.5 to 1. Moreover, the absolute gap has

Table 1. Unemployment Rates of Men Aged 16 and Older, by
Race and Hispanic Origin, 1954–1985

	White	Black[a]	Hispanic All[a]	Mexican	Puerto Rican	Cuban
1954	4.8	10.3	—	—	—	—
1955	3.7	8.8	—	—	—	—
1956	3.4	7.9	—	—	—	—
1957	3.6	8.3	—	—	—	—
1958	6.1	13.7	—	—	—	—
1959	4.6	11.5	—	—	—	—
1960	4.8	10.7	—	—	—	—
1961	5.7	12.8	—	—	—	—
1962	4.6	10.9	—	—	—	—
1963	4.7	10.5	—	—	—	—
1964	4.1	8.9	—	—	—	—
1965	3.6	7.4	—	—	—	—
1966	2.8	6.3	—	—	—	—
1967	2.7	6.0	—	—	—	—
1968	2.6	5.6	—	—	—	—
1969	2.5	5.3	—	—	—	—
1970	4.0	7.3	—	—	—	—
1971	4.9	9.1	—	—	—	—
1972	4.5	9.3	—	—	—	—
1973	3.8	8.0	6.7	—	—	—
1974	4.4	9.8	7.3	—	—	—
1975	7.2	14.8	11.4	—	—	—
1976	6.4	13.7	10.8	9.8	15.9	12.6
1977	5.5	13.3	9.0	8.5	13.9	8.0
1978	4.6	11.8	7.7	7.1	12.5	7.1
1979	4.5	11.4	7.0	6.6	11.5	6.6
1980	6.1	14.5	9.7	9.6	13.1	9.0
1981	6.5	15.7	10.2	10.0	14.2	9.1
1982	8.8	20.1	13.6	13.9	17.3	10.8
1983	8.8	20.3	13.5	14.6	17.0	11.6
1984	6.4	16.4	10.5	10.9	12.5	8.6
1985	6.1	15.3	10.2	10.5	13.0	7.5

[a]Before 1972, black refers to black and other nonwhite workers. Dashes indicate data not available.

SOURCES: U.S. Department of Labor (1982, pp. 518–527; 1985, pp. 27–29, 71–73); U.S. Bureau of Labor Statistics (1986, pp. 197–198).

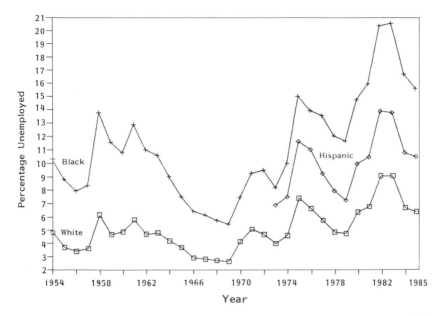

Figure 1. The unemployment rate among men aged 16 and over, 1954–1985. For sources, see Table 1. Key: White = –□–, Black = –+–, Hispanic = –◇– .

increased from an average of about 3 percentage points in the 1960s to more than 9–12 points in the 1980s (for a similar observation, see Farley, 1984).

Our observation of Hispanic unemployment rates is limited to the economic roller coaster years of the last decade—it is unclear what "normal" patterns might have been in the 1950s and 1960s. In general, male Hispanic unemployment rates are intermediate between those of white and black men. Among Hispanics, Puerto Rican men have the highest levels—a bit above black men in the late 1970s and a bit lower in the early 1980s. Mexican men have lower levels of unemployment than Puerto Rican men, and Cuban men have the lowest of the Hispanic groups—although the latter group's levels are still above those of white men.

Unemployment is highest among young workers, particularly teenagers (Bowers, 1979). As entrants to the labor force with little prior job experience, young workers might be expected to experience above-average levels of joblessness. Moreover, young members of the labor force are selective of those who discontinue their schooling at younger ages and thus may be most likely to experience employment problems. Even given these qualifications, the levels and trends in youth unemployment (age groups 16–19, 20–24, and 25–34) in Table 2 present a dismal picture.

In the mid-1950s, teenage unemployment rates were almost equal for white

Table 2. Unemployment Rates of Men by Race and Hispanic Origin;
Selected Age Groups, 1954–1985

	Ages 16–19			Ages 20–24			Ages 25–34		
Year	White	Black[a]	Hispanic[a]	White	Black	Hispanic	White	Black	Hispanic
1954	13.4	14.4	—	9.8	16.9	—	4.2	10.1	—
1955	11.3	13.4	—	7.0	12.4	—	2.7	8.6	—
1956	10.5	15.0	—	6.1	12.0	—	2.8	7.6	—
1957	11.5	18.4	—	7.0	12.7	—	2.7	8.5	—
1958	15.7	26.8	—	11.8	19.5	—	5.6	14.7	—
1959	14.0	25.2	—	7.5	16.4	—	3.8	12.3	—
1960	14.0	24.0	—	8.3	13.1	—	4.1	10.6	—
1961	15.7	26.8	—	10.1	15.3	—	4.9	12.9	—
1962	13.7	22.0	—	8.1	14.6	—	3.8	13.0	—
1963	15.9	27.3	—	7.8	15.6	—	3.9	9.5	—
1964	14.7	24.3	—	7.4	12.6	—	3.0	7.6	—
1965	12.9	23.3	—	5.9	9.3	—	2.6	6.2	—
1966	10.5	21.3	—	4.1	7.9	—	2.1	4.9	—
1967	10.7	23.9	—	4.2	8.0	—	1.9	4.4	—
1968	10.1	22.1	—	4.6	8.3	—	1.7	3.9	—
1969	10.0	21.4	—	4.6	8.4	—	1.7	3.4	—
1970	13.7	25.0	—	7.8	12.6	—	3.1	6.1	—
1971	15.1	28.8	—	9.4	16.2	—	4.0	7.5	—
1972	14.2	31.7	—	8.5	14.9	—	3.4	7.2	—
1973	12.3	27.8	19.0	13.2	8.2	3.0	6.2	5.0	
1974	13.5	33.1	19.0	7.8	16.2	9.9	3.6	8.1	5.5
1975	18.3	38.1	27.6	13.1	24.7	16.3	6.3	12.7	9.6
1976	17.3	37.5	23.3	10.9	22.6	16.0	5.6	12.0	8.1
1977	15.0	39.2	20.9	9.3	23.0	11.7	5.0	11.8	7.9
1978	13.5	36.7	19.7	7.7	21.0	9.4	3.8	9.8	6.6
1979	13.9	34.2	17.5	7.5	18.7	9.2	3.7	9.6	5.3
1980	16.2	37.5	21.6	11.1	23.7	12.3	5.9	13.4	8.2
1981	17.9	40.7	24.3	11.6	26.4	14.2	6.1	14.4	9.0
1982	21.7	48.9	31.2	14.3	31.5	18.3	8.9	20.1	12.5
1983	20.2	48.8	28.7	13.8	31.4	17.1	9.0	19.4	11.6
1984	16.8	42.7	25.3	9.8	26.6	12.7	6.2	15.0	—
1985	16.5	41.0	24.7	9.7	23.5	13.0	5.7	13.8	—

[a]Before 1972, black refers to black and other nonwhite workers.
SOURCES: U.S. Department of Labor (1982, pp. 518–527; 1985, pp. 71–73); U.S. Bureau of Labor
Statistics (1985, pp. 157–158; 1986, pp. 201).

and black men. Mare, Winship, and Kubitshek (1984) caution against a benign
interpretation of this equivalence (or narrow differential). Lower levels of school
enrollment and military participation meant that young black workers had more
years of job experience than young white workers in the 1950s. Over time, the
underlying racial differential in the labor market was unmasked as white and

black youth experienced comparable levels of school enrollment and military service. Note that for men above age 20, black unemployment rates have always exceeded white rates.

Another analysis points to population redistribution between and within regions as the primary explanation for the widening of black-white teenage unemployment rates (O'Neill, 1983). Historically, most black youths lived in the South, especially in the rural South, where blacks were concentrated in agriculture and racially segregated sectors of employment. In these settings, open unemployment was low. Over the last few decades, the black population has been redistributed from rural to urban areas within the South and from the South to the rest of the country. Outside the South, especially in large Northern cities, black teenage unemployment rates have always been much higher than white levels. The consequence has been that high black teenage unemployment has become the dominant national pattern. The recency of this pattern should not obscure the fact that black youth have always experienced higher unemployment if they competed in the same labor market with white youth.

The rise in youth unemployment during the recessions of the 1970s and 1980s were unprecedented, especially for minorities. White teenage males hit a peak of 18% unemployment in 1975 and then more than 20% in the 1982–1983 recession. For black teenage males, the unemployment rate has been above 20% since 1957. In the early 1970s, the black teenage rate rose from the low to mid-20% range (where it had been for most of the prosperous 1960s) to the mid- to high 30% range. Only modest declines were registered in the late 1970s, before the recessions of the early 1980s raised black male teenage unemployment to almost 50%. Even in 1985 the rate is over 40%—about 25 percentage points above the comparable white rate. The Hispanic male teenage unemployment rate followed a similar trajectory, with values intermediate between the white and black levels, although closer to the white figures.

Although the reported unemployment rates for young men beyond the teenage years (age categories 20–24 and 25–34) are considerably below the teenage rates, the patterns and the widening black-white differential are even more disturbing. By the time that men are in their early twenties, upwards of 80% are in the labor force, and virtually all men are engaged in their work careers by their late twenties. Unemployment can no longer be explained as a transient problem of first-time jobseekers. For white men, the cyclical patterns move in the expected directions, but within a defined range. For example, the 20- to 24-year-old white-male unemployment rate broke the 10% mark in 1958, 1961, and 1975–1976 and reached a maximum figure of 14% in 1982. By contrast, unemployment in the 20- to 24-year-old black male labor force rose to 23% in 1975, and hit 31% in 1982–1983. For 25- to 34-year-old black men, the peaks for the same years were 12% and 20%, whereas the comparable white figures did not rise above 10%.

To summarize, the impact of economic downturn is not shared equally.

Black and Hispanic men are especially vulnerable. Whereas youthful workers in all groups face the highest unemployment rates, the figures for minority men in the formative years of their careers reached record levels. What was considered high unemployment in the 1950s is now quite ordinary, and the levels of unemployment reached during the 1982–1983 recession were unimaginable only a decade earlier.

THE TREND IN LABOR FORCE NONPARTICIPATION

Advocates against government intervention in labor markets typically argue that rises in unemployment are not a serious problem. They claim that unemployment rates are inflated because of an increase in "secondary" workers—women and teenagers—who do not have to support families. Besides, the welfare state alleviates the economic distress of unemployment. They also argue that a real problem is minimum wage laws that discourage employers from creating new jobs. All of these claims are open to challenge. Here, I simply note that the standard measure of open unemployment is a minimal indicator of the degree of labor underutilization. Workers who can find only part-time work or jobs that are below their skill levels (regardless of wages) are counted as fully employed, even if they are actively seeking alternative employment.

A serious weakness of the standard indicator of unemployment is that it excludes the passive unemployed—those who have given up on the job search because they think their prospects are so bleak. Although this weakness has long been recognized, it was usually considered a relatively minor issue. As remunerative work was both a normative and an absolutely essential role for adult men, open unemployment probably represented almost all jobless men. But that has changed in the last two decades. As open unemployment has reached new heights, the ranks of the passive unemployed have grown apace. Without a good behavioral indicator of passive unemployment, I use the rate of labor force nonparticipation as a crude proxy.

Table 3 presents the CPS annual time series of labor force participation rates (LFPR) by selected age groups for black and white men. These rates are simply the ratio of the civilian labor force to the civilian population. Not all labor force nonparticipants are idle or members of the passive unemployed; older labor-force nonparticipants may be retired and others may have full-time family responsibilities. In this analysis, I focus on men in the early stages of the life cycle, where regular employment is the normative pattern. Although increases in labor force nonparticipation of young adults might be explained by rising school enrollments, black and white differentials in LFPRs can still be meaningfully interpreted. For white and black teenagers, school enrollment rates are roughly comparable (although black youth are less likely to be enrolled in college), but

Table 3. Labor Force Participation Rates of Men by Race:
Selected Age Groups, 1954–1985

Year	Ages 16 and Over		Ages 16–17		Ages 18–19		Ages 20–24		Ages 25–34	
	White	Black[a]	White	Black	White	Black	White	Black	White	Black
1954	85.6	85.2	47.1	46.7	70.5	78.4	86.3	91.1	97.5	96.2
1955	85.4	85.0	48.1	48.2	71.7	75.7	86.5	89.7	97.8	95.8
1956	85.6	85.1	51.3	49.6	71.8	76.4	87.6	88.9	97.4	96.2
1957	84.8	84.3	49.6	47.5	71.5	72.0	88.6	89.6	97.2	96.1
1958	84.3	84.0	46.8	45.1	69.4	71.7	86.7	88.7	97.2	96.3
1959	83.8	83.4	45.4	41.7	70.3	72.0	87.3	90.8	97.5	96.3
1960	83.4	83.0	46.0	45.6	69.0	71.2	87.8	90.4	97.7	96.2
1961	83.0	82.2	44.3	42.5	66.2	70.5	87.6	89.7	97.7	95.9
1962	82.1	80.8	42.9	40.2	66.4	68.8	86.5	89.3	97.4	95.3
1963	81.5	80.2	42.4	37.2	67.8	69.1	85.8	88.6	97.4	94.9
1964	81.1	80.0	43.5	37.3	66.6	67.2	85.7	89.4	97.5	95.9
1965	80.8	79.6	44.6	39.3	65.8	66.7	85.3	89.8	97.4	95.7
1966	80.6	79.0	47.1	41.1	65.4	63.7	84.4	89.9	97.5	95.5
1967	80.6	78.5	47.9	41.2	66.1	62.7	84.0	81.2	97.5	95.5
1968	80.4	77.6	47.7	37.9	65.7	63.3	82.4	85.0	97.2	95.0
1969	80.2	76.9	48.8	37.7	66.3	63.2	82.6	84.4	97.0	94.4
1970	80.0	76.5	48.9	34.8	67.4	61.8	83.3	83.5	96.7	93.7
1971	79.6	74.9	49.3	32.4	67.8	58.9	83.2	81.5	96.3	92.9
1972	79.6	73.6	50.2	34.3	71.1	60.2	84.3	82.7	96.0	92.7
1973	79.4	73.4	52.7	32.3	72.3	61.2	85.8	83.7	96.2	91.8
1974	79.4	72.9	53.3	34.0	73.6	61.9	86.6	83.6	96.3	92.8
1975	78.7	70.9	51.8	29.8	72.8	57.2	85.5	78.7	95.8	91.6
1976	78.4	70.0	51.8	29.0	73.5	55.0	86.3	79.0	95.9	90.9
1977	78.5	70.6	53.8	30.2	74.9	58.0	86.8	79.2	96.0	90.7
1978	78.6	71.5	55.3	31.9	75.3	59.7	87.3	78.8	95.9	90.9
1979	78.6	71.3	55.3	30.7	74.5	58.1	87.6	80.7	96.0	90.8
1980	78.2	70.3	53.6	30.9	74.1	56.6	87.2	79.9	95.9	90.9
1981	77.9	70.0	51.5	29.2	73.5	55.0	87.0	79.2	95.8	88.9
1982	77.4	70.1	49.3	24.6	70.5	55.3	86.3	78.7	95.6	89.2
1983	77.1	70.6	46.9	24.7	71.3	55.0	86.1	79.4	95.2	89.0
1984	77.1	70.8	47.0	26.9	70.8	56.2	86.5	79.1	95.4	88.9
1985	77.0	70.8	48.5	29.8	71.2	60.0	86.4	79.0	95.7	88.8

[a]Before 1972, black refers to black and other nonwhite workers.
SOURCES: U.S. Department of Labor (1978, pp. 187–188; 1985, pp. 20–21); U.S. Bureau of Labor Statistics (1985, pp. 157–158; 1986, pp. 155–156).

for age 20 and above, white enrollment rates exceed black enrollment levels (Bruno, 1985, pp. 6–7).

In general, white male LFPRs show little relationship to the business cycle. For white men age 16 and above, there has been a slow decline in participation rates, from around 80–85% in the 1950s to about 77–78% in the 1980s. As there has been essentially no trend in the LFPR of white men in the 20–24 and 25–34 age ranges, the pattern for all adult men is largely a product of declines at older ages. For white male teenagers, there were modest increases in LFPRs in the 1970s, which were followed by modest declines in the 1980s. In general, the entire range of variation in LFPRs of white men has been fairly small.

The LFPRs for black men have followed a quite different historical trajectory. In the 1950s, black LFPRs were equal to or above the white rates for each age group. Since then, however, black LFPRs have fallen dramatically, especially for teenagers—the same age group with spectacular increases in unemployment rates.

In Table 3, the teenage population is separated into two groups: those aged 16–17 and 18–19. About half of high-school-age black youths (age 16–17) were in the labor force in the late 1950s. By the early 1960s, the rate had declined to about 40% and fluctuated around this figure for most of the 1960s. The LFPR of black men 16–17 years old declined slowly in the early 1970s, and then fell suddenly by 5 percentage points in 1975 and by another 5 points in 1982. With the exception of the last 2 years in the series (1984 and 1985), there has never been a "recovery" of LFPRs to previous levels. With equivalent levels of school enrollment (about 90% of those aged 16–17) for black and white youths, the explanation of the almost 20 percentage-point racial differential is not a product of the available "supply" of jobseekers (for a similar conclusion, see Freeman & Wise, 1982, p. 13). The same empirical patterns and interpretation fit the 18- to 19-year-old category. More than 40% of black men in this age group are out of the labor force, compared to less than 30% of the comparable age group of whites. This differential appeared in the late 1960s and has widened over the years, with some fluctuations.

For young men in their early twenties, the level of black labor-force participation was about equal to that of whites until the early 1970s (black rates did decline in the late 1960s, but they had been above white levels prior to that time). Then the 1975 recession produced a 1-year drop of 5 percentage points that put the black LFPR below 80%. A black–white differential of about 7 percentage points has persisted over the past decade (for the 20–24 age group). A similar differential—of 6 to 7 percentage points—exists in the LFPRs of white and black men aged 25–34. The differential emerged in the 1970s and has remained steady over the years.

The declining trend in labor force participation is a uniquely minority problem. Whereas open unemployment affects all segments of the population in a cyclical fashion, the increase of nonparticipation is not evident for white men, except at the oldest ages. For young black men, however, there have been steady declines in LFPRs, often ratcheted suddenly downward in recessionary years. Economic recovery rarely reverses the impact of a recession (for a similar finding, see Newman, 1979). Teenagers have been most affected, but there is a similar pattern, albeit less dramatic, for black men in their twenties.

DOES EDUCATION MATTER?

A frequent explanation for the deterioration of employment prospects of young minority men is that they lack skills. The implication of this interpretation is that employers do not discriminate on the basis of race but on the relevant criterion of job qualifications. This thesis can be investigated from a number of angles; here, I simply look at the links between education (attainment and enrollment) and the employment of blacks and whites. Education is assumed to be a central indicator of skill levels and job qualifications. Although the quantity and quality of schooling are different dimensions, years of schooling is probably highly correlated with other indicators that might be considered to represent the quality of schooling (see Duncan, 1969, pp. 664–670).

Table 4 presents the trend in median years of schooling of the white, black, and Hispanic male labor forces. Although not speaking directly to the question of relative employment prospects, these data show aggregate differences in educational levels over time. Basically, the trend is one of narrowing the gap in average educational attainment between majority and minority men in the labor force. In 1959, the difference in median years of schooling between black and white workers was more than 3 years. The current gap is less than a half a year of schooling between black and white men and less than a year of schooling between white and Hispanic men. In other words, as the employment situation has worsened between white and minority men, there has been a convergence in educational qualifications.

Table 5 establishes a more direct link between educational attainment and unemployment levels. These time-series data show the unemployment rate of white, black, and Hispanic workers within levels of educational attainment, but owing to the limitations of the published tabulations, unemployment rates cannot be disaggregated by age group or sex (all persons in the labor force aged 16 and above compose the population in this table).

These data show a marked change in the relative levels of black and white unemployment by educational attainment. Historically, that is, in the 1960s and early 1970s, significant black–white differences in unemployment were concentrated in the middle range of the educational ladder. In the lowest educational categories, blacks and whites had comparable unemployment rates (or only

Table 4. Median Years of Schooling
Completed by Members of the Civilian
Male Labor Force by Race and Hispanic
Origin: Selected Years, 1959–1984[a]

Year	White	Black	Hispanic
1959	11.8	8.1	—
1962	12.1	9.0	—
1964	12.2	9.7	—
1965	12.2	10.0	—
1966	12.3	10.0	—
1967	12.3	10.2	—
1968	12.3	10.7	—
1969	12.4	10.8	—
1970	12.4	11.1	—
1971	12.5	11.4	—
1972	12.4	11.5	—
1973	12.5	11.9	—
1974	12.5	12.1	10.8
1975	12.6	12.1	11.0
1976	12.6	12.2	11.3
1977	12.6	12.1	11.4
1978	12.6	12.2	11.3
1979	12.7	12.2	11.3
1980	12.7	12.3	11.7
1981	12.7	12.3	11.6
1982	12.7	12.4	12.0
1983	12.8	12.4	12.1
1984	12.8	12.4	12.0

[a]Before 1977, black refers to black and other
nonwhite workers. Before 1972, data are based
on men aged 18 and above; for 1972 and later,
data are based on men aged 16 and above.
Dashes indicate data not available.
SOURCE: U.S. Department of Labor (1985,
pp. 166–168).

modest differences). For university graduates, unemployment was a rare event for both black and white workers (although the black rate was generally above the white level). In contrast, among workers with partial or completed high school education, or with some college, black unemployment rates were considerably higher than white levels.

With the recessions of 1975 and the early 1980s, unemployment has gone up for all groups, and black–white gaps have widened considerably (in absolute and sometimes in relative terms). For white workers, only that group with less

Table 5. Unemployment Rates (in Percentages) of Workers Aged 16 and Above, by Race, Hispanic Origin, and Educational Attainment: Selected Years, 1962–1984ᵃ

| | Years of schooling | | | | | | | | | | | | | | | | | |
| | Less than 5 years | | | 5–8 years | | | 9–11 years | | | 12 years | | | 13–15 years | | | 16+ years | | |
Year	White	Black	Hispanic	White	Black	Hispanic	White	Black	Hispanic	White	Black	Hispanic	White	Black	Hispanic	White	Black	Hispanic
1962	8.0	12.6	—	—	—	—	7.2	15.3	—	4.6	12.4	—	—	—	—	—	—	—
1964	9.3	7.8	—	—	—	—	6.4	12.5	—	4.3	10.1	—	—	—	—	—	—	—
1965	7.4	7.8	—	—	—	—	6.4	13.5	—	3.7	8.2	—	—	—	—	—	—	—
1966	6.1	5.5	—	4.5	6.6	—	4.5	9.7	—	2.8	7.0	—	2.8	6.3	—	1.0	1.9	—
1967	4.4	6.3	—	4.2	6.9	—	4.6	10.6	—	2.9	6.5	—	2.5	5.8	—	0.8	1.9	—
1968	5.4	4.9	—	4.0	5.7	—	4.6	9.8	—	2.7	6.7	—	2.5	3.9	—	1.0	1.6	—
1969	3.2	2.7	—	3.6	5.0	—	4.4	7.6	—	2.6	6.4	—	2.3	4.8	—	0.9	1.2	—
1970	5.3	5.7	—	4.7	5.2	—	5.7	9.5	—	3.6	7.2	—	3.7	6.1	—	1.5	1.4	—
1971	7.2	5.2	—	6.6	8.4	—	8.1	11.8	—	5.1	8.8	—	5.4	9.0	—	2.2	3.3	—
1972	5.9	6.6	—	6.5	9.4	—	9.2	15.5	—	5.1	9.6	—	4.5	9.7	—	2.5	2.8	—
1973	4.7	3.6	6.6	6.1	7.5	6.7	8.0	13.6	10.2	4.1	8.8	6.0	3.6	8.8	5.7	2.1	2.3	5.0
1974	5.4	3.9	6.5	5.7	8.5	9.0	8.7	14.7	12.2	4.3	8.9	7.1	3.9	6.9	5.0	1.8	3.4	4.8
1975	15.2	8.6	16.5	10.9	15.8	14.2	14.0	22.0	18.4	8.4	15.2	10.5	6.6	10.1	7.9	2.8	3.9	3.6
1976	8.6	8.2	9.4	10.0	10.4	12.3	12.6	19.0	15.5	7.5	14.3	11.6	5.7	12.5	8.2	2.8	3.0	4.4
1977	8.7	12.2	10.9	9.9	12.0	11.9	12.7	20.0	17.2	6.8	14.4	10.0	5.5	12.5	8.2	3.2	5.0	5.0
1978	7.6	8.2	10.5	8.3	8.9	10.0	10.7	21.6	14.0	5.5	12.7	7.4	4.1	10.4	7.3	2.3	4.7	7.3
1979	7.5	9.1	8.2	7.4	10.3	7.0	10.9	19.6	14.6	5.0	12.6	8.2	3.8	8.8	6.5	2.1	4.2	0.5
1980	8.7	8.5	9.2	9.8	11.6	12.8	11.6	20.5	14.3	5.9	13.1	7.1	4.4	10.8	5.9	1.9	4.4	0.4
1981	10.0	11.7	11.1	11.7	13.2	14.4	13.5	24.7	17.0	7.2	16.4	9.7	4.4	11.8	6.3	2.3	4.0	2.8
1982	15.2	23.4	16.2	13.2	16.1	15.4	17.0	24.1	21.8	9.1	20.7	11.4	5.8	15.8	7.1	2.9	8.3	4.9
1983	15.1	21.8	20.6	16.1	16.2	18.6	19.0	29.5	23.9	10.3	22.8	14.4	7.0	17.3	10.9	3.4	8.5	6.8
1984	12.9	15.7	17.8	12.2	16.7	12.9	15.2	27.3	18.4	7.4	18.3	9.6	5.1	12.0	7.2	2.6	6.3	3.5

ᵃBefore 1977, black refers to black and other nonwhite workers. Before 1972, data are based on persons aged 18 and above; for 1972 and later, data are based on persons aged 16 and above. Dashes indicate data not available.
SOURCE: U.S. Department of Labor (1985, pp. 170–171).

than a high school education has experienced double-digit unemployment rates. For black workers, this level has been reached by high school graduates and even those with some college. Black college graduates have also experienced record unemployment rates—generally more than double white rates. Differences in educational attainment cannot account for the widening gaps in unemployment between black and white workers (for a similar conclusion, see U.S. Commission on Civil Rights, 1982, p. 43).

Finally, the question of the link between educational enrollment and labor force participation is addressed in Table 6. This table compares the LFPRs of white, black, and Hispanic men in three young age groups (16–17, 18–19, 20–24) distinguished by enrollment status. A cross-tabulation of both characteristics allows us to consider how much of the trend towards "dropping out" of the labor force is independent of change in enrollment levels.

First, let us consider those currently enrolled in school. High-school-age (ages 16–17) enrolled white men exhibit an erratic labor-force participation trend, which first rose during the 1970s (to a high of around 50%) and then declined in the 1980s. For black high-school-age students, labor force participation declined in the 1960s, picked up a bit in the early 1970s, then plummeted with the 1975 recession. Another upturn occurred during the recovery of the late 1970s, followed by a downturn slide with the deep recession of the early 1980s. In 1983, a black high school student was three times less likely to be in the labor force than a white student.

For the white students aged 18–19 and 20–24, there have been moderate rises in LFPRs over the last two decades; about half of these students were in the labor force in 1983. These rates may be affected by the omission in the CPS of college students who live in institutional settings (dormitories). Few effects of recession years are evident for white students. Overall, black students in these same ages have experienced a net decline of about 10 percentage points over the same period, although there were fairly wide year-to-year fluctuations. In terms of black–white LFP differentials, the gap for 18- and 19-year-old students is very wide (almost 2 to 1 in 1983), but is only about 10 points for students aged 20–24. It is more difficult to discern a clear picture of the LFPRs of Hispanic students, not only because of the volatile trend (perhaps due to a small sample base), but also because of the ethnic heterogeneity of this population. In general, the LFPRs of Hispanic students have declined, but not as much as those of black students. For the teenage years, the LFPRs of Hispanic students are below whites. But for the 20–24 age category, Hispanic students have the highest rate of labor force participation. Hispanic students, like black students, are much more vulnerable than are white students to a sudden downturn in labor force participation during a recession.

Among the nonenrolled youth, there are too few cases of black and Hispanic 16- and 17-year-olds to be tabulated; hence our comparisons are limited to

Table 6. Labor Force Participation Rates of Men by Race, Hispanic Origin, and School Enrollment: Selected Age Groups, 1964–1983

| | Enrolled — Ages 16–17 | | | Enrolled — Ages 18–19 | | | Enrolled — Ages 20–24 | | | Not enrolled — Ages 16–17 | | | Not enrolled — Ages 18–19 | | | Not enrolled — Ages 20–24 | | |
Year	White	Black	Hispanic	White	Black	Hispanic	White	Black	Hispanic	White	Black	Hispanic	White	Black	Hispanic	White	Black	Hispanic
1964	32.8	30.4	—a	35.7	38.9	—	47.3	—	—	74.9	—	—	92.3	90.2	—	96.9	94.3	—
1965	38.0	31.1	—	36.6	32.0	—	49.2	—	—	81.2	—	—	91.2	91.4	—	96.4	95.7	—
1966	39.9	28.9	—	38.9	25.0	—	46.6	—	—	76.4	—	—	89.2	84.9	—	98.0	96.1	—
1967	41.8	35.0	—	41.3	31.3	—	49.0	55.8	—	75.6	—	—	87.8	88.3	—	96.9	92.8	—
1968	41.1	27.8	—	43.6	37.4	—	52.0	39.7	—	74.5	—	—	88.0	86.7	—	94.3	93.4	—
1969	42.6	28.5	—	43.6	42.7	—	52.3	45.1	—	78.4	—	—	89.4	82.2	—	95.3	94.8	—
1970	41.1	23.9	—	42.3	31.5	—	52.1	41.3	—	79.9	—	—	88.9	75.7	—	95.3	90.5	—
1971	42.8	23.2	—	44.1	36.0	—	53.8	39.0	—	77.1	—	—	88.9	86.9	—	94.5	91.0	—
1972	43.5	19.1	33.9	47.1	43.3	3.1	53.2	53.2	—	76.1	—	—	91.1	81.5	91.2	95.6	90.5	96.0
1973	47.9	21.8	32.1	47.7	30.6	55.7	55.3	50.0	—	79.5	—	—	90.3	88.1	87.3	95.1	90.5	92.0
1974	46.3	26.8	31.9	46.1	35.0	50.5	56.4	50.7	68.1	79.1	—	—	90.2	87.3	89.1	95.9	91.7	91.0
1975	46.0	16.9	30.3	43.8	32.2	45.8	52.0	44.5	56.7	77.2	—	—	92.7	81.6	92.9	94.9	84.9	91.7
1976	46.4	22.8	32.9	46.8	35.8	45.0	56.7	49.2	60.6	76.1	—	—	90.9	75.8	88.6	95.6	84.3	91.9
1977	49.9	22.8	35.8	48.2	38.7	62.1	55.8	40.6	51.5	77.3	—	—	93.3	82.6	92.0	95.7	88.7	95.7
1978	50.7	24.2	39.5	51.2	33.1	54.2	57.8	37.6	72.9	73.4	—	—	94.0	80.1	94.1	95.6	88.6	94.5
1979	50.4	21.8	30.2	45.0	28.9	41.6	58.6	53.9	67.6	72.6	—	—	91.3	81.2	94.0	95.5	87.7	94.5
1980	47.5	25.8	31.2	48.2	32.3	51.7	56.4	47.5	70.7	74.9	—	—	91.7	75.0	87.0	95.2	86.8	92.2
1981	47.1	18.0	34.9	47.7	28.8	31.1	56.1	50.2	60.7	73.9	—	—	90.9	74.9	89.7	95.0	86.2	92.4
1982	42.7	18.5	22.9	46.1	29.4	32.2	57.6	53.0	61.2	76.6	—	—	87.6	71.4	84.2	94.6	86.5	90.0
1983	40.0	13.6	22.5	50.0	26.7	40.7	57.2	46.2	62.4	63.5	—	—	89.2	72.2	93.3	94.6	84.1	93.1

aBefore 1972, black refers to black and other nonwhite workers. Dashes indicate data not available.

SOURCE: U.S. Department of Labor (1985, pp. 141–143).

nonstudents aged 18–19 and 20–24. For men in these populations, nonparticipation in the labor force does indicate a phenomenon of real concern. For whites and Hispanics, upwards of 90% of nonenrolled young men are in the labor force. There are year-to-year fluctuations, but little sign of a trend. This is not the case for young black men, whose participation rates began to edge downward in the 1960s, especially among 18- and 19-year-olds. But the 1975 recession was a turning point; black rates declined and experienced only a modest recovery before the recession of the 1980s hit again. In 1983, over a quarter of black nonenrolled men aged 18–19 were not in the labor force, and more than 15% of the 20–24 age category were in a similar position.

These figures of "hidden" unemployment are on top of the record levels of unemployment reported earlier. And these data are conservative estimates of the situation because those missed in the CPS (the undercount) are even more likely to be marginal to the labor force.

CONCLUSIONS

The employment problem is not unique to minorities. In absolute numbers, there are many more unsuccessful white than minority jobseekers. But in relative terms, the proportion of minority workers afflicted is much greater. The peak rates of unemployment and labor force nonparticipation among black men resemble conditions at the depth of the Great Depression. To use a medical analogy, the extent of joblessness among young black men can be considered a social epidemic. Similar to the physiological process of one illness leading to other diseases, the lack of decent jobs often leads to other social pathologies. Poverty, poor housing, children without resident fathers, and the hustling of illicit goods are some of the related problems that tear at the social fabric of minority communities.

Is joblessness of young men really the source of this tangled web of problems? Although I have no new evidence on the social epidemiology of unemployment, family formation, and low incomes, the analysis of Elliot Liebow (1967) in *Tally's Corner* provides a convincing interpretation that joblessness is the key causal factor. The question of joblessness is of particular significance, as some researchers have pointed to the narrowing black–white earnings gap among employed workers (Smith & Welch, 1986) as a harbinger of black progress in the American economy. However, this trend of "success" for employed black workers has paralleled a trend in the deterioration of economic and social conditions for minority men at the bottom of the hierarchy—a finding that reinforces the "polarization" thesis of William Julius Wilson (1980) and others (see Farley, 1984, pp. 9–10).

There are several angles from which to view the problem of unemployment.

Most arresting is the cyclical problem that seems to be in an upward spiral. In the 1960s, economists spoke of economic fine-tuning and the end of the periodic boom-and-bust of an uncontrolled market economy. Then came the troubled 1970s, with a fairly modest recession at the beginning of the decade, followed by the 1975 recession, which broke all the standard yardsticks of labor market failure for the post–World War II era. Most recently, the 1982–1983 recession made the 1975 downswing look modest in comparison. There is little current talk of economic fine-tuning or of returning to an era of stable low unemployment.

The second dimension of the unemployment crisis is the secular drift upward in unemployment rates through good and bad times. Each peak is higher than the last and "recoveries" are never quite complete. To be sure, this interpretation of a long-term trend rests on the experiences of the 1970s and 1980s, not of the 1950s and 1960s. Another critical element of growing unemployment is the rise of labor force nonparticipation among young minority men. Although most concentrated among the teenage years, this pattern has spread into the ranks of men in their twenties. This dimension of joblessness is "hidden" because persons out of the labor force are not counted as unemployed.

Although white men have not escaped either the cyclical or secular patterns of rising unemployment, their levels are modest compared to Hispanic and most especially to black men. Not only do black men have unemployment rates twice (or greater) that of white men, but the problem of labor force nonparticipation is entirely a minority phenomenon.

Explaining the widening differential between white and black men is more difficult than documenting it. There does not appear to be any evidence for the thesis that black youths are unwilling to accept menial work (Borus, 1982). Nor are the patterns explained by educational attainment or by changing levels of school enrollment. As employment prospects have widened since the mid-1960s, educational credentials have converged between black and white men in the labor force. More education is associated with lower unemployment, but black unemployment rates are higher at every educational level. Nor do differences in school enrollment appear to be the answer. Unemployment rates and levels of nonparticipation have risen for black students and also for black youths who are not enrolled in school.

The looming question, then, is what *does* explain the intertemporal differences in nonparticipation among minority men. A potential explanation resides in the influence of economic growth on overall employment opportunities. Management of the economy as seen from the corporate boardroom or government offices may appear to be color-blind. However, the data presented here show that black workers are more vulnerable to cyclical downturns than white workers, hence the consequences of economic decline are disproportionately borne by minorities, especially black men. More to the point, if aggregate economic growth has limited the employment prospects for all men, it is not readily evident why black men have been more affected by cyclical fluctuations.

An alternative explanation for the increasing levels of nonparticipation among blacks is that changes in the locational distribution of employment opportunities have concentrated joblessness among minority men. This interpretation, first put forth by John Kain (1968) and more recently discussed by John Kasarda (1986) and William Julius Wilson (1987) (see Chapters 9 and 10 in this volume), certainly deserves careful empirical scrutiny. Are black workers concentrated in jobs or locations that limit their employment opportunities or put them at greater risk when the economy turns sour? (See Kain, 1968; Straszheim, 1980.) Or do employers selectively hire white workers if they can no longer hire minority workers for a lower wage (Shapiro, 1984)? Or do our black workers lack the social networks that could help locate good jobs? The research literature does not provide conclusive findings. But answering these questions must become a priority on the agenda for researchers and for policymakers who seek to cure the epidemic of minority joblessness.

APPENDIX

The Labor Force Concept and the Measurement of Joblessness

The definitions of employment and unemployment are subject to considerable confusion and debate. Part of the confusion arises from a lack of awareness of the important distinction between unemployment and nonparticipation in the labor force. To be counted as unemployed, individuals without work must be actively seeking a job. To merely want a job, without actually searching for one, leaves a person in the "out of the labor force" category.

In spite of considerable debate, most evaluations have reaffirmed the basic labor force concept and the standard indicators of employment and unemployment (National Commission on Employment and Unemployment Statistics, 1979). Since the 1940s, the U.S. Department of Labor and the Bureau of the Census have utilized a set of standard procedures to measure labor force activity through household surveys (Hauser, 1949; U.S. Bureau of the Census, 1976). Basically, in response to a question on activity during the previous week (7 days), individuals are sorted into the economically active population (the labor force) or economically inactive population (out of the labor force). The labor force consists of those working or seeking work (employed and unemployed). Employment is defined by work for pay or profit (of marketable goods or services) for at least 1 hour during the preceding week. This rather minimalist definition of employment helps to ensure a conservative estimate of labor underutilization (Bancroft, 1958, Appendix C).

The unemployment category includes only those who are not employed and have made active efforts to seek work in the last 4 weeks. In addition to wage and salary workers and the self-employed, the employed category includes unpaid persons working for at least 15 hours in a family enterprise, and persons who have jobs, but did not work last week because of vacation, illness, a labor–management dispute, bad weather, or other personal reasons (Wolfbein, 1964, p. 20). On the other side, the unemployment category includes persons who did not seek work because they were temporarily laid off or were waiting to begin a new job in the next 30 days.

A simple tree diagram of the standard labor-force categories is shown for men and women in Figure A. The population counts (in thousands) are from the 1980 census, and are percentaged on the base of the immediately preceding category (the one to the left). Three-quarters of men, but only half of women, were in the labor force in 1980. For men, especially young men, service in the armed forces is an important option (1.5 million men were in the armed forces in 1980). As military service represents a withdrawal from the conventional labor market, almost all research focuses on the civilian labor force. This tendency is reinforced with reliance on the CPS for most labor force analyses. As mentioned in the text, the CPS universe is limited to the household population, which excludes members of the armed forces living on military bases.

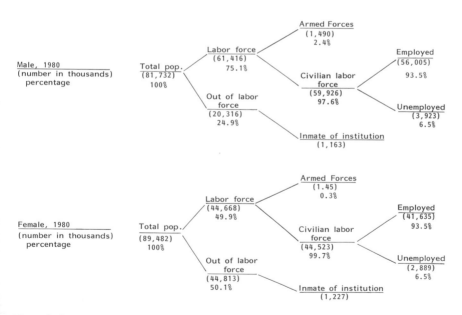

Figure A. Standard labor force classifications, men and women aged 16 and over, 1980. SOURCE: U.S. Bureau of the Census (1983, p. 26).

The "out of the labor force" population is a composite of persons in a variety of nonremunerative roles, such as student, homemaker, and retiree. Inmates of institutions (i.e., homes, schools, hospitals or wards for the mentally handicapped; hospitals or wards for chronic-disease patients; nursing or rest homes for the aged, and correctional institutions) are also a small segment of the "out of the labor force" population. For adult women, homemaking and child care responsibilities have traditionally represented alternatives to formal labor force participation. This is one reason why the study of women's labor force activities is more complicated than that of men. Only those in the labor force are eligible to be employed or unemployed. In 1980, the unemployment rate was 6.5% of the civilian labor force for both men and women. Sometimes there are

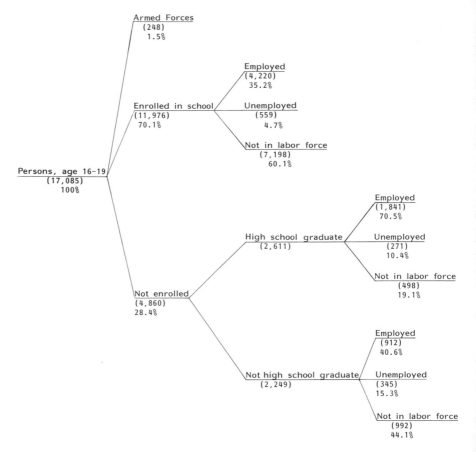

Figure B. School enrollment, labor force activity, and high school graduation status of youth aged 16–19, 1980. SOURCE: U.S. Bureau of the Census (1983, p. 71).

efforts to count the "passive unemployed"—those who have given up on searching for work because they believe there are no available opportunities (Finegan, 1979). But the passive unemployed are not included in the standard measures of the labor force or unemployment.

Another issue of some confusion is the joint relationship between school enrollment and labor force activity. Although the student and worker roles are generally thought to be mutually exclusive, there is, in fact, considerable overlap. Figure B shows a tree diagram of enrollment status and labor force activity for the population (both sexes) aged 16 to 19—the age range of the highest overlap. For this age group in 1980, 70% were still in school (either high school or college), whereas 28% were not enrolled; the balance was in the armed forces. Of enrolled youth, three-fifths were out of the labor force, presumably engaged in full-time study, but over one-third of students were also working in paid employment. Nonstudents are divided into two categories: high school graduates (or higher), and non–high school graduates (dropouts). These two groups—of approximately equal size—have quite different labor market experiences. More than 70% of nonenrolled high school graduates were employed (the balance was unemployed or out of the labor force), whereas only 40% of the high-school dropouts were employed.

Those who were not enrolled, not working, and not looking for work present an anomaly for labor force analysis. Typically, this population is excluded from most studies because they are "out of the labor force." But the increase of labor force nonparticipation among young minority men is a topic of growing significance.

ACKNOWLEDGMENTS

For their critical comments on an earlier version of this paper, I thank Avery Guest, Ronald G. Ehrenberg, Edward P. Lazear, and Jonathan Leonard.

REFERENCES

Bancroft, G. (1958). *The American labor force.* New York: John Wiley.

Borus, M. (1982). Willingness to work among youth. *Journal of Human Resources, 17,* 581–593.

Bowers, N. (1979). Young and marginal: An overview of youth employment. *Monthly Labor Review, 102* (October), 4–16.

Bruno, R. (1985). *School enrollment: Social and economic characteristics of students: October 1981 and 1980.* Current Population Reports, Series P-20, No. 400. Washington, DC: GPO.

Citro, C. F., & M. L. Cohen, Eds. (1985). *The bicentennial census: New directions for methodology in 1990.* Washington, DC: National Academy Press.

Duncan, B. (1969). Trends in output and distribution of schooling. In E. B. Sheldon and W. E. Moore, Eds. *Indicators of social change: Concepts and measurements.* New York: Russell Sage.

Ehrenberg, R. G. (1980). The demographic structure of unemployment rates and labor market transition probabilities. In R. G. Ehrenberg, Ed. *Research in labor economics* (Vol. 3). Greenwich, CT: JAI Press.

Farley, R. (1984). *Blacks and whites: Narrowing the gap.* Cambridge: Harvard University Press.

Finegan, T. (1979). The measurement, behavior, and classification of discouraged workers. In National Commission on Employment and Unemployment Statistics, Eds. *Counting the Labor Force: Concepts and Data Needs* (Vol. 1). Washington, DC: GPO.

Freeman, R. B., & H. J. Holzer, Eds. (1986). *The black youth employment crisis.* Chicago: University of Chicago Press.

Freeman, R. B., & D. Wise, Eds. (1982). *The youth labor market problem.* Chicago: University of Chicago Press.

Hauser, P. M. (1949). The labor force concept and gainful workers—Concept, measurement, and comparability. *American Journal of Sociology, 54,* 338–355.

Kain, J. (1968). Housing segregation, Negro employment and metropolitan decentralization. *Quarterly Journal of Economics, 82,* 175–197.

Kasarda, J. D. (1980). The implications of contemporary distribution trends for national urban policy. *Social Science Quarterly, 61,* 373–400.

Lichter, D. T. (1988). Blacks and whites: Narrowing the unemployment gap in U.S. cities. *American Journal of Sociology,* in press.

Liebow, E. (1967). *Tally's corner: A study of Negro streetcorner men.* Boston: Little, Brown.

Mare, R. & C. Winship. (1984). The paradox of lessening racial inequality and joblessness among black youth: Enrollment, enlistment, and employment, 1964–1981. *American Sociological Review, 49,* 39–55.

Mare, R., C. Winship, & W. N. Kubitschek. (1984). The transition from youth to adult: Understanding the age pattern of employment. *American Journal of Sociology, 90,* 326–358.

National Commission on Employment and Unemployment Statistics. (1979). *Counting the labor force.* Washington, DC: U.S. Government Printing Office.

Newman, M. J. (1979). The labor market experience of black youth. *Monthly Labor Review, 102* (October), 19–27.

O'Neill, D. M. (1983). Racial trends in teenage unemployment. *Journal of Human Resources, 18,* 295–305.

Passel, J., & J. G. Robinson. (1984). Revised estimates of the population in the 1980 census based on demographic analysis. In *American Statistical Association, 1984 proceedings of the section of social statistics.* Washington, DC: American Statistical Association.

Plotnick, R. D., & F. Skidmore. (1975). *Progress against poverty: A review of the 1964–1974 decade.* New York: Academic Press.

Rees, A. (1986). An essay on youth joblessness. *Journal of Economic Literature, 24,* 613–618.

Ross, A. M., & H. Hill, Eds. (1967). *Employment, race, and poverty.* New York: Harcourt, Brace, and World.

Shapiro, D. (1984). Wage differentials among black, Hispanic, and white young men. *Industrial and Labor Relations Review, 37,* 570–581.

Siegel, J. S. (1974). Estimates of coverage of the population by sex, race, and age in the 1970 census. *Demography, 11,* 1–23.

Smith, J. P., & F. R. Welch. (1986). *Closing the gap: Forty years of economic progress for blacks.* R-3330-DOL. Santa Monica, CA: Rand Corporation.

Smith, S. J. (1986). *Worklife estimates: Effects of race and education.* Bulletin 2254. Washington, DC: Bureau of Labor Statistics, U.S. Department of Labor.

Straszheim, M. R. 1980. Discrimination and the spatial characteristics of urban labor markets for black workers. *Journal of Urban Economics, 7,* 119–140.

U.S. Bureau of the Census. (1976). *Concepts and methods used in labor force statistics derived from the current population survey.* Current Population Reports, Series P-23, No. 62. Washington, DC: U.S. Government Printing Office.

U.S. Bureau of the Census. (1983). *1980 census of the population, Vol. 1: Characteristics of the population.* (No. PC80-1-C1). Washington, DC: U.S. Government Printing Office.

U.S. Bureau of Labor Statistics. (1985). *Employment and Earnings, 32*(1).

U.S. Bureau of Labor Statistics. (1986). *Employment and Earnings, 33*(1).

U.S. Commission on Civil Rights. (1982). *Unemployment among blacks, Hispanics, and women.* Washington, DC: U.S. Commission on Civil Rights.

U.S. Department of Labor. (1978). *Employment and training report of the President.* Washington, DC: U.S. Government Printing Office.

U.S. Department of Labor. (1982). *Labor force statistics derived from the current population survey: A databook* (Vol. 1, Bulletin 2096). Washington, DC: U.S. Government Printing Office.

U.S. Department of Labor. (1985). *Handbook of labor statistics.* (Bulletin 2217). Washington, DC: U.S. Government Printing Office.

Wilson, W. J. (1980). *The declining significance of race: Blacks and changing American institutions* (2nd Ed.). Chicago: University of Chicago Press.

Wilson, W. J. (1987). *The truly disadvantaged: The inner city, the underclass, and public policy.* Chicago: University of Chicago Press.

Wilson, W. J., & R. Aponte. (1985). Urban poverty. *Annual Review of Sociology,* 11, 231–258.

Wolfbein, S. (1964). *Employment and unemployment in the United States.* Chicago: Science Research Associates.

4

Minorities and Homelessness

Peter H. Rossi

Homelessness is a manifestation of extreme poverty that particularly affects poor persons who are not members of family households. As minorities make up more than their proportionate share of the extremely poor, we can also expect that homelessness will also affect minorities to much the same disproportionate extent as does poverty. This paper will review the existing empirical evidence about homelessness and minority status, drawing heavily on a recently completed intensive survey of homeless persons in Chicago.[1]

HOMELESSNESS IN AMERICA

Since the early 1980s, the plight of homeless persons in America has been given a great deal of attention in the media[2] and in our major legislative bodies. There are many good reasons for this heightened attention, among which the most important are the undeniably dreadful living conditions of the homeless and the correspondingly high level of public sympathy for those living under such conditions of deep privation. In a nation that pays so much attention to its housing and devotes so large a portion of personal income to housing and its accoutrements, it is appalling to realize that some persons do not have *any* place of their own in which to carry on the usual comforting domestic routines and to take their nightly rest. Homelessness evokes both sympathy for the obvious suffering involved and a sense of outrage at whatever and whoever has allowed this condition to happen.

---

[1]A full report of the study is contained in Rossi, Fisher, and Willis (1986).

[2]The rather sudden welling up of concern can be indexed by the number of listings under "homelessness" in the *Reader's Guide to Periodical Literature*. In 1975, there were no listings; in 1981, 3; in 1982, 15; in 1983, 21; and in 1984, 32.

PETER H. ROSSI • Social and Demographic Research Institute, University of Massachusetts, Amherst, Massachusetts.

Although the shame that widespread homelessness can and does exist in our society worries all who have the least shred of conscience, the prevalence of this condition, the factors that produce it, and the remedies that should be applied are not at all clear and obvious. In short, the problem of homelessness, although clearly present at unacceptable levels, is only dimly and imprecisely known.

An important issue is the extent to which homelessness is a manifestation of one or another of a variety of social and personal problems. Is homelessness primarily a problem of poverty, a housing problem, an employment problem, a condition created by deinstitutionalization, a manifestation of the breakdown of family life, a symptom of the inadequacies of our public welfare system, or primarily a manifestation of any of the myriad other social problems that currently worry our society? The important point, of course, is not which of these explanations is the "correct" one. There is some evidence that each of them is true to a degree. The more important question is, "to what specific degree?" In other words, how much of the current problem of homelessness in America can be attributed to each of the many causal factors?

Estimates of the total size of the homeless population in the country vary from about a quarter million to upwards of 3 million (Cuomo, 1983; U.S. Department of Housing and Urban Development, 1984). Similarly wide variations exist in the estimate of the homeless populations of cities and states.

Although some attention has been paid to the composition characteristics of the homeless population, by and large such studies have been based on partial coverage of the homeless. Nevertheless, all empirical studies show that minority groups are strongly overrepresented, in part reflecting the characteristic ethnic composition of the city being studied. In New York, blacks and Puerto Ricans constitute more than a plurality of the homeless in shelters. In places like Phoenix, Arizona, Hispanics predominate. Although minorities are overrepresented among the homeless compared to their share of the total population, it is not at all clear whether that overrepresentation would also be apparent if the comparison were made to the composition of the extremely poor. In other words, an important issue is whether the ethnic composition of the poor represents the economic condition of minorities or whether minorities *per se* are especially selected into the homeless state.

Definitions of Homelessness

Even the very definition of the condition of homelessness itself has yet to be widely agreed upon (Baxter & Hooper, 1981; Crystal, Goldstein, & Leavitt, 1982). Homelessness is not an all-or-none binary condition, but a continuum. Consequently, it is easy to achieve agreement on the extremes of the range from homed to homelessness, but there is much disagreement on where the boundary between the homed and the homeless should be placed. A very general definition on which there is some consensus defines homelessness as a condition that describes persons who do not have customary and regular access to a conventional dwelling, mainly those who are members of households that do not rent or own a conventional dwelling.[3] Thus, persons found sleeping in abandoned buildings and who do not have an apartment or house they could go to are clearly homeless. At the other extreme, persons in households who own their own homes are clearly homed. But there are many instances between these extremes around which disagreement may arise.

The ambiguities of homelessness center on two critical components of the definition given above, namely: (a) what defines a *conventional dwelling unit,* and (b) what defines *customary and regular access.* Conventional dwellings surely include apartments, houses, and mobile homes that are parked in a mobile home park. But does the concept of conventional dwelling unit include hotel rooms, especially in so-called SROs (single-room-only hotels), rented rooms in private dwellings, beds in dormitory-like accommodations, vans, tents, or shacks made of scrap materials? Similarly, questions can arise over the interpretation of the term *customary and regular access.* Someone who owns her or his own home has customary access to that place, as does someone who is currently a member of that household. But is someone homed or homeless who has been given temporary permission to share a conventional dwelling by its owner? And, what period of time constitutes "temporary?" For example, if a divorcing adult child is offered temporary shelter by his or her parents, "for as long as you like," does that constitute being homed or being homeless? In a sense, all these ambiguous cases are ones in which there is an element of homelessness in that the persons involved do not have a conventional dwelling to which they can consistently and regularly go. At the same time, such persons are also homed in the sense of having shelter of some sorts for at least a time.

Additional ambiguities are easily encountered. For example, some of the shelters for the homeless ask for small payments from persons applying for shelter, but usually forego payment if the homeless person cannot pay the fee. Does that payment constitute rent? If so, should paying occupants still be considered homeless? Comparable ambiguities arise concerning persons who are in other institutional settings: Should general hospital patients who do not have conventional dwelling arrangements to return to be considered homeless? Or, the inmates of jails and prisons in comparable circumstances?

These definitional ambiguities are not simply scholastic issues. First, important social-policy issues are involved, among which the most important concerns what should constitute the floor of housing adequacy and decency

---

[3]Including single-person households.

below which no member of our society should be permitted to sink without being offered some better alternative.[4] If we set the standard that every household—including one-person households—should be able to live in an apartment or house of their own, then the definition of homelessness is enlarged to include many of the ambiguous instances listed above.[5] If we accept a lower standard, which includes as adequate housing, doubling-up, or single-room hotel accommodations, then the definition of homelessness is narrowed.

Second, the amount and extent of homelessness is enlarged or limited according to whether one advocates a more generous or a less generous standard of housing adequacy. Much of the controversy concerning the size of the American homeless population is fueled by differences in this definition. The well-publicized and highly controversial 1984 report of the U.S. Department of Housing and Urban Development, containing national estimates of between 250,000 and 500,000, is based on a definition of homelessness that includes only persons in shelters or living out on the streets, in contrast to the much larger national estimates advanced by the advocates of the homeless who claim 2.5 to 3 million, using a much more generous definition of homelessness.[6] The current controversy[7] surrounding the estimates of the Chicago homeless population published by my associates and myself (Rossi, Fisher, & Willis, 1986) is also focused in large part on definitional issues.

In dealing with these definitional problems, we have found it useful to distinguish between (a) the literal homeless, persons who clearly do not have access to a conventional dwelling and who would be homeless by any conceivable definition of the term, and (b) the precariously (or marginally) housed, persons with tenuous or very temporary claims to a conventional dwelling of more or less marginal adequacy. This distinction, of course, does not solve the definitional problem, although it does more clearly specify subpopulations of likely policy interest. The Chicago Homeless Study data reported in this paper refer to the literal homeless of the city of Chicago, that subset of the ill-housed

[4]Note that the emphasis in this statement is on "being offered" better housing opportunities, ruling out the alternative of coercing persons to accept such opportunities.

[5]In Initiative 17, passed (November, 1984) in the District of Columbia, the principle was advanced that every person in the District was entitled to housing, expressing in that form a very generous definition of adequate housing. The initiative was subsequently struck down in the federal court in 1985.

[6]It is not entirely clear what definition of homelessness is used by the advocates, although it is clear that this definition covers doubled-up families, temporarily homed persons, and persons living in rented rooms.

[7]Our surveys support an estimate of a nightly average of approximately 2,700 homeless persons and an annual prevalence of about 7,000 homeless persons, whereas "guesstimates" of local experts on homelessness in Chicago are from 10,000 to 25,000. This extremely wide discrepancy is generated, we believe, largely by differences in the definitions of homelessness involved in the test sets of estimates, as well as the greater amounts of uncertainty surrounding "guesstimates."

poor who are the most seriously in need and whose conditions most closely approximate the common, public understanding of "who is homeless."

The choice of this literal homelessness as the operational definition for the Chicago study was not intended to deny either the importance or the extent of the precariously homed, but was governed primarily by logistic reasons. More inclusive definitions of homelessness move inexorably toward including most, if not all, of the bottom layers of the poor, whether homed or not, leading to operational definitions that enlarge the scope of corresponding empirical research beyond what can reasonably be accomplished with always scarce resources. Indeed, most actual empirically based attempts to estimate the homeless through direct counts have been restricted operationally to persons living on the streets (or in public places) and in shelters for the homeless, whatever the nominal definition of homelessness.[8] The logistics of counting those temporarily housed and doubled-up imply research efforts that are too expensive to accomplish.[9] It is operationally far easier to count only persons housed in shelters and persons living on the streets or in public places than to implement operationally a definition that includes doubled-up families and residents in SROs. The consequence is that empirically based estimates of the homeless tend to focus on those literally homeless, and therefore to produce lower estimates.

CHARACTERISTICS OF PERSONS LITERALLY HOMELESS

Considerable insight into literal homelessness can be gained by considering the social characteristics of literally homeless persons as shown in empirical research.

The Data Base

Almost all of the data to be presented in this section come from a recent set of surveys conducted in 1985 and 1986 on the homeless of Chicago (Rossi, Fisher, & Willis, 1986). The data derive from two probability samples of literally homeless persons taken in the fall of 1985 and winter of 1986, each con-

---

[8]For example, an attempt to count all the homeless in Nashville, Tennessee, used the following nominal definition of homelessness: homelessness included people who literally had no "roof over one's head" as well as the more encompassing definition, "homelessness was diminished safety, comfort, and privacy—a social disaffliction" (Wiegard, 1985, p. 35). The operational definition of homelessness employed in the enumeration consisted of all persons out on the streets, in public places or in shelters between the hours of 3:30 a.m. and 6 a.m.

[9]In order to enumerate the doubled-up population, it would be necessary to sample dwelling units, locating those inhabited by two or more households. This would require an extensive survey, as doubled-up households can be expected to be a relatively rare occurrence.

stituting unbiased samples of shelter residents and of homeless persons found in public places, abandoned buildings, living on the streets, hallways, and so on.[10] In addition, we will consider findings from other empirically based studies, noting whenever such studies report findings that differ substantially from the Chicago patterns.

Although the term *literally homeless* denotes with some precision the population with which the Chicago study is mainly concerned, it is not without some linguistic clumsiness. Thus, when referring to the subjects of the Chicago study, we will often use the term *homeless* with the understanding that its empirical referent is the literally homeless.

A Collective Portrait of the Homeless

There are four overall distinctive characteristics of the homeless: First, Chicago's minorities are heavily overrepresented among the homeless. This overrepresentation is particularly striking for blacks and Native Americans. Literal homelessness, however, is a leveling condition: Among the homeless there are few striking racial or ethnic differences.

Second, the homeless are extremely poor, with income levels close to zero. Correspondingly, their ties to the labor market are either nonexistent or within the lowest levels of the occupational hierarchy. Neither have the homeless managed to connect effectively with the income transfer programs of the public welfare system.

Third, the homeless are also family-less. Most are single-person "households," consisting of persons who have either never married or whose former marriages have long since broken. Although most have family and other relatives, these kinship ties are currently tenuous. In addition, there is considerable evidence that they have been rejected by their families or vice versa.[11] It is also consistent with this familyless pattern that the overwhelming majority of the homeless are men. In general, the homeless come close to being social isolates, having few ties with either relatives or friends.

Fourth, the homeless are characterized by high levels of disability. Large proportions are physically ill, show signs of mental illness, and signs of present

---

[10]The surveys were undertaken by (a) sampling all shelters for the homeless in Chicago, interviewing a systematic sample of persons resident in the shelters chosen; and (b) searching blocks selected in a stratified probability samples of blocks, entering all places to which access was possible, and screening all persons encountered for homelessness. Shelter surveys were conducted at hours when the shelters had closed for the night. Street surveys were conducted between midnight and 6 a.m. to make screening more efficient.

[11]Family is defined here as parents, siblings, spouses (current and previous) and children.

or former alcoholism. Correspondingly, large proportions have been institutionalized or have been in jail or prison.

The overall characteristics of the homeless, as described above, cannot be fully appreciated without considering specific details, as shown in the next sections of this chapter.

Race and Ethnicity

The self-reported racial/ethnic compositions of the Chicago homeless are shown in Table 1, as well as the 1980 census distributions.[12] It appears that almost all racial and ethnic groups are represented among the homeless, but some are overrepresented compared to their presence in the general population. Blacks constitute about one-third of the 1980 Chicago census population, but slightly more than half (53%) of either the shelter or street populations. (If we add to that percentage those who consider themselves to be black Hispanics, the proportion black goes up slightly, to 54%.)

Perhaps the ethnic/racial group most overrepresented among the homeless is American Indians, who constitute 7.1% of the street, 3.5% of the shelter samples, and 5.1% of the total homeless, but only 0.1% of the Chicago census population.[13]

About one in three of the homeless are whites (29% of the street and 32% of the shelter samples), indicating that whites are underrepresented among the homeless as compared to their proportion (55%) in the general adult population. Also underrepresented among the homeless are the 7% who are Hispanics, as compared to the 14% reported in the 1980 Chicago census.

It should be noted that there are no significant differences between the shelter sample and the street sample with respect to ethnicity, although it does appear that American Indians are particularly numerous in the street sample and Hispanics appear to be particularly numerous in the shelter sample.

Nor are there many striking differences in the demographic compositions of the ethnic components of the literal homeless, as Table 2 shows. Three out of four are men. Only Native Americans deviate strongly from that gender pattern, about half being from each gender group. The homeless cluster around age 40,

---

[12]Respondents were read a list of ethnic/racial categories and asked which one of the groups on the list they considered themselves to be. The list read to them corresponds to the categories in Table 1. In addition, interviewers also rated the race/ethnicity of each respondent, with high agreement between the self-reports and the interviews' reports (gamma = .89).

[13]Overrepresentation of American Indians among the homeless was found in both fall, 1985 and winter, 1986 surveys, leading to greater confidence in the findings concerning the degree to which Native Americans are overrepresented. Nevertheless, the small numbers involved clearly suggest caution in interpreting these findings.

Table 1. Racial and Ethnic Comparison of the Homeless
Samples and the 1980 Chicago Population (Percentages)

Race or ethnicity	Street sample	Shelter sample	Weighted total	1980 Chicago census
Total Hispanic	4.0	9.3	6.9	14.0[a]
Hispanic white	3.0	7.5	5.5	—[a]
Hispanic black	1.0	1.8	1.4	—[a]
Black American	55.6	50.8	53.0	35.5
American Indian	7.1	3.5	5.1	0.1
Asian or Pacific	1.0	0.4	0.7	2.3
White	28.9	32.1	30.7	55.1
Other	3.3	3.4	3.3	7.0
Don't know	0.0	0.5	0.3	—
Unweighted number	(165)	(557)	(722)	

[a]The U.S. Census does not provide separate counts of white and black
Hispanics. The Hispanic proportion shown in the census counts over-
laps with the other groups shown.

with an underrepresentation of the very young and the very old adults (compared
to the Chicago adult population). However, there are some departures from the
average age of 40: Whites tend to be somewhat older (average, 45 years) and
Hispanics considerably younger (average, 33 years).

The homeless are strikingly different from the general adult population of
comparable ages in their current marital status, a great majority of the latter being
married. In contrast a majority, 57%, of the homeless had never been married
and fewer than one in ten were currently married (not indicated by Table 2). Only
whites and Native American homeless differed from this pattern, less than half of
each never having been married.

Table 2. Some Sociodemographic Differences

	Hispanics	Blacks	Native Americans	Whites	Others	Total
Gender						
Male (%)	70.2	77.7	52.8	75.7	81.1	75.5
Age						
Average years	32.5	39.0	38.3	45.6	34.0	40.3
Marital status						
Never married (%)	61.7	62.7	48.7	44.2	72	56.6
Total number	(49)	(385)	(36)	(220)	(28)	(718)

The full meaning of the racial/ethnic distribution among the homeless samples is fraught with ambiguity. Although blacks and American Indians are clearly overrepresented among the homeless, it is not at all clear whether it is the socioeconomic conditions under which such groups live that generated their overrepresentation, or some other factors, for instance, that relate to differences in kinship structures or in the incidence of disabling conditions.

Income and Employment

A major reason why persons are homeless is that their incomes are so low they cannot afford to purchase conventional housing. It is also likely that low income is a consequence of homelessness, as few employers would welcome new employees whose appearances are below their employment standards and who may not be able to provide an address.

As a measure of income, we asked each person interviewed how much cash income he or she received in the month prior to the interview. The resulting data are shown in Panel A of Table 3, separately for our Phase I (fall, 1985) and Phase II (winter, 1986) surveys.

Cash income levels in both surveys were appallingly low. Almost one in five (18%) had no income at all during the last month. Half had incomes below $100, and the average monthly income was only $168. There are simply no humane standards under which most of the income levels reported can be considered adequate. There are also no standards under which the modal, median, or

Table 3. Cash Income Received Last Month

A. Last month's income for total sample

Dollar amount received	Phase I	Phase II	Total
None	16.9%	19.1%	18.1%
Mode	$0.00	$0.00	$0.00
Median	$130.61	$79.90	$99.85
Mean	$181.25	$156.90	$168.39
Unweighted number	(372)	(350)	(722)

B. Income differences by ethnic groups

Income last month	Hispanics	Blacks	Native Americans	Whites	Others	Total
Average	$138	$197	$97	$145	$129	$169
Total number	(49)	(385)	(36)	(220)	(28)	(718)

average income levels can be considered adequate to sustain any reasonable standard of living in Chicago. The modal income was $0.00, clearly impossible to live on. The median income amounted to less than $3.33 per day, hardly enough to buy one adequate meal per day. The average income amounted to $5.61 per day, clearly insufficient for either adequate daily food or adequate shelter, and obviously inadequate to cover both food and housing. Average monthly rent for SRO accommodations in Chicago, the least expensive accommodations available for single persons, was $175 in 1985, clearly more than either the median or mean income of the homeless.

These low cash-income levels also condition the physical location of the homeless. Few, if any, can afford to travel far or frequently even within Chicago. Public transportation fares in Chicago are now $0.90 per trip, constituting a heavy charge for persons whose average daily incomes are less than $6.00. Therefore, the homeless congregate close to the shelters and soup kitchens upon which they are highly dependent.

Panel B displays average last month's incomes for ethnic groups. Although average incomes varied by as much as $100 (blacks compared to Native Americans), these differences were not statistically significant. In any event, none of the racial groups approached reasonably adequate monthly income levels.

The Chicago homeless managed to get by largely through in-kind donations of food, clothing, and shelter. More than half (55%) of the previous 7 days' sleeping arrangements was provided by homeless shelters and some small amount of temporary housing was provided by relatives and friends (6%). The rest of the time, the homeless either made use of the inadequate shelter provided by public access places (29%) or rented rooms (4%).

In-kind donations of meals and clothing, and participation in the food stamp program also helped to supplement the inadequate income levels of the homeless. Seventy-two percent had received at least one free meal over the previous month—one wonders why this proportion is not closer to 100%. One in four (24%) participated in the federal food stamp program.[14] And four in ten received free clothing, most likely from the shelters. In short, the Chicago homeless had to rely on social service organizations to satisfy their most basic needs.

A checklist asking whether or not the homeless received any income from a variety of sources provided information on how they acquired cash income. The resulting data are shown in Table 4. Surprisingly, the most frequently cited source was employment: One in three (32%) claimed to have received some

---

[14]An interesting issue is how food stamps helped the homeless, most of whom did not have access to facilities in which to prepare food or utensils in which to cook. Of course, some food products that can be purchased need little or no preparation, for example, bread, cookies and crackers, fruit, cheese, and milk. Furthermore, food stamps can be converted into cash, although not legally. Finally, some of the shelters that serve family groups do provide some cooking facilities.

Table 4. Sources of Cash Income Last Month
(Percentages)

Source	Phase I	Phase II	Total
Employment	32.2	30.7	31.6
General assistance	21.8	22.5	22.1
Handouts	22.7	18.1	20.6
Friends	18.9	10.0	14.9
Family and relatives	10.0	11.2	10.2
Swaps and trades	12.7	6.9	9.6
Gifts	11.4	6.9	9.4
Other sources	10.4	7.3	9.0
Supplemental security income	8.6	4.6	6.8
Social security	8.3	4.9	6.8
Disability	5.6	2.6	4.2
AFDC	5.3	7.5	6.3
Unemployment insurance	2.2	0.9	1.6
Unweighted number	(372)	(350)	(722)

income the previous month from employment. Given the low levels of income reported in Table 3, the employment in question was understandably intermittent, casual labor with accompanying very low pay rates. Slightly more than one in five (22%) received some income from General Assistance, a surprisingly low level, as almost all of the homeless were eligible for participation in the Illinois General Assistance program.[15]

Another one in five received cash in the form of handouts, mainly from public begging. It is also likely that the gifts, reported as an income source by 9% of the homeless, may have consisted of handouts. Adding these two sources together, handouts and gifts were sources of income for about one in three of the homeless. Again, despite the prevalence of these sources, the generosity of donors did little to provide an adequate income flow.

The remaining income sources are cited by small minorities of the homeless. Friends and relatives provided gifts (respectively to 15% and 10% of the homeless). Perhaps the most telling of all are the low levels of receipt of income from pensions, disability payment programs, unemployment benefits, and AFDC. These findings have two somewhat contradictory implications. On the one hand, the findings indicate the extent to which the homeless were overlooked

[15]There are virtually no requirements for eligibility under the Illinois General Assistance program other than having a monthly income below $154 and no assets. There are no minimum residence requirements and no requirements to have a permanent address.

by these major income-maintenance programs. The homeless caught in our survey may not have known about the programs, never applied, were discouraged from applying by the administering agencies, or were judged ineligible. On the other hand, receiving benefits under these programs may have provided sufficient income to take many recipients out of the homeless group. Hence, the homeless in our survey may simply have been those who were unable to qualify for income support programs and to maintain their eligibility for long periods of time.

Despite the fact that jobs are a frequent source of income for the homeless, their employment histories show that they had not held any but intermittent jobs for long periods of time. Asked when they last held down a ''steady job'' for more than 3 months, most of the homeless have not held such jobs since more than several years ago. Table 5 shows that the average number of months elapsed since the homeless last held a steady job is 55, or about 4.5 years. The median number of elapsed months (40) is not much different, indicating that half have been without steady employment for up to 3.3 years and half more than that time. Finally, it should be noted that the modal length of time elapsed since leaving their last steady jobs is 120 months or 10 years, one in five homeless having held their last steady job 10 or more years ago.

As Panel B of Table 5 shows, there are marked (and statistically significant) differences among the various ethnic groups in average months since their last steady jobs. Native Americans have been without steady jobs for the longest period, 66 months or 5.5 years, closely followed by blacks (60 months or 5 years) with Hispanics not far behind (55 months or 4.6 years). In contrast, the white homeless have been without steady work for only 46 months (3.8 years).

It is very instructive to compare the findings shown in Table 5 with the length of time reported being homeless, as shown in Table 6. The homeless have

Table 5. Time Elapsed since Last Steady Job

	A. Total sample		
Number of months	Phase I	Phase II	Total
Mode	120.0	120.0	120.0
Median	49.4	35.3	40.0
Mean	56.4	53.1	54.9

		B. Ethnic variation				
	Hispanics	Blacks	Native Americans	Whites	Others	Total
Average months	54.5	59.6	66.0	46.0	45.0	54.8

Table 6. Length of Time Currently Homeless

| | A. Total sample | | |
Months	Phase I	Phase II	Total
0–1	10.4	15.4	12.7
2–3	18.4	19.4	18.9
4–6	16.7	12.3	14.7
7–12	13.9	14.8	14.3
13–24	15.7	12.6	14.3
25–48	12.0	12.3	12.1
49–119	5.8	8.6	7.0
120 and over	7.1	4.6	5.9
Unweighted number	(372)	(350)	(722)
Mode (months)	4.0	1.0	2.0
Median (months)	7.9	7.3	7.6
Mean (months)	22.4	21.3	21.9

| | | B. Ethnic variation | | | | |
| | | | Native | | | |
	Hispanics	Blacks	Americans	Whites	Others	Total
Average months	16.6	20.1	18.0	27.1	22.4	22.0

been without steady employment for much longer periods of time than they have been homeless. The median time homeless was 7.6 months, in contrast to the median of 40 months passed since their last steady employment. *In short, the homeless have lived on inadequate personal incomes literally for years before becoming homeless.*

Unfortunately, we did not gather any information on how they managed to remain homed for the years of being unemployed. We can only speculate that they managed to do so mainly through the generosity of family and perhaps friends, supplemented by casual employment that did not qualify as a "steady job." But such generosity apparently has limits, and the long-term unemployed eventually found themselves without access to a dwelling.

This pattern also means that few of the homeless were rendered homeless immediately or shortly after the loss of employment. Homelessness is apparently the end state of a long process that may begin with the loss of a steady job, but is not often immediately precipitated by that loss.

Note also that the distribution of lengths of time homeless has a complicated shape. About one in three homeless have been in that condition for less than 3 months, but another one-third have been homeless longer than 18 months. It appears that the homeless are highly heterogeneous in this respect, a very large proportion being homeless for short periods of time and a large proportion being apparently "permanently" homeless, having been in that condition for years.

Panel B of Table 6 shows the ethnic variation in average time homeless. Although there are differences as large as 10 months (between whites and Hispanics), these differences were not large enough to reach statistical significance ($p = .07$). Whites have been homeless on the average longer than any other ethnic group, but by amounts less than a year. As whites are, on average, older than the other ethnic groups, this pattern of time homeless is consistent with the interpretation that whatever recent increases have occurred among the literal homeless has been contributed by nonwhites and Hispanics.[16]

Gender Differences within Race and Ethnicity

Within minority groups, gender differences are often large, indicating that homelessness may have different meanings for minority women as contrasted to men. Table 7 contrasts men and women within each of the ethnic groups. The base numbers for women are entirely too small to sustain any firm statements about Hispanics and Native Americans, but the gender contrasts for whites and blacks are on somewhat firmer grounds.

Several important findings are shown. First, women are much less likely than men to be homeless alone. Almost all men are homeless by themselves (ranging from a low of 94% to a high of 98%), women much less so. In almost every case (over 95%), the persons with the homeless are their children. About one-third of black women have their children with them, a proportion that rises to 50% for Hispanic women and 25% for Native American women. Fewer of the white women (one in four) have their children with them. Two out of three of the homeless families were single-parent families, the majority of whom were black.[17] At least in Chicago, the problem of homeless families is one that primarily involves black single-parent households.

Overall, women have been homeless for shorter periods of time than men. This gender difference is marked in all ethnic groups except blacks, where the difference is only 2 months.

A final gender difference to be noted is in average age: Among Hispanics and blacks, homeless women are younger than homeless men. Among Native

---

[16]What little historical evidence exists also bears this out. The black and Hispanic proportions of New York's shelter population has increased drastically since the early 1980s. A 1958 study of homeless men in Chicago (Bogue, 1963) found very few blacks in Chicago's inexpensive Skid Row "hotels."

[17]Of the 75 homeless family groups in our sample, two out of three were single-parent families, and of the single-parent families two out of three were headed by black women.

Table 7. Gender Differences within Homeless Members of Minority Groups

	Hispanics	Blacks	Native Americans	Whites	Others
A. Average age (years)					
Men	36	40	35	46	32
Women	24	35	42	46	39
B. Time homeless (months)					
Men	22	21	20	31	25
Women	4	19	15	14	12
C. Percentage homeless alone					
Men	94	98	97	97	98
Women	50	68	75	82	73
Total men	(35)	(297)	(19)	(166)	(23)
Total women	(14)	(84)	(17)	(50)	(5)

Americans and "others," women are older than men, and among whites, both sexes are of the same average age.

Social Isolation

Not only are the homeless outside of households in which there are other adults, but their contacts with family and friends are infrequent. Table 8 presents the proportions of the homeless who have relatives and friends and the proportions that maintain minimum contact levels (visiting, writing, or phoning at least once every few months) with such persons.

The critical set of findings is contained in Panel C, showing that one in three of the homeless in Chicago did not maintain even minimal contact with their families and that one in four did not have minimal contacts with either family or friends. Unfortunately, we have not been able to find comparable statistics for the general population, and can therefore only surmise that these proportions are much lower than would be found in the general population.

Note that young homeless women are the least isolated homeless group. It should be borne in mind, however, that many of the young women are homeless single parents whose children are with them in the shelters. Their low levels of isolation from family reflects the fact that they are in daily contact with their children. Indeed, it many respects, this group is quite different from the typical homeless, being much more likely to be homeless for a short period of time, to be homeless accompanied by other family members (usually their infant children), and to reject their previous households rather than having been rejected by them.

Table 8. Social Contacts (Percentages)

	Younger than 40		40 and Older		
	Men	Women	Men	Women	Total
A. Family of orientation (parents, siblings and other relatives) 1. Has live members of family of orientation	92.6	94.1	86.0	76.0	88.3
2. Is in contact with some member	68.2	73.9	50.8	45.6	59.6
B. Family of procreation (spouse and children) 1. Has live members of family of procreation	43.8	79.8	55.5	61.2	54.8
2. Is in contact with some member	29.1	67.5	25.6	31.6	32.8
C. Isolation measures 1. Not in contact with any relatives, spouse, or children	28.4	8.7	41.5	47.9	33.3
2. Not in contact with family and has no friends	20.9	6.5	26.7	40.9	23.7

D. Ethnic differences in social contacts

	Hispanics	Blacks	Native Americans	Whites	Others
1. Not in contact with relatives	31.7	25.2	20.1	47.9	40.3
2. Not in contact with friends or relatives	20.1	20.1	4.0	31.6	33.2

The last panel of Table 8 shows that there were strong ethnic differences in degrees of isolation. Whites were the most isolated of all the groups (48% having no contacts with any relatives and 32% having no contacts with either relatives or friends), Native Americans the least (20% and 4%, respectively). Blacks and Hispanics were in between those two groups. It is difficult to interpret these ethnic differences in levels of isolation, although all appear to be excessively high.

THE PREVALENCE OF DISABILITIES

Physical Health

The precise assessment of the health status of any population would require medical examinations, and is beyond the resources ordinarily at the command of social researchers. The best approximation to medical examinations are self-reports, a procedure that may overlook many conditions that do not produce painful symptoms or incapacities. In addition, the medical conditions may be inaccurately or vaguely reported. Nevertheless, conditions that are painful or that hinder the full functioning of the individual are likely to be reported.

The Chicago Homeless Survey used two approaches in ascertaining the health status of individuals. In Phase I, we asked those interviewed whether or not they were subject to medical conditions that impaired their ability to work.[18] In Phase II, we asked for a global health rating,[19] an approach that had been used in several health status surveys of homed populations and therefore provided a comparative framework for interpreting findings.

Table 9 presents the findings on self-reported health status, as measured in the Phase II survey. About one in five homeless (18%) reported themselves to be in "excellent" health, with an additional 46% reporting "good" health. If we take these two categories as reports of at least the absence of serious impairments to functioning, about two out of three (63%) of the Chicago homeless reported themselves to be in that condition. Homeless persons reporting "fair" (25%) or "poor" health (11%) total more than one in three (37%).

Because self-assessments of health status have been obtained from the homed, it is possible to compare the Chicago homeless with a national sample of American adults, as shown in the last line of Panel A. A 1982 national survey sponsored by the Robert Wood Johnson Foundation found only 18% of American adults who claimed "fair" or "poor" health status, about half the level found among the Chicago homeless. Clearly, the Chicago homeless reported considerably lower health-status levels than the homed. Nor are the Chicago homeless likely to be different in health status from the homeless in other cities: A recent report (Robertson & Cousineau, 1986) of a survey of Los Angeles homeless claimed 34% reporting their health as "fair" or "poor."

Table 9 also contains some data on the relative health status of subgroups among the homeless: Although the homeless interviewed in shelters did not differ significantly from those interviewed "on the streets," as shown in Panel

---

[18]The question asked was "Do you have any serious illnesses or physical conditions that prevent you from working?" This was followed by "What are your serious illnesses or physical conditions?"

[19]The item used in Phase II was "Would you say your health, in general, now is excellent, good, fair, or poor?"

Table 9. Self-Reported Health Status (Phase II only; Percentages)

A. Health status by gender and age

	Younger than 40		40 and Older	
	Males	Females	Males	Females
Excellent	24.0	24.4	10.2	19.9
Good	47.9	46.7	43.1	44.5
Fair	20.7	26.6	29.9	22.3
Poor	7.4	2.2	16.8	13.3
	Chicago Homeless	National Sample[a]		
Fair and poor combined	36.6	18.0		

B. Health status by ethnicity

	Hispanics	Blacks	Native Americans	Whites	Others
Fair or poor health	40.0	36.5	38.5	36.6	28.6

[a]As reported for the adult U.S. population (1982) in the Robert Wood Johnson Foundation, *Special Report*, No. 1, 1983. The contrasts would be even greater if standardized for age and gender distribution differences.

A, there were some strong differences by age. Homeless men and women over age 40 reported high levels of "poor" and "fair" health (46% and 36%, respectively), when compared to their under-40 counterparts (28% and 29%). Note, however, that all age groups reported lower levels of health status than the 1982 national sample.

As shown in Panel B of Table 9, ethnic differences in self-reported health status are small and do not reach conventional statistical significance levels. All ethnic groups suffer from high levels of self-reported poor health.

All told, the data presented above substantiate a characterization of the homeless as a population that reported a moderate level of healthiness, but contained a sizable minority with serious chronic conditions, some of which ordinarily require continual medical care and attention. Based on the self-reports, it appeared that between one-fourth and one-third of the Chicago homeless have such conditions.

Depression and Demoralization

The Phase II Chicago survey included six items drawn from the CES-D Scale, developed by the Center for Epidemiologic Studies at the National Institute of Mental Health, to measure levels of depression in community surveys. The scale relies on respondent self-reports (as opposed to ratings made by clinicians) to assess the extent to which feelings of depression are present in communities and in subpopulations of communities (Radloff, 1977). The scale quite accurately captures the presence of depressed symptoms, but it is not designed to discriminate among clinical subcategories of depression, such as major depression and minor depression; nor is it able to distinguish between primary depression (where depression is the diagnosis) and secondary depression (resulting from or accompanying some other mental illness).

Some researchers have suggested that high scores on the CES-D and other depression scales indicate, besides depression, a sense of *demoralization* (Link & Dohrenwend, 1980), that is, feelings of hopelessness and despair concerning one's prospects in the future, including the effects of neglect by social welfare organizations. The lack of institutional supports, especially if they are sorely needed, is thought to be sufficiently stressful to precipitate the physiological changes in the functioning of the brain that constitute a depressive disorder. If the homeless condition can be said to engender mental illness, demoralization would appear to be the most likely mechanism through which it has this effect, for the homeless lack the daily resources that others can take for granted.

There are 20 items on the full CES-D Scale, as originally devised. They are designed to cover components of depressive symptoms identified in the clinical literature, including depressed mood, feelings of guilt and worthlessness, feelings of helplessness and hopelessness, psychomotor retardation, loss of appetite, and disturbance of sleep. Because it was not possible to administer all 20 items, a subset of 6 was selected that appeared to cover the range of depressive symptoms, and 4 of them seemed well-suited to serve as indicators of the concept of demoralization described above.

The CES-D Scale has been used with many populations. Perhaps the best source of data for comparison with our homeless sample is HANES, the Health and Nutrition Examination Survey, conducted by the National Center for Health Statistics. No attempt was made in our comparison to match the Chicago homeless with the HANES national sample in terms of age, sex, and race.

We compared the national average scale scores computed from the HANES survey to comparable scores derived from the Chicago homeless. We found the strongest differences in the items which were most closely related to demoralization. "Feeling unhappy about the way one's life is going" showed the largest difference: 86% of the respondents in the national sample said they never felt their life had been a failure, but only 25% of the Chicago homeless said they never felt unhappy with the way their life was going. It is clear that the homeless were generally quite dissatisfied with their condition.

The demoralization of the homeless showed itself with special strength in the three items measuring depression, loneliness, and worry about the future. The differences from the national survey for each of these items were fairly large. About two-thirds of the national sample (67%) said they never felt depressed, but just over one-third (35%) of the homeless reported never feeling depressed. Similarly, about three-fourths of the national sample reported not feeling lonely, but the corresponding percentage of the homeless was 40%. More than half (58%) of the national sample reported no concern about the future, but only 29% of the homeless were similarly unconcerned.

In the HANES survey, the CES-D scores on each item of the full scale of 20 items were summed to form a summary total score for each individual surveyed. In order to compute a comparable score for the 6 items used in the Chicago Homeless Study, the average scores for the 6 items used were adjusted and projected to account for the shortness of the scale.[20] The resulting adjusted score was 19.199, 10.70 points higher than the national estimate. The computed adjusted projected summary score can be taken as a crude estimate of what the CES-D-Scale score would have been if all 20 items in the scale had been given to the Chicago homeless. This score is useful for comparative purposes because with the full scale a cutoff point of 16 has been established to distinguish cases that require clinical attention from those that are less serious.[21]

The homeless in Chicago were, on average, beyond the 16-point cutoff. If we take a comparable cutoff point on the short scale, we find that nearly one-half (47%) of the Chicago homeless had a total unadjusted score equivalent to the CES-D score of 18. By contrast, only 16% of the respondents in the HANES survey had a CES-D-Scale score of 16 or more. Clearly, levels of depression among the Chicago homeless are magnitudes higher than in the national adult population.

Every ethnic group in the homeless sample showed a much larger proportion of clinically depressed persons than the national average. The depression level was highest for Native Americans and lowest for whites, but none of these differences was significant statistically.[22] The circumstances of the homeless

---

[20]The sum (over 20 items) for the HANES survey is 8.495. As only a subset of the 20 CES-D items are used in this study, the sum of the six items must be projected by a factor of 20/6 or 3.333 to estimate the CES-D Scale score. For the HANES survey the projected sum is 9.417. The projection is 10.9% greater than the national estimated CES-D Scale score based on all 20 items (mean = 8.495). To make the homeless estimates roughly comparable with the national data, the projected sum is multiplied by a factor of .902.

[21]Weissman, Sholomskas, Pottenger, Prusoff, and Locke (1977) found that the 16-point cutoff is very sensitive in that more than 90% of those who are clinically depressed score higher than 16 on the CES-D Scale. But the scale is only moderately specific, because from 56% to 86% of those who are not clinically depressed still have scores higher than 16 on the CES-D Scale. One should be cautious, therefore, in using this cutoff point to estimate the number of homeless who need professional treatment for depression.

[22]Note that the CES-D Scale was used only in the winter, 1986 survey, and hence the numbers of persons in each ethnic group is small.

were apparently sufficiently uniform across ethnic groups to obscure whatever ethnicity may contribute to depression and demoralization.

Psychotic Symptoms

The Phase II survey provided a rough measure of the presence of psychotic symptoms in the form of five items taken from the Psychiatric Epidemiology Research Interview (PERI). Developed by Dohrenwend and his associates (1980), the PERI consists of 30 scales measuring symptoms of mental illness. These scales showed "a superior ability to differentiate a sample of well respondents from the community from respondents in a sample of psychiatric patients" (Dohrenwend, Dohrenwend, Link, & Levav, 1983, p. 1178). The five items used in the Phase II survey were taken from the eight-item PERI scale, "False Beliefs and Perceptions." They were (a) hearing voices; (b) fearing harm from others; (c) having visions; (d) possessing special powers; (e) being controlled by external forces.

Respondents were asked to report how often they had experienced these symptoms over the past year. This time frame is longer than that for the CES-D items (where the time frame was 1 week), because psychotic symptoms often occur in acute "episodes" of fairly short duration. Respondents were cautioned not to report symptoms that occurred while drinking alcohol or taking drugs.

The responses of the Chicago homeless to these five measures were compared with a sample of 267 (nonhomeless) residents in Washington Heights, a neighborhood in New York City. The comparison data, provided by Bruce Dohrenwend, were taken from the PERI Methods Study (Dohrenwend, Shrout, Egri, & Mendelson, 1980). Washington Heights is an ethnically diverse neighborhood of Manhattan that includes a wide range of incomes. We can assume it is fairly representative of the population living in the inner city of a large metropolitan area.

On every measure the residents of Washington Heights had lower average scores than the Chicago homeless. But two of the differences were small, and not statistically significant. These were (a) hearing voices (mean = .36 versus mean = .47, a difference of .11); and (b) feeling that one has special powers (mean = .37 versus mean = .47, a difference of .10). The remaining differences were large and statistically significant. The homeless were more likely to report having visions (difference = .30) and feeling that uncontrollable forces had taken over their minds (difference = .21). The largest difference (.44 points) was in the feeling that others want to harm or hurt the respondent.

Ordinarily, visual hallucinations occur less frequently than auditory hallucinations. This pattern occurred as expected in the Washington Heights population (mean of hearing voices = .36; mean of seeing visions = .18), but not in the homeless sample, where the average scores on the two measures were virtually equal (mean = .470 and mean = .474). Similarly, the delusion that one's mind is controlled by outside forces was the rarest of all in the Washington Heights sample (and among patients with psychosis generally), where it occurred about one-third as often as hearing voices (mean = .13 versus mean = .36), but in the Chicago homeless sample feelings of thought control occurred with a frequency that was 70% that of hearing voices (mean = .34 versus mean = .47).

On the other hand, paranoid delusions among the Chicago homeless occurred in superabundance. The mean score on fear of harm was twice as high as the mean score for hearing voices (.98 versus .47). In the Washington Heights sample, the mean score for fearing harm was only one and a half times as great as the mean score for hearing voices (.54 versus .36). It may well be that the fear of harm reported by some of the homeless is not delusional, but reflects the greater risk of theft, assault, and robbery that the homeless face.

All five items correlate rather well with each other, with correlations ranging between .39 and .69, and averaging .45, indicating that the homeless tend to have multiple psychotic symptoms. This pattern, coupled with the higher average scores of the Chicago homeless on all five items, suggests that the mental illnesses characterized by psychosis were both more prevalent *and more severe* among the homeless than they were in the settled community. It appears that the chronically mentally ill with the highest levels of impairment were selected into the homeless condition.

Although firm norms have not yet been computed for the PERI scale and its derivatives, we can use a somewhat arbitrary criterion to determine the level of psychotic symptoms among the Chicago homeless. Using the Washington Heights study as a standard and setting the cutoff score at two standard deviations above the mean of that sample, we find that about one-third of the homeless show scores that are above that cutoff point. In short, one out of three of the homeless currently show strong signs of psychotic thinking.

In terms of ethnic differences in psychotic thinking among the Chicago homeless, the pattern was similar to that shown with respect to depression and demoralization. All of the ethnic groups showed higher levels of psychotic thinking than the Washington Heights adult domiciled population. Native Americans showed the highest level, more than half (54%) showing high levels of psychotic thinking. At the other extreme, whites showed the lowest level (25%). Hispanics and blacks were at intermediate levels.

Institutionalization Experiences

Being homeless may be traumatic and unpleasant enough, but homelessness is not the only unpleasant event this group has experienced. Significant proportions have been in jail or prison, others have been the victims of drug and alcohol

Table 10. Institutionalization Experiences of the Homeless (Percentages)

Type of institutionalization	Hispanics	Blacks	Native Americans	Whites	Others	Total
Detoxification	17.9	32.2	26.3	40.0	28.2	32.2
Mental hospital	18.2	23.4	9.6	23.7	48.0	23.1
Prison	7.8	21.6	11.9	8.1	33.4	16.6
Jail	27.6	48.2	36.3	28.8	57.2	40.7
Probation	19.2	33.1	19.8	22.0	48.7	28.3
Number	(49)	(383)	(36)	(220)	(28)	(716)

abuse, and still others have had one or more episodes as patients in mental hospitals. The relevant data are shown in Table 10.

One in three have been in detoxification units for alcohol or drug abuse, indicating that at least this proportion have suffered from that affliction. Unfortunately, we did not collect information on current levels of drug or alcohol abuse, but the detoxification instances were frequent enough to infer very high current levels.

Ethnic differences in experiencing detoxification were statistically significant. Two out of five whites had been in a detoxification center at one extreme, whereas less than one in five Hispanics (18%) had that experience.

One in four (23%) have had at least one episode of mental hospitalization. Levels of mental hospitalization among the general adult population are magnitudes smaller: Epidemiological studies place the prevalence of past hospitalizations in the general population at 3% or below.

This high level of mental hospitalization is consistent with the evidence on current mental illness in the previous section, where we showed that the homeless have very high levels both of depression and indications of psychotic thinking.

Although ethnic differences in mental hospitalizations are statistically significant, such differences are not very large. Blacks, "others," and whites show the highest level of previous mental hospitalizations, Hispanics and Native Americans the lowest. It should be noted that this ordering does not follow closely that of the measures of current mental illness presented in the last section, in which Native Americans had the highest levels of current mental illness.

The Chicago homeless have also been in trouble frequently with the criminal justice system. Forty-one percent have spent some time (defined as a stay of more than 3 or 4 days) in a city or county jail, presumably serving time for some minor infraction or awaiting indictment and/or trial on some offense. Twenty-eight percent have been sentenced by a court and then given probation, typical treatments for first-offense convictions for all but the most serious offenses. Finally, 16.5% have served sentences in a federal or state prison following conviction on a felony offense. As in most states, prison sentences are rarely given for first offenses; these sentences most likely represent just one in a series of felony convictions.

Ethnic differences in criminal justice experiences are very large and highly significant statistically. All of the ethnic groups have higher levels of such experiences than would be found in the general adult population. "Others" and blacks showed the highest levels of criminal justice contacts. One in five blacks have been in prison, almost half have been in jail, and one in three have been on probation. "Others" have slightly higher levels. In contrast, less than one in ten whites have served prison time, slightly more than one in four Hispanics have been in jail and less than one in five Hispanics have been placed on probation.

The Accumulation of Disabilities

The various disabilities discussed in this section are considered jointly in Table 11. Very few (17%) of the homeless have escaped having one or another disability. Slightly more than one in three have suffered three or more disabilities and more than half (57%) have had one or two. These data provide some clues as to why some of the homeless are in that condition. There are significant proportions showing signs of disabilities arising out of substance abuse or chronic illness (and possibly both). Another large proportion have been in trouble with the law and suffer from the restrictions on opportunities that follow on felony convictions. In addition, these are clues to why their families and friends have seemingly turned away from them and why they are family-less.

Although all of the ethnic groups have a large number of reported problems, some clearly have more than others. In particular, Native Americans have very high problem levels—85% have two or more problems. In contrast, whites appear to have very few, with only 52% reporting two or more.

THE SOCIAL-STRUCTURAL ROOTS OF HOMELESSNESS

Earlier in this chapter, we advanced the general thesis that homelessness is a manifestation of extreme poverty. Thus, the structural roots of homelessness are those conditions that create extreme poverty in general and, in particular, force the manifestation of poverty in housing arrangements. In this interpretation, the high levels of disability conditions of the homeless and their household status are regarded as factors that identify those persons who are likely to become extremely poor, and therefore these disabilities affect the incidence of homelessness, that is, who becomes homeless.

Table 11. Reported Health, Mental Health, and Crime Problems (Percentages)

Number of problems[a]	Hispanics	Blacks	Native Americans	Whites	Others	Total
0	20.7	13.1	7.7	24.6	14.3	17.2
1	17.3	25.6	7.6	23.7	28.6	23.7
2	34.5	26.1	30.8	25.4	28.6	26.9
3	6.9	13.7	15.4	10.0	14.2	12.0
4	13.8	9.7	23.0	9.1	7.2	10.2
5 or more	6.9	11.4	15.4	7.3	7.1	9.9
Number	(27)	(164)	(12)	(102)	(13)	(319)

[a]Problems consist of the following: Self-reported "fair" or "poor" health, having been institutionalized for mental illness, sentenced by a court, having been in a detoxification center for alcohol or drug abuse, above-average score on CES-D, and above-average score on psychotic thinking scale.

The Urban Housing Stock

The stock of housing available in American urban places has become increasingly out of the reach of persons in extreme poverty. In city after city, the stock of inexpensive housing suitable for single-person households has declined drastically in the last decade. For example, in Chicago the number of single-person accommodations (single rooms renting for less than $50 per week, small apartments renting for less than $75 per week, dormitory accommodations in inexpensive "hotels" renting for less than $30 per week) has declined by 22% between 1980 and 1983. Proportionate declines of similar magnitudes have been reported for Detroit, New York, and Philadelphia.

The reasons for the decline in the housing stock available to the extremely poor are well-known: Urban renewal, gentrification, the demolition of inexpensive housing, and a general upsurge in the price of housing have been the main processes that have shrunk the housing stock available to the extremely poor.

The decline in the housing stock available to poor persons affects the extremely poor in two ways. First, most single-person households who are homeless simply cannot afford to pay market prices for housing. Second, the poor multiple-person households who might share their housing with persons currently homeless are hard pressed to find adequate housing for themselves. For example, the parental household which might have been able to accommodate an adult child in a housing market that offered housing of adequate size at an affordable price may now find it impossible to find such housing.

Changes in Household Composition

The last few decades have also seen a rise in the number of single-person households, a result, in part, of the changes in marriage and divorce patterns and, in part, in the reduction of inexpensive large housing units. Young people are marrying at a later age, more marriages end up in divorce and fewer inexpensive housing units are large enough to accommodate multiple adults in the same unit. In addition, there is some evidence that we are changing our norms concerning the appropriateness of adult children remaining in their parental households. More single persons are ''on their own,'' a structural development that leads to a greater number of households that are more vulnerable to catastrophic changes in economic circumstances. A multiple-adult household can act as a buffer against catastrophic economic losses of any single adult in that household by absorbing the loss of income on the part of any single adult contributor to the household income. If a spouse loses a job, the other spouse may increase his or her income-producing activity. Or a child going to school might leave school to find employment and contribute to the household income. If an adult child suffers a period of unemployment, parents can still provide housing and food, at least for a while. But a single-person household suffering a job loss through illness or being laid off may find that the ability to hold on to housing comes rapidly to an end.

Holes in the Welfare Net

Our public welfare system was designed to provide help to persons who are unable to obtain adequate income by their own efforts. The welfare system, however, regards some persons as being more worthwhile helping than others. Consequently, those who are not regarded as worthwhile are concentrated among the homeless because they are ineligible for income transfer programs or are eligible only for programs that do not provide payments sufficient to take them out of the extremely poor category. Particularly unwelcome are single men in their productive years, the modal type among homeless persons. There are very few persons over 65 among the homeless, mainly because most are eligible for at least minimum OASI payments, a level of income that is sufficient to take them out of the category of the extremely poor. Similarly, the few single parents accompanied by children who are among the homeless stay in that condition for only short periods until they can become eligible for AFDC payments, also sufficient to take them out of the extremely poor category. As we saw above, there are also very few persons among the Chicago homeless who are on disability payment programs: These programs are usually generous enough to bring their participants out of the extremely poor category.

Persons who are not eligible to participate in any of the federally funded income-transfer programs are totally dependent on state and locally funded in-

come transfers. Some states are relatively generous both in their eligibility requirements for state programs; others are quite penurious. For example, the
Illinois General Assistance program is a relatively generous one, covering all
persons earning less than $154 per month who have no assets. In contrast, the
state of Alabama has no general relief program at all and even restricts eligibility
for Medicaid only to families who are on AFDC.

Statutory generosity, however, is often not matched in operational generosity: Most of the Chicago homeless were eligible for General Assistance, but
only 20% were receiving any payments. The gap between statutory eligibility
and actual participation is brought about by the discretion allowed to the operating agents of the Welfare Department who seemingly are unwilling to enroll
"able-bodied" males in the General Assistance program.

In addition, many of the Chicago homeless were likely to be eligible to
participate in disability programs. Many were veterans (of the Vietnam encoun-
ter) and therefore eligible for Veterans Administration payments. Others had
severe mental health problems and would be likely to qualify as chronically
mentally ill and therefore eligible for disability programs administered through
the Social Security Administration. We can only speculate why they were not
enrolled in the disability programs for which they were eligible: A reasonable
surmise is that here, too, administrative discretion allowed the agency to discriminate against men between 30 and 50.

One cannot discuss the problems of homelessness without any mention of
the deinstitutionalization of the mentally ill and its contribution to the problem.
There is no doubt that before 1970 many of the persons presently homeless
would have been found in state mental hospitals. Indeed, one in four of the
currently homeless in Chicago have passed at one time or another through a
mental institution. Others show levels of depression, substance abuse, or psychotic thinking that in the period before deinstitutionalization would have
brought them into a state hospital. However unpleasant mental hospitals may
have been, they may also be regarded as part of the welfare net, providing
minimum subsistence, housing, and care for extremely poor persons who had the
requisite disabilities. This welfare support is no longer as freely available.

Variations in the Strength of Kinship Ties

In a recent study of General Assistance participants in Chicago, Stagner and
Richman (1985) found that most of the participants managed to get by on the
$154-per-month payments because they were living with kin, mainly with their
parental families or adult siblings. In effect, their kin were partially subsidizing
their rent and possibly their food costs as well. One may speculate that kinship
obligations felt toward children and siblings helped to sustain these relationships. We have some hints in the Chicago data that this pattern of subsidy

can go on for some years, but eventually comes to an end. As we saw above, the typical homeless person has been without a steady job for far longer than he has been homeless, suggesting that there is a limitation on the obligations that one feels toward kin. When you consider as well that the disabilities suffered by the homeless are not exactly pleasant ones to live with, then the rejection of the homeless by their parental families and other kin become even more understandable. A chronic mentally ill, alcoholic, or petty criminal person would surely strain the binding obligations of kinship ties, possibly already strained by the resource limitations of poverty itself.

Studies of felt kinship obligations (Rossi & Rossi, 1986) are consistent with our findings on these patterns of living. Male relatives are less obligating than female. Indeed, the two kin categories that evoke the strongest sense of obligation are widowed mothers and unmarried daughters. Unmarried sons are considerably lower in the strength of the obligations they invoke. We can only speculate at this point on what variations in kinship strength accompany ethnicity, noting that Hispanics are consistently underrepresented among the homeless whereas blacks are overrepresented.

Among the Chicago homeless, blacks and Native Americans appear to be conspicuously overrepresented. In large part, this pattern of overrepresentation reflects the ethnic composition of the unaffiliated extremely poor. The exceptional ethnic group are the Hispanics who, despite their poverty, are underrepresented among the homeless. Unfortunately our data do not allow us reasonably to address two critical questions: First, are blacks and native Americans represented among the homeless to the extent that they make up the extremely poor segment of Chicago's population? Second, what accounts for the ability of Hispanics to avoid literal homelessness?

I conclude that homelessness in our society is the result of the failure of institutions to provide for the familyless poor, especially unaffiliated males. Minorities are overrepresented in this category because of the greater prevalence of poverty among them. Disabled persons are also overrepresented among the homeless because their disabilities make them less attractive as family members and because their disabilities reinforce their poverty.

Acknowledgments

The research reported in this chapter was funded in part by grants from the Pew Memorial Trust, the Robert Wood Johnson Foundation, and the State of Illinois Department of Public Aid.

REFERENCES

Baxter, E. & K. Hooper. (1981). *Private lives/public spaces: Homeless adults on the streets of New York City.* New York: Community Service Society, Institute for Social Welfare Research.

Bogue, D. A. (1963). *Skid row in American cities*. Chicago: Community and Family Study Center, University of Chicago.

Crystal, S., M. Goldstein, & B. Leavitt. (1982). *Chronic and situational dependence: Long-term residents in a shelter for men*. Report prepared for Human Resources Administration of the City of New York, New York.

Cuomo, M. M. (1983). *1933/1983—never again: A report to the national governors' task force on the homeless*. Portland, Maine.

Dohrenwend, B. S., B. P. Dohrenwend, B. Link, & I. Levav. (1983). Social functioning of psychiatric patients in contrast with community cases in the general population. *Archives of General Psychiatry*, 40, 1174–1182.

Dohrenwend, B. P., P. E. Shrout, G. Egri, & F. S. Mendelshon. (1980). Nonspecific psychological distress and other dimensions of psychopathology. *Archives of General Psychiatry*, 37, 1229–1236.

Link, B., & B. P. Dohrenwend. (1980). Formulation of hypotheses about the true prevalence of demoralization in the United States. In B. P. Dohrenwend, B. S. Dohrenwend, M. S. Gould, B. Link, R. Neugebauer, & R. Wunsch-Hipsig (Eds.), *Mental illness in the United States: Epidemiologic estimates*. New York: Praeger.

Radloff, L. S. (1977). The CES-D Scale: A self-report depression scale for research in the general population. *Applied Psychological Measurement*, 1, 385–401.

Robertson, M., & M. R. Cousineau. (1986). Health status and access to health services among the urban homeless. *American Journal of Public Health*, 76, 561–563.

Rossi, P. H., & A. S. Rossi. (1986). *The structure of American kinship norms*. Amherst, MA: Social and Demographic Research Institute.

Rossi, P. H., G. A. Fisher, & G. Willis. (1986). *The condition of the homeless of Chicago*. Amherst, MA, and Chicago, IL: Social and Demographic Research Institute and National Opinion Research Center.

Stagner, M., & H. Richman. (1985). *General assistance profiles: Findings from a longitudinal study of newly approved recipients*. Chicago: National Opinion Research Center, University of Chicago.

U.S. Department of Housing and Urban Development. (1984). *A Report to the Secretary on the homeless and emergency shelters*. Washington, DC: Office of Policy Development and Research.

Weissman, M. M., D. Sholomskas, M. Pottenger, B. A. Prusoff, & B. Z. Locke. (1977). Assessing depressive symptoms in five psychiatric populations: A validation study. *American Journal of Epidemiology*, 106, 203–214.

Wiegard, R. B. (1985). Counting the homeless. *American Demographics*, 7, 34–37.

5

Poverty and Immigration in the United States: 1960–1980

LEIF JENSEN

Since the mid-1960s, the United States has experienced another great wave of immigration. This new immigration, distinguished by the predominance of persons from Asian and Latin American countries (Borjas & Tienda, 1987), resurfaced concerns that the United States was admitting too many individuals who were prone to be chronically poor and dependent on social services. Despite the explosive growth of the immigration literature over the past 10 to 15 years, very few studies have investigated immigrants' use of social services (Blau, 1984; Jensen, 1988; Simon, 1980; Tienda & Jensen, 1986) and no recent study has compared trends in poverty among immigrants admitted since 1965 relative to those admitted prior to 1965. Accordingly, this chapter documents the level and trends in poverty among immigrants using census data from 1960, 1970, and 1980.

The assertions that immigrants tend to be poor and dependent on income transfer programs (e.g., welfare) have frequently been voiced in policy circles to support a more restrictive immigration policy. Such assertions also are evident in U.S. public opinion polls. A recent CBS News/New York Times poll (New York Times/CBS News, 1986) revealed that, for many, the words "poor" and "welfare" are the first to come to mind in response to the word "immigrant." Those data also showed that almost half of the adults interviewed felt that the majority of immigrants wind up on welfare. It is little wonder that a plurality of the opinion poll respondents favored an overall reduction in immigration.

Theoretically, there is reason to expect greater poverty among recent immigrants than among all other immigrants or natives. Assimilation theory (Gordon, 1964) posits a period of social and economic adjustment during which new

LEIF JENSEN • Income and Well-Being Section, Economic Research Service, U.S. Department of Agriculture, Washington, D.C.

immigrants are apt to be dislocated from the economy. In time, the acquisition of the host country's language and culture enhances immigrants' ability to obtain adequate employment. Thus, while initial periods of poverty might be anticipated, the percentage of immigrants who are poor should decline in time. To the extent that immigrants are an economically select group, possessing if nothing else the daring and entrepreneurial spirit required to immigrate (Chiswick, 1979), their poverty experiences may be more temporary than chronic, as suggested by Segalman and Basu (1981).

This chapter fills a significant research gap by examining changes in poverty among recent immigrants, and highlighting changes since the sweeping immigration reforms of 1965. The following section describes baseline trends in poverty since 1960, comparing immigrants of Asian, Hispanic, black, and white origins. It is followed by an analysis of the individual, familial, and contextual determinants of poverty risks which emphasizes nativity differentials, and distinctions between recent and prior immigrants. The final section summarizes the key findings and reflects on their policy implications. To avoid deflecting attention from the substantive issues addressed, the technical and methodological issues are discussed in an appendix.

BASELINE TRENDS IN POVERTY AMONG IMMIGRANTS

Table 1 documents basic trends in poverty for the period 1959–1979. This table reports poverty rates for native and immigrant families, and disaggregates the latter into years-since-immigration categories. The first row of this table shows a downward trend in poverty rates among all families. Most of this decline took place between 1959 and 1969, when poverty rates fell from 18.0% to 10.6%. The progress against poverty during the 1960s has been attributed to a number of factors, particularly the expansion of cash assistance programs (Blumberg, 1980)[1] and a relatively strong economy (O'Hare, 1985). Poverty rates continued to improve slowly during the 1970s, as evidenced by the decline to 9.3% by 1979.

The next two rows of Table 1 report poverty rates separately for native and immigrant families. Native families exhibit the same monotonic decline in poverty observed for all families. Immigrant poverty declined between 1959 (15.6%) and 1969 (12.9%), but rose during the 1970s, reaching 14% by 1979. It

---

[1]One might speculate that part of the rapidity of this decline may be accounted for by the strong economy and very low unemployment rate in 1969. Unemployment in 1969 was only 3.5% (Ehrenberg & Smith, 1982). However, the 1959 and 1979 unemployment rates were likewise rather low (5.5% and 5.8%, respectively). Unfortunately, I do not have nativity-specific poverty rates for the intercensal periods and thus cannot determine the linearity of the decline in poverty over the 1960s.

Table 1. Poverty Rate (Percentage) for Families
by Immigration Cohort and Year

Head's nativity and years since immigration	1959	1969	1979
All families[a]	18.0	10.6	9.3
All natives[a]	18.2	10.4	8.9
All immigrants[a]	15.6	12.9	14.0
0–5 years[a]	16.8	17.1	27.7
Over 5 years[a]	15.6	12.4	11.7
0–5 years		15.9	26.7
6–10 years		11.1	15.0
11–20 years		8.2	11.8
Over 20 years		11.5	7.0

[a]Includes Puerto Ricans.
SOURCE: U.S. Bureau of the Census, 1960, 1970, and
1980 Public Use Samples.

appears that immigrant families did not share in the progress against poverty experienced by native families.

Within-year differences between immigrants and natives show that poverty among immigrant families was below that of natives in 1959 only (15.6% versus 18.2%). Sometime during the 1960s, this differential reversed itself. The poverty rate for immigrant families exceeded that of natives by 24% (2.5 percentage points) in 1969 and 57% (5.1 percentage points) in 1979.

Thus far I have established that the decline in poverty among immigrant families during the 1960s was considerably slower than that for natives. Whereas poverty among natives continued to decline until 1979, immigrant poverty increased. Some insight into these observations can be obtained by comparing various years-since-immigration categories (the last six rows of Table 1). The steady and dramatic *increase* in poverty among recent immigrant families (those with heads who arrived five or fewer years before the census) is striking. Poverty rates for these families increased from 17% to 28% over the period. The sudden increase in poverty among recent arrivals between 1969 and 1979 is all the more impressive because it occurred during a period when poverty rates for all families declined. Although the increase in poverty among recent immigrants is an important cause of the overall rise in immigrant poverty during the 1970s, the most recent immigrants are not solely responsible for this increase. Two other duration groups—those who immigrated 6–10 and 11–20 years before the census—also had higher poverty rates in 1979 compared to 1969. Nevertheless, the sharp rise in poverty among recent immigrants requires closer scrutiny.

Table 2 presents poverty rates for recent immigrants by race/ethnicity and year. Four basic racial and ethnic groups are identified—non-Hispanic whites, blacks, Asians, and Hispanics—based on the characteristics of heads. Table 2 also includes the relative racial/ethnic composition of recent immigrants under the columns headed "Percentage of recent immigrants."

Besides establishing the importance of the changing racial/ethnic composition of recent immigrants on the overall increase of poverty among them, Table 2 provides clues as to why poverty increased continuously between 1959 and 1979 for families headed by recent immigrants. First, despite the fact that they represent a decreasing proportion of all recent immigrants, the poverty rate for recent white immigrants increased more than threefold between 1959 and 1979. This result supports Keely's (1975) assertion of a gradual decline in the economic viability of white immigrants. As white families constituted a sizable proportion of all recent immigrant families as late as 1980 (31%), their increased poverty rate had a strong positive impact on the poverty rate for all recent immigrants.

That the increase in poverty among recent white immigrant families was an important contributor to the increase among all recent immigrant families is reaffirmed by the following exercise. Replacing the 1979 white poverty rate (23.7%) with their rate in 1959 (7.6%) yields a weighted average for all recent immigrants in 1979 of only 22.5%, which compares to the observed value of 27.7%. In other words, regardless of the shift in the racial/ethnic composition of immigrants, had poverty among recent white immigrants not increased, the poverty among all recent immigrants in 1979 would have been almost 20% lower than actually observed.

The effects of the sudden increase in poverty among recent white immigrants were partly offset by their declining representation among all recent arriv-

Table 2. Poverty Rate for Families Headed by Recent Immigrants

	1959		1969		1979	
	Percentage in poverty	Percentage of recent immigrants	Percentage in poverty	Percentage of recent immigrants	Percentage in poverty	Percentage of recent immigrants
White	7.6	66.3	10.7	46.4	23.7	31.5
Black	12.5	1.2	13.5	4.9	27.2	5.6
Hispanic[a]	35.6	29.1	24.8	39.9	32.5	34.5
Asian	35.7	3.4	17.7	8.7	26.1	28.4
Overall/total	16.7	100.0	17.1	99.9[b]	27.7	100.0

[a]Includes Puerto Ricans.
[b]Does not sum to 100 due to rounding error.
SOURCE: U.S. Bureau of the Census, 1960, 1970, and 1980 Public Use Samples.

als. Applying the 1979 poverty rates to the 1959 racial/ethnic distribution of recent immigrants yields an overall rate of 26.4%—not appreciably different from the actual 1979 rate of 27.7%. In other words, despite popular concern that the shift toward Third World countries of origin was a direct cause of the rising poverty observed among recent immigrants, my standardization exercise indicates that had the origin composition not changed since 1959, poverty rates among recent immigrants would still have increased to the levels they eventually did. Again, this is largely due to the sudden increase in poverty among all recent immigrants—whites included.

A second reason why poverty increased among recent immigrants between 1959 and 1979 can be traced to the changed composition of recent cohorts. Although poverty decreased between 1959 and 1969 for Hispanic and Asian families, these groups (especially Hispanics) had comparatively high poverty rates throughout the period and made up twice the share of all recent immigrants in 1969 as compared to 1959. Finally, poverty increased between 1969 and 1979 among all four racial/ethnic groups of recent immigrants.

To summarize, these descriptive tables firmly document that poverty among immigrants did increase, and that much of this rise was due to the higher rate among recent arrivals. Our tabulations disaggregated by race and ethnicity captured part of the effect of the changing composition of immigrants after the 1965 immigration reforms. Of course, there are several other factors that could account for the increase in immigrant poverty. These include: individual factors, such as age and education; family characteristics, such as headship configuration and economic dependency; and locational factors, such as rural versus urban residence. Using a multivariate framework, I consider the relative importance of each of these factors in the next section.

MULTIVARIATE MODELS OF POVERTY AMONG FAMILIES

In this section, I use multivariate logistic regression analysis[2] to pursue two broad goals. One is to verify the conclusions drawn from the descriptive tabulations, and the second is to explore the unique effect of immigrant status as one among a number of individual, family, and contextual correlates of poverty.

---

[2]Because the dependent variable is a dichotomy—a family either is or is not in poverty—logistic regression analysis is used. Unlike ordinary least-squares regression, logistic regression provides unbiased and efficient estimates for equations with dichotomous dependent variables (Hanushek & Jackson, 1977). The parameter estimates of logit models reflect the effect of a unit change in the independent variable on the log of the odds of being in poverty. To provide more intuitively meaningful results, these logit coefficients are transformed to reflect the effect of a unit change in the independent variable on the probability of being poor (Petersen, 1985). Maximum likelihood estimates of logit parameters were computed using the GLIM system (Baker & Nelder, 1978).

Table 3. Logistic Regression of Poverty on Individual and Family Characteristics, Pooled by Race/Ethnicity[a]

	Model 1		Model 2		Model 3		Model 4	
	L	P	L	P	L	P	L	P
Intercept	−1.01		2.08		−2.51		−2.52	
	(.04)		(.22)		(.30)		(.28)	
1969	−.57	−.053	−.51	−.048	−.72	−.063	−.74	−.064
	(.05)		(.06)		(.06)		(.08)	
1979	−.80	−.068	−.51	−.048	−.69	−.061	−.70	−.062
	(.05)		(.06)		(.07)		(.08)	
Family head variables								
Prior immigrant	−.15	−.016	−.35	−.035	−.00^b	−.000	.02^b	.002
	(.05)		(.06)		(.07)		(.12)	
Recent immigrant	.53	.073	.31	.040	1.04	.169	.54^b	.075
	(.09)		(.10)		(.12)		(.29)	
Black			1.20	.204	1.01	.163	1.02	.165
			(.06)		(.08)		(.08)	
Mexican			.73	.108	.64	.092	.64	.092
			(.08)		(.09)		(.09)	
Puerto Rican			1.01	.163	1.03	.167	1.05	.171
			(.12)		(.14)		(.14)	
Other Hispanic			.54	.075	.40	.053	.42	.056
			(.09)		(.10)		(.10)	
Japanese			−.17^b	−.018	−.00^b	.000	−.00^b	−.000
			(.20)		(.22)		(.22)	
Chinese			−.01^b	−.001	.21^b	.026	.19^b	.023
			(.20)		(.22)		(.22)	
Other Asian			.65	.094	.64	.092	.57	.080
			(.15)		(.16)		(.17)	
Education			−.15	−.016	−.12	−.013	−.12	−.013
			(.01)		(.01)		(.01)	
Secondary occupation			.02^b	.002	.32	.041	.32	.041
			(.06)		(.06)		(.06)	

Models based on logistic regression permit an assessment of several correlates of poverty and the possibility of changes in these relationships over time. The first set of equations (Table 3) predict poverty from year of observation, race/ethnicity, and immigrant status. These equations offer a more rigorous test of the assertion, first addressed in the descriptive tabulations, that the new immigrants have become increasingly poverty prone.

Another series of logit models establish the role of immigrant status as one among many variables determining poverty. The predictor variables include both individual-level (e.g., education) and family-level (e.g., headship configuration)

Table 3. (*continued*)

	Model 1		Model 2		Model 3		Model 4	
	L	P	L	P	L	P	L	P
Family head variables, cont.								
Age			−.09	−.010	−.04	−.005	−.04	−.005
			(.01)		(.01)		(.01)	
Age squared			.82	.125	.23	.029	.23	.029
			(.08)		(.10)		(.10)	
Family and contextual variables								
Dependency rate					.04	.005	.04	.005
					(.00)		(.00)	
Spouse absent					1.34	.236	1.34	.236
					(.06)		(.06)	
Extended family					−.68	−.061	−.69	−.061
					(.08)		(.08)	
Southern residence					.69	.101	.69	.101
					(.06)		(.06)	
Nonmetropolitan residence					.73	.108	.73	.108
					(.06)		(.06)	
Interaction terms								
Prior immigrant, 1969							.07[b]	.008
							(.15)	
Recent immigrant, 1969							.35[b]	.046
							(.34)	
Prior immigrant, 1979							−.13[b]	−.014
							(.16)	
Recent immigrant, 1979							.74	.110
							(.32)	
−2 log (likelihood ratio)	13210		11590		9338		9329	
Degrees of freedom	13985		13974		13969		13965	

[a]L = Logit coefficient (standard errors in parentheses); P = probability change (reflects the change in the probability of being in poverty resulting from a unit change in the independent variable) computed at P′ = .1323 (see Petersen, 1985).
[b]Parameter estimate not significant at .05.

variables. These models, both pooled and disaggregated by race/ethnicity, ask: Are families headed by immigrants more or less likely than those headed by natives to be poor, net of other determinants of poverty? Are recent immigrant families particularly likely to be poor? Has this changed since the 1965 legislative reforms? Before presenting empirical results, I discuss the conceptual framework underlying the multivariate models of family poverty.

Conceptual Background

My models of family poverty draw on the status attainment (Blau & Duncan, 1967) and human capital (Becker, 1975) perspectives of socioeconomic attainment.[3] I assume that employment is the primary source of family income, and that there is a market for labor in which people are remunerated in direct proportion to their productivity. This value is determined by workers' skills, education, and other human capital characteristics. In the context of poverty, I predict that, *ceteris paribus,* families with heads who are lacking in human capital will be more likely than others to be in poverty.[4]

Additional characteristics of heads included in the logistic regressions are age,[5] race/ethnicity, and nativity (see Appendix Table A for operational definitions). Because earnings and total income tend to increase with age (Ehrenberg & Smith, 1982), age of head should lower poverty among families.[6] It is also important to control for age to differentiate, albeit crudely, between aging and assimilation effects. Whereas income increases with age, it often declines among the aged (Atchley, 1978), hence including the square of head's age captures the nonlinear effect of age on poverty.[7]

Race and ethnicity are defined differently in these multivariate models than in the descriptive tables. Hispanics and Asians are disaggregated into three ethnic groups each: Mexicans, Puerto Ricans, and Other Hispanics for the former, and Japanese, Chinese, and Other Asian for the latter. Thus the eight-category version of race/ethnicity identifies whites (the reference category), blacks, and the three Hispanic and three Asian groups.

Head's nativity is used to define the nativity of the entire family. Immigrant status also is defined somewhat differently from its definition in Table 1. Because of the lack of detail on years-since-immigration in the 1960 census, a

---

[3]See Jensen (1987) for a more thorough description of the conceptual framework underlying these models of poverty.

[4]By stressing the importance of human capital attributes, I am not dismissing structural explanations for poverty. Rather, my empirical formulations acknowledge the structural barriers that can prevent individuals from attaining the human capital needed to lift them out of poverty. To deny the importance of human capital for earnings determination would err in the opposite direction. Such characteristics, therefore, warrant inclusion in models of poverty. In the analyses below, I restrict my consideration to the individual characteristics of the head of the family.

[5]Those who are under 18 are excluded from this analysis, and any heads who are 100 or more years of age are recorded as 99.

[6]Many of the hypothesized effects in this section are based on previous research on status and income attainment research. Because income is negatively related to poverty, I hypothesize that most of the significant predictors of income will likewise be significant for poverty, but of opposite signs.

[7]In order to bring the mean for this variable in line with those of the other independent variables employed, head's age-squared is divided by 1,000. A reduced need for income among the aged has been factored into the absolute poverty lines used here (Orshansky, 1965).

three-category nativity variable is employed. The reference group is all families with native-born heads. To them, I compare immigrant families headed by those who arrived more than 5 years before the census (prior immigrants) and those who arrived 5 or fewer years before (recent immigrants).

In addition, my models include other family characteristics. Assuming that families are income-sharing units, family poverty partly hinges on its ability to commit additional workers to the labor force, and its economic commitment to dependent members. Also, to account for the macroeconomic context, I have included two ecological variables that influence poverty risks: residence in the South[8] and in nonmetropolitan areas.[9]

Aside from heads' characteristics and residential variables, several family characteristics directly influence the economic well-being of family units. Three of the most important are headship configuration, extended family structure, and economic dependency. Tying these indicators together is the fundamental assumption that the ability and tendency for families to commit workers to the labor force is of overwhelming importance in determining families' poverty risks (Gans, 1982).

Headship configuration is singularly important among the family variables that define poverty risks. For a variety of reasons, families headed by married couples are far less apt to be poor than those headed by a single parent (Schiller, 1980). Spouse-absent families should experience higher poverty rates, *ceteris paribus,* than intact families.

Extended families, those in which adult relatives of the head are present (other than spouse and children), have greater flexibility in allocating labor resources (Tienda & Angel, 1982; Angel & Tienda, 1982). Such families have an enhanced ability to commit workers to the labor force, if necessary. Thus, I predict a negative effect of extended family status on poverty. Also, I expect that families will be poor in direct proportion to their economic dependency, that is, to the degree that a large number of family members depend on the income produced by a small number of workers. Accordingly, the dependency rate,

[8]Southern states include Alabama, Arkansas, Delaware, District of Columbia, Florida, Georgia, Kentucky, Louisiana, Maryland, Mississippi, North Carolina, Oklahoma, South Carolina, Tennessee, Texas, Virginia, and West Virginia.

[9]An area is considered metropolitan if it lies within the confines of a Standard Metropolitan Statistical Area (SMSA). For my purposes, nonmetropolitan areas lie outside of SMSAs; the reference group consists of families within SMSAs. Due to data suppression to protect the anonymity of the respondents to the 1960 and 1970 censuses, certain states had areas in which the metro/nonmetro variable was missing. Where possible, I assigned the nonmetro code to those living in rural areas and the metro code to those living in urban areas. In states where both the urban/rural and metro/nonmetro variables were suppressed, I assigned all residents of that state to either the metro or nonmetro groups. These included Rhode Island and Delaware (metro), and Hawaii, Nevada, North Dakota, and Utah (nonmetro). In 1980, there was no suppression of the metro/nonmetro variable. This operationalization maximized comparability under the existing data constraints.

defined as the number of nonworkers as a percentage of total family size, should have a negative direct effect on family poverty.

Empirical Results

To test whether immigrant poverty increased significantly over time, net of changes in cohort composition, the following analyses are pooled across the year of observation. That is, data from the 1960, 1970, and 1980 family files were concatenated to form a single data file.[10] Year of observation is then included in these models as a predictor, with the year 1959 serving as the reference category. The desired test for temporal changes in immigrant poverty inheres in the interaction terms between year of observation and immigrant status.

Table 3 presents a progression of four hierarchical models of poverty among families pooled across racial/ethnic groups. In Model 1, the negative estimates for the year of observation confirm that families were less likely to be poor in 1969 and 1979 than they were in 1959. The relative magnitudes of these estimates reflect the rapid decline in poverty during the 1960s and abated decline during the 1970s. An example will illustrate the interpretation of the transformed logit coefficients under column P. The probability that a family was poor in 1969 was .053 less than in 1959, after controlling for immigrant status.

Model 1 also shows that, controlling for the overall decline in poverty over the 1960 to 1980 period, recent immigrants were significantly more likely, and all other immigrants were significantly less likely, than natives to be in poverty. This accords with the image of immigrants starting from humble origins, but enjoying upward socioeconomic mobility as they have time to adjust to the U.S. economy.

Throughout I have speculated about the reasons for higher poverty among recent arrivals. Alternative explanations include the shift in the racial/ethnic composition of recent immigrants, their youth, their relative lack of formal education, or their concentration in secondary labor market occupations. To account for these possibilities, Model 2 includes race/ethnicity, education, secondary occupation, age, and age-squared. The effects for the eight-category race/ethnicity variable conform to our expectations. Compared to families headed by whites (the reference group), blacks, Mexicans, Puerto Ricans, Other Hispanics, and Other Asians were significantly more likely to be poor. This effect is especially pronounced among blacks and Puerto Ricans. As expected, among all Hispanics, Puerto Ricans have comparatively high poverty rates. No

---

[10]Whereas the years of observation were 1960, 1970, and 1980, because poverty status is based on family income in the previous year, families would have been poor in 1959, 1969, and 1979, respectively.

groups were significantly less likely than whites to be poor (the negative terms for Japanese and Chinese families failed to reach significance).

The effects for the other independent variables also generally conform to expectation. Families with heads who were older and better educated were less likely to be poor, other things being equal. Moreover, the positive and significant effect for age-squared supports the hypothesis that, whereas the probability of poverty generally decreases with age, it increases among the aged. The most important result of Model 2, however, is that the inclusion of race/ethnicity, education, and age do not fully explain the effect for recent immigrants. Whereas the effect for recent immigrants is attenuated somewhat, it is still positive and statistically significant.[11] Along with the negative term for prior immigrants, Model 2 continues to show that recent immigrants were more likely, and all other immigrants less likely, than their native counterparts to be poor. This result is consistent with assimilation theory, which posits an initial period of economic adjustment, during which immigrants are more prone to poverty.

Model 3 in Table 3 introduces the family and contextual variables. The effects of these variables on family poverty likewise conform to expectation. Families with greater economic dependency—with a greater percentage of non-workers—were significantly more likely to be poor. In terms of family structure, families in which the spouse of the head was absent were more likely and extended families were less likely to be in poverty. The former effect is particularly strong. Other things being equal, the probability that a family was poor increased by .236 if it was headed by a single adult. Finally, the two contextual terms also behave as expected. Families living in the South and those in non-metropolitan areas were significantly more likely to be poor, *ceteris paribus*. Both these effects are of similar magnitude, increasing the probability of poverty by about .10.

Model 3 reveals a suppression of the effect for recent immigrants. Adding the family and contextual terms to the equation produces a sizable increase in the positive effect of recent immigrant status on poverty. This result is explained by the means for recent immigrants on the five family and contextual variables. [Table available from author upon request.] In comparison to natives, recent immigrants had lower economic dependency, were more likely to be in extended families, and were less likely to live in the South and in nonmetropolitan areas. The suppression effect means that if recent immigrants did not differ from natives in their lower dependency and their greater propensity to be extended, to

---

[11]An intermediate model (not shown) that included only the period, nativity, and race/ethnicity terms revealed that race/ethnicity did not attenuate the positive and significant effect for recent immigrants. This solidifies the conclusion that the changing racial/ethnic composition of recent immigrants played no part in their rise in poverty.

live in the South and in rural areas, recent immigrant poverty would be even higher than the observed average. Thus, controlling for these variables increased the main effect of recent immigration status on poverty.[12]

A similar story arises for previous immigrants as well (those who arrived over 5 years prior to the census). The main effect for prior immigrants in Model 2 is negative and significant, suggesting that previous immigrants were less likely to be in poverty than natives, after controlling for the individual characteristics of the family head. When the five family and contextual terms are entered (Model 3), the main effect for prior immigrants attenuates to zero. Measures of central tendency indicate that these immigrant families were somewhat more likely than natives to be in extended families and were far less apt to live in the South and in nonmetropolitan areas (they did not differ with respect to dependency or headship). Again, because these characteristics tend to reduce poverty risks, they help explain the lower poverty rate among previous immigrants compared to natives revealed in Model 2.

The final model in Table 3 introduces the interaction between nativity status and year of observation. This model determines whether recent immigrants in 1979 were particularly likely to be poor, net of the other variables in the equation. These variables include several human capital, family, and contextual characteristics that could account for the higher incidence of poverty in the later period. However, the interaction term for recent immigrant in 1979 is positive and significant. Compared to recent immigrants in 1959 or 1969, those in 1979 were especially likely to be poor. This result indicates that neither a deterioration in immigrant "quality" nor an increase in the percentage of nonwhites accounts for the disproportionately high poverty rates among recent immigrants in 1979.

Table 4 examines the question of changes in immigrant poverty over time separately for the four basic racial/ethnic groups. Among white families, Table 4 upholds previous findings that poverty among recent immigrants increased substantially over time. The terms for recent immigrants in both 1969 and 1979 are positive and significant; other things being equal, recent white immigrants in 1969 and 1979 were more likely to be in poverty than their statistical counterparts in 1959.

A similar conclusion applies to black families. The strong and positive effect of recent immigrant in 1969 and recent immigrant in 1979 interactions suggest that recent black immigrant families have become increasingly likely to be poor, controlling for many factors affecting poverty. Here, however, poverty among prior black immigrants likewise increased over time. This secular in-

---

[12]Auxiliary analyses (not shown) revealed that dependency and extension were the two variables largely responsible for the suppression. This implies that the extended family structures, and the greater proportionate labor-force commitment that typify recent immigrants, is important for keeping many of them out of poverty. Were it not for these family structures and residence preferences, recent immigrant poverty would be considerably greater.

crease is not explained by a deterioration in the background characteristics of black immigrants as they have been purged of the influence of education and secondary labor-market occupation.

Table 2 documented that Hispanic immigrant families were not largely responsible for the steady increase in poverty among recent immigrants over the period 1959–1979. This finding is important, because Hispanics have been identified as disproportionately responsible for "the immigrant problem" (Cafferty, Chiswick, Greeley, & Sullivan, 1983). Results from the logit model of poverty among Hispanic families (Table 4) confirm the conclusion drawn from Table 2. Although recent Hispanic immigrants were significantly more likely than their native counterparts to be poor (evidenced by the main effect for recent immigrants), none of the interaction terms between immigrant status and the year of observation reached statistical significance. Unlike white and black families, recent Hispanic immigrant families did not experience a steady increase in poverty, other things being equal. This model also reveals that compared to Mexicans and Other Hispanics, Puerto Ricans were significantly more likely to be in poverty.

The model for Asian families in Table 4 shows that, in general, Asian immigrant families, particularly recent arrivals, were more likely to be poor than U.S.-born Asians. This result is manifest in the positive and significant main effects for immigrant status. Other things being equal, the probability that a recent Asian immigrant family was in poverty exceeded that among natives by .242. The interaction terms in this model suggest that, after controlling for numerous determinants of poverty, there was no intertemporal increase in the propensity of recent Asian immigrant families to be poor. Previous Asian immigrants, however, were less likely to be poor in 1969 and 1979 compared to 1959. Coefficients associated with year-of-immigration interactions for prior arrivals are negative and significant.

The other variables in these models behaved as expected. For example, for all four racial/ethnic groups, families with better educated and older heads were less likely, and those with heads engaged in secondary occupations were more likely, to be in poverty. Parameter estimates for family economic dependency, headship configuration, extended structure, and nonmetropolitan and Southern residence likewise conformed to expectations.

To summarize, Tables 3 and 4 presented multivariate models of poverty among families. The intent was to document the net propensity of immigrant families to be poor and to determine whether a secular increase in poverty could be confirmed in this multivariate context. They also established how these findings differed across the four race/ethnic groups. These models showed that, other things being equal, (a) families with heads who were better educated and older (but not aged) were less likely to be poor; (b) families with heads who had a secondary occupation or who were black, Mexican, Puerto Rican, or Other

Table 4. Logistic Regression of Poverty on Individual and Family Characteristics: White Black, Hispanic, and Asian Families[a]

	Whites		Blacks		Hispanics		Asians	
	L	P	L	P	L	P	L	P
Intercept	−2.28		−1.49		−2.17		−1.45	
	(.43)		(.31)		(.27)		(.40)	
1969	−.71	−.050	−.92	−.169	−.69	−.101	−.29	−.023
	(.11)		(.08)		(.09)		(.17)	
1979	−.70	−.049	−1.08	−.190	−.52	−.080	−.17	−.014
	(.12)		(.08)		(.10)		(.17)	
Family head variables								
Prior immigrant	−.00[b]	−.000	−.86	−.160	.13[b]	.024	.74	.089
	(.20)		(.32)		(.10)		(.17)	
Recent immigrant	−1.19[b]	−.070	−4.93	−.335	.59	.121	1.54	.242
	(1.05)		(2.40)		(.19)		(.33)	
Mexican					.06	.011		
					(.06)			
Puerto Rican					.43	.086		
					(.09)			
Japanese							−.36	−.028
							(.10)	
Chinese							.05[b]	.005
							(.09)	
Education	−.14	−.012	−.13	−.028	−.14	−.024	−.11	−.010
	(.01)		(.01)		(.01)		(.01)	
Secondary occupation	.57	.066	.38	.089	.42	.083	.44	.047
	(.12)		(.07)		(.06)		(.09)	
Age	−.04	−.004	−.04	−.009	−.04	−.007	−.09	−.008
	(.01)		(.01)		(.01)		(.01)	
Age squared	.26[b]	.027	.23	.053	.19[b]	.036	.68	.080
	(.14)		(.11)		(.10)		(.14)	

Asian (compared to white) were more likely to be poor; (c) families with single heads, nuclear (versus extended) structures, southern and nonmetropolitan residence, or with greater economic dependency ratio were more likely to be poor; (d) recent immigrants had higher poverty rates than natives; (e) poverty among recent immigrants would be even higher were it not for their lower dependency rates, greater prevalence of extended structure, and residence outside of southern and nonmetropolitan areas as compared to natives; (f) families who were immigrants, but not recent immigrants, were less likely than natives to be poor, but this was likewise accounted for by their family structure and residential preference; (g) recent immigrants in 1979 were particularly likely to be poor; and, (h) this increase over time in the net propensity of recent immigrant families to be poor obtained for whites and blacks.

Table 4. (Continued)

	Whites		Blacks		Hispanics		Asians	
	L	P	L	P	L	P	L	P
Family and contextual variables								
Dependency rate	.04	.004	.04	.009	.04	.007	.04	.004
	(.00)		(.00)		(.00)		(.00)	
Spouse absent	1.47	.231	1.37	.330	1.33	.302	1.04	.140
	(.11)		(.06)		(.06)		(.09)	
Extended family	−.83	−.056	−.55	−.110	−.46	−.072	−.50	−.037
	(.14)		(.08)		(.07)		(.10)	
Southern residence	.33	.035	.69	.166	.80	.171	.36	.038
	(.09)		(.07)		(.06)		(.11)	
Nonmetropolitan	.77	.096	.87	.211	.60	.124	.09[b]	.008
residence	(.08)		(.08)		(.07)		(.10)	
Interaction terms								
Prior immigrant, 1969	.06[b]	.006	.94	.229	−.05[b]	−.009	−.50	−.037
	(.25)		(.41)		(.13)		(.23)	
Recent immigrant, 1969	2.48	.477	5.62	.655	.16[b]	.030	−.29[b]	−.023
	(1.12)		(2.43)		(.24)		(.39)	
Prior immigrant, 1979	−.39[b]	−.031	1.19	.289	−.03[b]	−.005	−.87	−.056
	(.28)		(.35)		(.14)		(.21)	
Recent immigrant, 1979	2.84	.561	5.83	.656	.09[b]	.017	−.10[b]	−.009
	(1.12)		(2.41)		(.25)		(.35)	
−2 log (likelihood ratio)	4251		7148		9854		5794	
Degrees of freedom	8849		8268		11939		11945	

[a]L = Logit coefficient (standard errors in parentheses); P = probability change (reflects the change in the probability of being in poverty resulting from a unit change in the independent variable) computed at P′ = .1038 for whites; .3382 for blacks; .2344 for Hispanics; and .1006 for Asians (see Petersen, 1985).
[b]Parameter estimate not significant at .05.

DISCUSSION AND CONCLUSIONS

Since the mid-1960s, the United States has experienced a new immigration. A fundamental cause of this wave was the 1965 legislation that replaced a discriminatory quota system of immigration with a more equitable worldwide distribution of visas. This legislation also rearranged the priorities under which immigrants were admitted, giving preference to those wishing to rejoin kin over those entering on the merits of their occupational skills. This new immigration has therefore been characterized by (a) an increase in the flow of immigration; (b) an increase (decrease) in the percentage of immigrants entering under the family reunification provisions (entering with needed occupational skills); (c) an increase in the percentage arriving from less developed countries (especially from Asia and Latin America); and, (d) an increase in the percentage of immigrants who are nonwhite.

Echoing the past, these changes resurfaced popular concern that the country was admitting, to an increasing degree, too many immigrants destined for the bottom of the stratification system. To establish the validity of this concern, this chapter sought to document trends in the level of poverty among immigrant and native families during the 1960–1980 period.

Descriptive analyses revealed that poverty among U.S. families declined precipitously during the 1960s, but this decline was far less impressive among immigrant families. Poverty among all families continued to decline between 1969 and 1979, but increased slightly among immigrant-headed families during this time span. Whereas poverty roughly halved among native families between 1959 and 1979, it declined by only 10% among immigrant-headed families.

Poverty increased among immigrant families between 1969 and 1979. Results for specific years-since-immigration categories revealed that recent immigrants—those who arrived 5 or fewer years before the census—had by far the sharpest rise in poverty. Although poverty among those who had been in the United States from 6 to 10 and 11 to 20 years before the census also increased somewhat, I conclude that the post-1965 immigrants were primarily responsible for the rise in immigrant poverty between 1969 and 1979. Poverty among immigrants did increase as the new immigration proceeded.

Poverty among the most recent arrivals increased considerably between 1969 and 1979 and among all four racial/ethnic groups: non-Hispanic whites, blacks, Asians, and Hispanics. Despite popular allegations that part of the deterioration in the economic status of succeeding waves of immigrants was due to the changing social/ethnic composition of immigrants, my results reveal that recent white immigrant families were a prime contributor to the overall rise in poverty among recent arrivals. Thus, the increase in poverty among recent immigrants was not entirely compositional. Aggregate poverty rates increased among all groups of recent immigrants, even whites, which supports the idea that the emphasis on family reunification and deemphasis on job skills was a contributing factor.

Multivariate analyses confirmed that poverty among recent immigrants increased. That is, after controlling for the year of observation and race/ethnicity, recent immigrants in 1979 were significantly more likely to be poor than their counterparts in 1969 or 1959. Furthermore, this surge was not explained by a shift in the racial/ethnic composition of immigrants.

A justification for the more comprehensive models of absolute poverty was to determine whether the rise in recent immigrant poverty could be explained by household head, family, and residence characteristics. The pooled models revealed that recent immigrants in 1979 were more likely to be poor than their counterparts in 1969 and 1959. Disaggregating by race/ethnicity, a significant increase in absolute poverty was indicated for white and black recent immigrant families. Although much of the clamor over the new immigration has been in reaction to a flood of Hispanic and Asian immigrants, white and black recent immigrant families had the sharpest increase in poverty. This is a robust finding, as it held true in both the descriptive and multivariate analyses.

There is strong evidence that poverty among immigrants increased as the new immigration unfolded. Historically, the United States has been less concerned with poverty, *per se,* among immigrants, than with the presumed utilization of public assistance programs by immigrants (Jensen, 1987). The rise in poverty suggests an associated increase in the number of immigrants in need of cash assistance. However, other work (Tienda & Jensen, 1986) has shown that recent immigrants are less likely than otherwise comparable natives to use public assistance—especially in 1980 (Jensen, 1988). Whereas the potential demand for welfare income among recent immigrants increased over the past 20 years, this has been offset to some degree by an increased reluctance on their part to receive welfare income. Despite the increase in poverty, their aggregate use of welfare income remains in question.

ACKNOWLEDGMENTS

An earlier version of this chapter was presented at the 1987 Annual Meeting of the Population Association of America in Chicago, Illinois. This research was conducted while the author was supported by an NICHD training grant (HD-07014) awarded to the Center for Demography and Ecology at the University of Wisconsin-Madison. A grant to the Center for Demography and Ecology from NICHD (HD-05876) provided computational support. The University of Wisconsin-Madison College of Agriculture and Life Sciences provided institutional support as did a grant from the U.S. Department of Health and Human Services to the Institute for Research on Poverty. I benefited from the helpful comments of Marta Tienda, Gary Sandefur, Larry Bumpass, Karl Taeuber, and W. Lee Hansen. Remaining errors are my own. Data files were created with the programming assistance of Franklin W. Monfort and Cheryl Knobeloch. The technical and clerical expertise of Susan Walsh, Gary Heisserer, Diane Duesterhoeft, and Sarah Rudolph is most gratefully acknowledged.

APPENDIX: TECHNICAL AND OPERATIONAL PROCEDURES

This study of poverty among immigrants from 1960 to 1980 uses a repeated cross-sectional design. Use of the 1960, 1970, and 1980 Public-Use Samples of the U.S. Census ensured an adequate number of cases and maximized com-

parability of measurements over time. From these files, stratified subsamples
were drawn to provide an adequate representation of race/ethnic and nativity
groups. In each year, as many family households as possible, but not exceeding
10,000, were sought for each of the following groups: foreign Asian, foreign
Hispanic, foreign black, other foreign, native Asian, native Hispanic, native
black and other native. These files contain data on the family household head,
the head's spouse (if present) and a wide variety of household-level items. The
latter were either in the PUS household record or were computed from the
household-specific individual records.

    Family households compose the units of analysis in this chapter. The family
is defined as persons residing in the same household who are related by blood,
marriage, or adoption. Nonfamily households (persons living alone or households in which the head is unrelated to all other individuals) and persons living in

Table A. Definitions of Variables Used in Multivariate Analyses of Poverty

Variable	Definition
Family head characteristics	
Age	Age of head in years, 18–99
Age squared	Head's age squared, divided by 1000
Education	Grades of schooling completed by head
Secondary occupation	Head has secondary labor market occupation[a] coded 2; 1 otherwise
Race/ethnicity (4 categories)	1 = Head is non-Hispanic white
	2 = Head is non-Hispanic black
	3 = Head is Hispanic
	4 = Head is non-Hispanic Asian
Race/ethnicity (8 categories)	1 = Head is non-Hispanic white
	2 = Head is non-Hispanic black
	3 = Head is Mexican
	4 = Head is Puerto Rican
	5 = Head is Other Hispanic
	6 = Head is Japanese
	7 = Head is Chinese
	8 = Head is Other Asian
Hispanic ethnicity	1 = Head is Other Hispanic
	2 = Head is Mexican
	3 = Head is Puerto Rican
Asian ethnicity	1 = Head is Other Asian
	2 = Head is Japanese
	3 = Head is Chinese
Nativity	1 = Head is native
	2 = Head is prior immigrant (immigrated over 5 years before)
	3 = Head is recent immigrant (immigrated up to 5 years before)

Table A. *(Continued)*

Variable	Definition
Family characteristics	
Headship configuration	1 = Family, both spouses present
	2 = Spouse-absent family
Extended family	Adult relative of head (except spouse or child) present coded 2; 1 otherwise
Dependency rate	Number of nonworking family members as a percentage of total family members
Other independent variables	
Southern residence	Family resides in Southern state coded 2; 1 otherwise (where Southern states are AL, AR, DE, DC, FL, GA, KY, LA, MD, MS, NC, OK, SC, TN, TX, VA and WV)
Nonmetropolitan residence	Family resides in a nonmetropolitan area coded 2; 1 otherwise
Year of observation	1 = 1960
	2 = 1970
	3 = 1980
Dependent variables	
Absolute poverty	Total family income less than poverty threshold coded 1; 0 otherwise

[a]Based on Osterman's (1975) definition of secondary labor market occupation.

group quarters are excluded. In all, I analyze 38,161; 41,905; and 45,822 families in 1960, 1970, and 1980, respectively. These data are weighted in the descriptive tabulations. However, to ensure reliable tests of statistical significance, I use unweighted data in the multivariate analyses. Auxiliary tabulations revealed that nonfamily households compose less than one-fourth (23%) of all households and that there were negligible differences in the prevalence of nonfamily units according to nativity or race.

Special precautions were taken to maximize the comparability of measures across time. For example, rather than using the absolute poverty cutoffs supplied in the 1970 and 1980 censuses (which differ slightly from each other and from those used in 1960), I employed poverty thresholds calculated for 1959, intended for use with the 1960 census (Orshansky, 1965). These cutoffs were inflated via the Consumer Price Index to form the poverty thresholds in 1969 and 1979. The operational definitions of all variables used in the analyses throughout are detailed in the Appendix table.

In the ensuing analyses, families are defined as immigrant or native based on the immigrant status of the household head. An immigrant family's years since immigration is likewise determined by the head. In 1960, and for Puerto

Ricans in all 3 years, a lack of data on detailed years since immigration forced a reliance on the variable defined as residence 5 years ago. Immigrants who lived abroad 5 years before the census were defined as recent immigrants, while immigrants who lived in the United States 5 years prior were defined as prior immigrants.

Because the United States exercises a degree of sovereignty and jurisdiction over the Commonwealth of Puerto Rico, those born on this island are legally regarded as native U.S. citizens (Nelson & Tienda, 1985). However, in many respects island-born Puerto Ricans resemble immigrants. Puerto Ricans on the island are physically and often culturally distant from mainstream U.S. society, and the causes and consequences of their migration to the mainland resemble those of other immigrant streams. Some writers have chosen to regard island-born Puerto Ricans as natives, not immigrants (Cafferty *et al.*, 1983). Still others have faced this dilemma by ignoring Puerto Ricans altogether (Simon, 1984; Blau, 1984). However, as Puerto Ricans have been shown to have high levels of poverty and welfare receipt (Tienda & Angel, 1982; Tienda, 1984; Bean & Tienda, 1987), they are critical to the focus of this research and their omission could distort the findings. Moreover, because they so resemble other immigrant streams, I have chosen to define Puerto Ricans who were born outside the United States as immigrants, with the understanding that this is technically imprecise. The empirical results on Puerto Ricans should be interpreted in this light. Finally, because Puerto Ricans are considered U.S. citizens, those born on the island are not asked year of immigration in the census. Still, I was able to define recent Puerto Rican "immigrants" as those who did not reside in the United States 5 years prior to the census.

REFERENCES

Angel, R., & M. Tienda. (1982). Determinants of extended household structure: Cultural pattern or economic need? *American Journal of Sociology, 87*, 1360–1383.

Atchley, R. C. (1978). Aging as a social problem: An overview. In M. Seltzer, S. Corbett, & R. Atchley (Eds.), *Social problems of the aging: Readings*. Belmont, CA: Wadsworth Publishing Company.

Baker, R. J., & J. A. Nelder. 1978. *The GLIM system, release 3, generalized linear interactive modelling*. Oxford: Numerical Algorithms Group.

Bean, F. D., & M. Tienda. (1987). *The Hispanic population of the United States*. New York: Russell Sage.

Becker, G. S. (1975). *Human capital: A theoretical analysis with special reference to education*. Chicago, IL: University of Chicago Press.

Blau, F. (1984). The use of transfer payments by immigrants. *Industrial and Labor Relations Review, 37*(2), 222–239.

Blau, P. M., & O. D. Duncan. (1967). *The American occupational structure*. New York: John Wiley.

Blumberg, P. (1980). *Inequality in an age of decline*. New York: Oxford University Press.

Borjas, G., & M. Tienda. (1987). The economic consequences of immigration. *Science*, 235 (Feb. 26), 613–620.

Cafferty, P. S., B. R. Chiswick, A. M. Greeley, & T. A. Sullivan. (1983). *The dilemma of American immigration: Beyond the golden door*. New Brunswick, NJ: Transaction Books.

Chiswick, B. R. (1979). The economic progress of immigrants: Some apparently universal patterns. In W. Felner (Ed.), *Contemporary economic problems*. Washington, DC: American Enterprise Institute.

Ehrenberg, R. G. & R. S. Smith. (1982). *Modern labor economics: Theory and public policy*. Glenview, IL: Scott, Foresman.

Gans, H. J. (1982). *The urban villagers: Group and class in the life of Italian-Americans*. (Updated and expanded edition). New York: The Free Press.

Gordon, M. (1964). *Assimilation in American life: The role of race, religion, and national origins*. New York: Oxford University Press.

Hanushek, E. A., & J. E. Jackson. (1977). *Statistical methods for social scientists*. New York: Academic Press.

Jensen, L. (1987). *The new immigration: Implications for poverty and public assistance utilization*. Unpublished Ph.D. thesis in Sociology, University of Wisconsin at Madison.

Jensen, L. (1988). Patterns of immigration and public assistance utilization, 1970–1980. *International Migration Review*, forthcoming.

Nelson, C., & M. Tienda. (1985). The structuring of Hispanic ethnicity: Historical and contemporary perspectives. *Ethnic and Racial Studies, 8*(1), 49–74.

New York Times/CBS News. (1986). "Immigration survey." The New York Times/CBS News Poll, June 19–23.

O'Hare, W. P. (1985). Poverty in America: Trends and new patterns. *Population Bulletin, 40*(3), 1–43.

Orshansky, M. (1965). Counting the poor: Another look at the poverty profile. *Social Security Bulletin*, 28 (Jan), 3–29.

Osterman, P. (1975). An empirical study of labor market segmentation. *Industrial and Labor Relations Review*, 28, 508–523.

Petersen, T. (1985). A comment on presenting results from logit and probit models. *American Sociological Review, 50*(1), 130–131.

Schiller, B. R. (1980). *The economics of poverty and discrimination* (3rd ed.). Englewood Cliffs, NJ: Prentice-Hall.

Segalman, R., & A. Basu. (1981). *Poverty in America: The welfare dilemma*. Westport, CT: Greenwood Press.

Simon, J. (1980). *What immigrants take from and give to the public coffers*. Final Report to the Select Commission on Immigration and Refugee Policy. Washington, DC: U.S. Government Printing Office.

Simon, J. (1984). Immigrants, taxes, and welfare in the U.S. *Population and Development Review, 10*(1), 55–69.

Tienda, M. (1984). The Puerto Rican worker: Recent evidence and future prospects. In *Puerto Ricans in the mid-eighties: An American challenge*, National Puerto Rican Coalition (Eds.). Washington, DC: National Puerto Rican Coalition.

Tienda, M., & R. Angel. (1982). Headship and household composition among blacks, Hispanics and other whites. *Social Forces, 61*, 508–531.

Tienda, M., and L. Jensen. (1986). Immigration and public assistance participation: Dispelling the myth of dependency. *Social Science Research*, 15, 372–400.

II

Family and Intergenerational Processes

6

Poverty and the Family

JAMES P. SMITH

Until recently, poverty could be analyzed without paying major attention to the family. That is now no longer the case. Policy debates are increasingly centering around the family, and both major political parties are furiously attempting to formulate a family policy. Because of the long-term neglect of this topic by researchers, family policy is running far ahead of informed scholarship. At present, we do not even have good preliminary answers to the most basic issues: the causes of the declining black family, the feminization of poverty, and the rising numbers of children among the poor. We also know little about the consequences of those demographic changes in family composition on the distribution of economic rewards. This chapter attempts to examine some of those consequences.

The chapter is organized in three sections. The first describes the changing division of the American family between the poor, the middle class, and the affluent. Throughout this section, my depiction of the rise of the middle class since 1940 and the decline in family poverty, racial, and ethnic differences are highlighted. Particular attention is paid to the increasing divergence between intact families (those with both spouses present) and female-headed families. In view of the purpose of this volume, portraits of long-term changes in family poverty are provided for white, black, and Hispanic families. Because of the diversity among Hispanics, separate portraits are provided for Mexicans and Puerto Ricans. The second section examines the people who live in these families, investigating in particular the implications of changing family rates on the feminization of poverty. The final section deals with the basic issue of the role played by the breakup of the family, especially the black family, on rates of family poverty.

JAMES P. SMITH • The RAND Corporation, Santa Monica, California.

AMERICA DIVIDED: THE POOR, THE MIDDLE CLASS, AND THE AFFLUENT

From the first attempts to measure poverty, debate has continued on whether the measure should reflect absolute or relative deprivation. The official government statistic is based on an absolute concept, so that the income necessary to escape poverty is adjusted upward over time only by the rate of inflation. Critics of the official statistics contend that poverty is a relative concept that should be defined according to the average income in that year. In this view, barring changing shapes of the distribution curve, the bottom quarter of the income distribution would always be classified as poor.

Neither extreme position is satisfactory. If the absolute income standard had been set 100 years ago, few would be poor today. Only 25 years after the poverty income threshold was established, one hears ever more persuasive calls for a revision of the values set in 1963. Similarly, the definition of the poor as the bottom quarter of the income distribution among both Ugandans and Americans does not allow economic growth to reduce poverty at all.

I have adopted a middle ground, using elements of both absolute and relative definitions. It turns out that my definition also corresponds more closely to popular notions of what poverty means. Surveys about the income required not to be poor indicate that many people believe the poverty threshold has increased 50 cents for every dollar increase in real income. Based on that observation, my definition of poverty increases the poverty threshold income by half a percent for every 1% growth in real income. More precisely, I start with the standard poverty-income thresholds jointly stratified by the number of persons and related children under 18 in the family. Assuming that those who set this standard hit the mark when the initial statistic was generated, these income thresholds were centered in 1963. Income cutoffs were then adjusted by half the real income growth rate or decline relative to 1963.[1]

The appeal of the poverty line owes a great deal to its simple separation of the poor from the rest of the population. Building on that simplicity, I divide families into three income classes: the poor, the middle class, and the affluent. The starting point for my affluence line is arbitrary; it was set to include the top 25 percent of white families in 1960 (the census year closest to establishment of the poverty line in 1963). Because the standard for affluence should grow at least

[1]Median white family income was used to compute the real growth rates. (Medians derived from calculations using decennial census tapes.) Income may be from any source (e.g., earnings, social security). At other points in the paper, the term *earnings* is used to refer to money received from a job. Family income refers to the total income from all family members. Throughout this chapter, unrelated individuals are not included. The 1940 census provides data only on earnings, not income.

Table 1. Income Groups of Families, 1940–1980
(Percentages)

	1940	1950	1960	1970	1980
All families					
Poor	34	22	15	11	11
Middle class	40	50	62	66	63
Affluent	26	28	23	23	26
White families					
Poor	31	18	12	9	9
Middle class	42	52	63	66	61
Affluent	27	30	25	25	30
Black families					
Poor	71	54	48	32	30
Middle class	26	42	49	59	59
Affluent	3	4	6	9	11
All Hispanic families					
Poor	55	43	32	23	23
Middle class	33	45	59	66	65
Affluent	12	12	9	11	12
Mexican families					
Poor	69	51	37	25	24
Middle class	26	41	56	66	68
Affluent	5	8	7	9	8
Puerto Rican families					
Poor	—[a]	38	32	33	39
Middle class	—	49	63	60	55
Affluent	—	13	5	7	6

[a]Sample size too small.
SOURCE: Computations from decennial census data.

as rapidly as real income, the 1960 cutoff is adjusted fully for real income growth to set the cutoffs in other years.[2]

To determine the long-term trends in numbers of poor families since 1940, Table 1 separates families into three income classes for the census years 1940–1980. In 1940, 34% of all families fell below the poverty cutoff,[3] lending some

[2]The affluent income cutoffs were 2.45 (1940), 2.80 (1950), 3.54 (1960), 4.09 (1970), and 4.25 (1980) times the poverty cutoffs in each year.
[3]Using the more conventional inflation-adjusted poverty cutoffs, 51% of all families were poor in 1940. 16% in 1960, and 9% in 1980. The cutoffs for white families were 48% in 1940, 13% in

posthumous support to Franklin Roosevelt's claim that one-third of his contemporary America was ill-fed, ill-clothed, and ill-housed. In that year, 4 in 10 American families belonged to the middle class and another quarter qualified as affluent. The class tensions of the Great Depression may have been exacerbated by the roughly equal size of these three economic groups. In particular, middle-class America was not much larger in numbers than the poor.

The real story since 1940 has been the spectacular reduction in the ranks of the poor. Between 1940 and 1960 alone, the percentage of all families in poverty was more than cut in half, to 15%; 20 years later, in 1980, one in every nine families was poor. The pace of change was, however, quite uneven. Between 1940 and 1960, 83% of the secular decline in poverty among families took place. Progress was so large during these years that the total number of poor families declined by more than a million. The gains continued, but at a much diminished pace, in the subsequent 20 years. In fact, with my measure the proportion of poor families remained unchanged during the 1970s. Many of the victories of the War on Poverty apparently took place 5 years before the war was officially declared. The relative performance across these decades offers important clues concerning the contributors to long-run reductions in poverty.

A corollary of the falling relative size of the poverty group was the emergence of a numerically dominant American middle class. Between 1940 and 1960, the proportion of families in the middle class grew about 10 percentage points per decade. With the end of the economic boom, middle-class growth slowed during the 1960s and declined slightly during the 1970s. In the last decade, the middle class has lost constituents because of growing numbers of affluent families. Reflecting the constancy in relative income inequality, the proportionate size of the affluent group was, however, the same in 1980 as in 1940.

Table 1 also demonstrates that since 1940 poverty rates have diminished sharply for families of both races. Reflecting their weight in the total population, secular trends among white family poverty moved in lockstep with rates for all families. Poverty was pervasive in the black community of 1940; 70% of all black families were then destitute, with little hope that their lot or even that of their children would soon improve. From this dismal starting point, progress in reducing black poverty is impressive. By 1960, for the first time in American history, the median black family was not poor. Fully 30% of 1980 black families were still part of the poor black underclass. But placed in historical perspective, such figures still represent enormous progress toward eradicating black family poverty. Political rhetoric on the race issue must eventually balance two compe-

---

1960, and 7% in 1980. These figures for black families were 87% in 1940, 47% in 1960, and 27% in 1980.

ling truths. America has made considerable strides in reducing black poverty, but by the standards of a just society, it remains at unacceptably high levels.

The numbers for black families in Table 1 simultaneously illustrate the persistence of black poverty, the growth of the black middle class, and the recent emergence of a nonnegligible black upper class. In 1940, by any definition, the overwhelming majority of black families were poor. The small black middle class consisted of only one in four black families. At the other extreme, very few black families were members of the economic elite. Placed in the perspective of black history, these 40 years were unique because of the emergence of a black middle class, whose members by 1980 constituted almost 60% of black families. In that year, one in every nine black families was affluent, a fourfold increase over 1940.

Table 1 also illustrates the changing economic status of Hispanic[4] families. Separate profiles are presented for two numerically large subgroups—Mexicans and Puerto Ricans. In 1940, the economic plight of Hispanics rested roughly midway between that of non-Hispanic white and black families. More than half of all Hispanic families were classified as poor, and only one in three as middle class in that year. Although Hispanics as a group fared somewhat better than black Americans in 1940, there was little difference between the living standards of blacks and Mexicans. Seventy percent of 1940 Mexican families had incomes below the poverty threshold, little different from the rate for black families.

As was true for other American families, economic growth lifted many Hispanic families out of poverty and into the middle class. By 1980, the aggregate poverty rate among Hispanics was 23%, and two-thirds of 1980 Hispanic families were members of the middle class. The pace of economic advancement was somewhat slower, however, among Hispanics than among our other groups. The Hispanic poverty rate in 1980 was 42% of its 1940 level; in contrast, among all white families, the 1980 poverty rate was 29% of its 1940 value. As was true

---

[4]Census families were identified as Hispanic if the head of the family was Hispanic. The head was determined to be Hispanic if he or she met any of the following general conditions: was born in Central or South America, Spain, Mexico, Cuba, Puerto Rico, or the Spanish-speaking Caribbean; parents were born in any of the above countries; has a Spanish surname; Spanish is/was spoken in the home (except 1950); the census identified this person as Spanish (1960, 1970, 1980); or the head identified himself or herself as Spanish (1980 only).

Spanish families were identified as Mexican if the family head was born in Mexico, the head's mother or father was born in Mexico, or if the family resided in one of the five southwestern states: Arizona, California, Colorado, New Mexico, or Texas.

Spanish families were identified as Puerto Rican if the family head was born in Puerto Rico, the head's mother or father was born in Puerto Rico, or if the family resided in New Jersey, New York, or Pennsylvania.

The assistance of Marta Tienda in this ethnic definition is gratefully acknowledged. See Chapter 2 by Tienda and Jensen in this volume for a more detailed discussion of income status of Hispanics.

for all white and black families, the decline in the fraction of Hispanic families who were poor stalled during the 1970s.

Our separate statistics for Mexicans and Puerto Ricans attests to the great diversity among Hispanics in their level of economic well-being and the rate by which it has improved over time. On the one hand, Mexicans represent an economic success story, as their economic gains were even more rapid than those of blacks. Whereas black and Mexican income levels in 1940 were roughly the same, poverty rates among Mexican families declined to one in four families in 1980, and almost 70% became fully accredited members of the middle class. In contrast, Puerto Ricans' economic status changed little in the 30 years after 1950. Indeed, their 1980 poverty rate of 39% is actually one percentage point higher than it was in 1950. Particularly disturbing is the deteriorating position of Puerto Ricans during the 1970s, as the proportion in poverty rose by six percentage points. These bleak statistics point to one of this nation's best-kept secrets— a widespread and rising incidence of poverty among Puerto Rican families.

Table 1 also demonstrates another distinctive feature of the economic changes of Hispanic families after 1940. Whereas the percentage of black families classified as affluent expanded fourfold between 1940 and 1980, there was no change in the percentage of Hispanic families who were affluent. The relative numbers of Hispanic families among the economic elite was one in eight in 1940, and remains at that same level today. Once again, this stable aggregate figure hides considerable subgroup heterogeneity, with significantly declining numbers of Puerto Ricans in the affluent group, whereas the relative percentage of affluent Mexicans has registered a modest increase.

THE GROWING ISSUE OF FEMALE-HEADED FAMILIES

Not all families participated equally in these long-term trends. A central issue of this chapter concerns the disparate record of female-headed as compared with intact families (both spouses present). Table 2 documents the well-known and dramatic changes in the makeup of American families. Between 1940 and 1960, there was rough stability in the proportion of all families headed by women, but with the rising incidence of unwed parenting and divorce, the fraction of such families rose after 1960 and at an accelerated rate during the 1970s. By 1980, women headed almost one in seven families, almost 70% larger than the 1960 proportion.

Although the social and economic forces driving this trend affected both races, they reached epidemic proportions among blacks. Throughout this period, black families were always more likely than white families to have an absent father. One in six black families was female-headed in 1940, twice the white

Table 2. Distribution of Families according to Headship,
1940–1980 (Percentages)

	1940	1950	1960	1970	1980
All families					
Intact	87.6	89.3	89.5	86.9	83.2
Female-headed	8.6	7.9	8.1	10.4	13.6
Male-headed	3.8	2.8	2.4	2.7	3.2
White families					
Intact	88.3	90.3	90.8	88.9	86.6
Female-headed	7.9	7.0	6.9	8.5	10.5
Male-headed	3.8	2.7	2.3	2.6	2.9
Black families					
Intact	79.4	79.0	75.7	67.4	54.4
Female-headed	15.7	17.2	20.7	28.1	38.2
Male-headed	4.9	3.8	3.6	4.5	7.4
All Hispanic families					
Intact	83.4	82.9	84.7	82.1	76.1
Female-headed	10.7	12.2	11.6	14.3	19.0
Male-headed	5.9	4.8	3.7	3.6	4.9
Mexican families					
Intact	82.8	83.0	85.4	83.2	79.5
Female-headed	11.5	12.0	11.1	13.0	15.3
Male-headed	5.7	5.0	3.5	3.8	5.2
Puerto Rican families					
Intact	83.1	79.9	80.0	70.6	60.9
Female-headed	12.0	17.2	15.6	25.4	34.2
Male-headed	4.8	2.3	4.4	4.0	4.9

SOURCE: Computations from decennial census data.

rate. This proportion jumped sharply after 1960; almost four in ten black families were so constituted in 1980. The deteriorating position of the black family cannot be passed off simply as part of a more general social phenomenon. An additional two percentage points of white families became female-headed after 1970. In that decade alone, the increase among black families was ten percentage points. Either unique factors influenced the black family, or racially common factors affected blacks more intensely.

Until 1970, there was rough stability in the proportion of Hispanic families headed by women. During the 1970s, the incidence of female-headed families rose until it represented almost 20% of all families in 1980. Once again the principal Hispanic story is that of considerable diversity. The eye-catching numbers are those of Puerto Ricans. In the 20 years after 1960, the incidence of female-headed families more than doubled until, by 1980, more than one in three Puerto Rican families were female-headed. Although this problem is usually cast as a black one, one could just as accurately portray the rising rates of female headship among Puerto Ricans as reaching epidemic proportions. In contrast, Mexican families have remained relatively stable, with a slight rise in the relative numbers of families headed by women during the 1970s.

Table 3 permits a comparison of intact and female-headed households by using the same three-way income division as Table 1. Some caution must be exercised in interpreting secular trends by family type. Because the composition of families changed so much over time, this table cannot tell us whether the condition of the remaining family members deteriorated when they became female-headed or whether most of these families came from the previously poor. Indeed, the evidence I present below indicates that both forces were at work— becoming a female-headed household diminishes total family income; the families that became female-headed were increasingly selected from families with lower income. With this cautionary note in mind, we examine the relative economic status of intact and female-headed families.

To take the good news first, the 40-year trend points to considerable long-term poverty decline among intact families of all demographic groups. One-third of these families were poor in 1940, but only 7% were poor by 1980. As has been the case throughout, much of the poverty reduction took place before 1960. However, the economic status of intact and female-headed families continued to diverge during the subsequent 20 years. As a result, the post-1960 decline in poverty rates (as well as the increase in affluence rates) was noticeably larger in families with both spouses present. In particular, the rise in rates of affluence among these families was unusually large during the 1970s.

The serious economic difficulties faced by many black families can hide an often overlooked group of black intact families who are doing quite well. In 1940, even their poverty rates hovered around 70%, attesting to pervasiveness of black poverty at that time. But among all the demographic subgroups this study examines, subsequent gains were largest among intact black families. Their poverty rates were cut almost in half between 1940 and 1960. Contrary to the aggregate trend for all black families, the proportionate rate of progress was larger between 1960 and 1980. Only 15% of intact black families had incomes below the 1980 poverty cutoff, as declining black poverty rates continued even during the stagnant 1970s.

The post-1960 era is especially remarkable for the spectacular rise in the fraction of intact black families in the elite class. Among such families, affluence rates doubled, and much of this rise took place in the 1970s. Two-thirds of intact black families were economically middle class, and one in six had an income large enough for membership in the affluent class. The emergence of this sub-

	1940		1950		1960		1970		1980	
	Intact	Female-headed	Intact	Female-headed	Intact	Female-headed	Intact	Female-headed	Intact	Female-headed
All families										
Poor	33	47	20	48	12	42	8	39	7	36
Middle class	40	36	51	37	64	47	66	53	64	58
Affluent	27	17	29	15	24	11	26	8	29	6
White families										
Poor	30	41	17	42	10	34	7	32	6	30
Middle class	41	39	52	40	64	52	67	58	64	62
Affluent	29	20	31	18	26	14	26	10	30	8
Black families										
Poor	69	81	49	76	39	69	21	58	15	53
Middle class	27	17	44	21	54	29	69	40	68	44
Affluent	4	2	7	3	7	2	9	2	17	3
All Hispanic families										
Poor	55	66	40	62	28	59	17	56	16	52
Middle class	34	24	47	30	62	38	70	41	70	44
Affluent	11	10	13	7	10	3	12	3	14	3
Mexican families										
Poor	70	77	53	67	33	68	20	57	19	52
Middle class	27	17	39	26	59	29	70	40	72	46
Affluent	4	6	8	7	7	3	10	2	9	2
Puerto Rican families										
Poor	—[a]	—	33	62	29	52	20	69	21	72
Middle class	—	—	52	38	66	46	71	29	70	26
Affluent	—	—	15	0	5	2	8	2	9	2

[a]Sample size too small.
SOURCE: Computations from decennial census data.

group of prosperous black families is especially notable when tracked against the corresponding white experience. Although white rates of affluence in husband-wife families were roughly stable, black rates increased fourfold. Among families of this type, the odds of achieving affluence were almost 7 to 1 in favor of whites in 1940; they dropped to 1.7 to 1 by 1980. Given the 70% poverty rates that prevailed in 1940, a dual black economic experience would have seemed farfetched then. Today, a two-tier black economic society is a reality, and black families with both mother and father present are the principal inhabitants of the prosperous world.

Unfortunately, there is a full complement of bad news to tell as well. Persons in female-headed families were always more likely to be poor and less likely to be included among the affluent. Their 1940 poverty rates were 47%, as compared with the overall rate of 34%. So many black families were poor in 1940 that the higher incidence of poverty in female-headed black families only shifts the issue to how much poorer these families were.

Although poverty rates decreased over time even for these families, the decline was quite modest compared with those of other family configurations. More than a third of all families headed by women remained poor in 1980. Average incomes of female-headed families failed to keep up with the economywide income growth, so that as a group their situation worsened relative to that of other families. Their deterioration is best read from the affluent column, which comes closest to measuring economic status relative to the mean. Of female-headed families, 17% had family incomes above the 1940 affluence line compared with about one in twenty families in 1980.

Table 3 also depicts the increasing concentration of black poverty in those families headed by women. Although a rising economic tide lowered these poverty rates as well, the generated waves were not large. More than two-thirds of black families headed by women were poor in 1960, and the median such family remains poor today.

The overall trends for Hispanics parallel those just described for other families. Among Hispanics, Table 3 indicates that the largest and most persistent improvement in reducing the ranks of the poor occurred among intact families. One in six intact Hispanic families was poor in 1980, compared to more than one in two in 1940. Table 3 isolates one reason why the representation of Hispanics within the elite has not accelerated. The sharp rise in the numbers of black families in this affluent class was due to a spectacular increase in the percentage of black intact families who were affluent (a 1980 rate of 17% compared to 9% in 1970). No such change took place among Hispanics, where there was only a slight rise in the percentage of affluent intact families.

The poverty problem has become increasingly concentrated in female-headed families. Our three-way income class division among all Hispanic families in

1980 is quite similar to that of black families. If one knows today that an Hispanic family is headed by a woman, the odds are better than even that such a family is poor. Puerto Ricans dominate the bad news. Seventy-two percent of all female-headed Puerto Rican families have needs-adjusted incomes below our poverty thresholds. This rate is almost 20 percentage points higher than the black rate in 1980 and an equal number of percentage points greater than the Puerto Rican rate in 1960. It is the deteriorating economic reality faced by an expanding number of female-headed families that is at the core of the declining relative economic position of Puerto Ricans.

The degree of overlap of family income distributions among intact and female-headed families portrays the expanding gap between these families. The overlap is described in Table 4, which lists the fraction of female-headed households with incomes exceeding three critical values in the intact-family income distribution: the bottom quartile, the median, and the top quartile. To illustrate, in 1940, 60% of white female-headed families had incomes in excess of the lowest quarter of intact families, and 37% had incomes larger than the average (median) white intact family. Because equality in the distributions would imply proportions of 75% and 50%, the family income distribution of female-headed families was below that of intact families in 1940.

The key point, however, concerns the extent to which the distributions have moved apart over the years. By 1980, only 18% of white female-headed families had incomes in excess of the median intact family, and little more than a third exceeded the bottom 25% of intact families.

Table 4. Overlapping Income Distributions of Female-Headed and Intact Families

| | Percentage of female-headed families whose income exceeds intact families' income | | | | |
	1940	1950	1960	1970	1980
Blacks					
Bottom quartile	62	49	47	38	36
Median	34	23	24	18	15
Top quartile	14	9	10	6	5
Whites					
Bottom quartile	60	50	48	43	37
Median	37	31	29	24	18
Top quartile	17	14	13	9	6

SOURCE: Computations from decennial census data.

Table 5. Income Groups by Gender, Race, and Hispanic
Ethnicity, 1940–1980 (Percentages)

	1940	1950	1960	1970	1980
All families					
Poor					
Women	34	23	15	11	11
Men	34	22	13	8	7
Middle class					
Women	40	50	52	65	63
Men	40	50	62	66	64
Affluent					
Women	26	27	23	24	26
Men	26	28	25	26	29
White families					
Poor					
Women	31	20	12	9	9
Men	31	19	11	7	6
Middle class					
Women	41	50	63	66	63
Men	41	51	62	66	63
Affluent					
Women	28	30	25	25	28
Men	28	30	27	27	31
Black families					
Poor					
Women	71	57	45	32	30
Men	70	52	39	26	22
Middle class					
Women	25	38	49	60	60
Men	26	41	54	64	64
Affluent					
Women	4	5	6	8	10
Men	4	6	7	10	14
All Hispanic families					
Poor					
Women	56	44	32	22	22
Men	56	42	28	18	16
Middle class					
Women	33	44	60	67	66
Men	32	45	62	70	70
Affluent					
Women	11	12	9	11	12
Men	12	13	10	12	14

Table 5. (Continued)

	1940	1950	1960	1970	1980
Mexican families					
Poor					
Women	70	56	37	25	23
Men	71	55	33	21	18
Middle class					
Women	26	36	56	66	69
Men	24	37	59	69	73
Affluent					
Women	4	8	7	9	8
Men	4	9	8	10	9
Puerto Rican families					
Poor					
Women	—[a]	44	30	31	38
Men	—	36	26	21	23
Middle class					
Women	—	45	65	61	56
Men	—	51	68	70	69
Affluent					
Women	—	11	5	8	6
Men	—	13	6	9	8

[a]Sample size too small.
SOURCE: Computations from decennial census data.

The Feminization of Poverty

These divergent trends across family types carry immediate implications for the people who live in these families. A direct corollary of the rising numbers of female-headed families is the feminization of poverty. Table 5 presents three-way income strata separately for adult men and women. In 1940, poverty was sex-neutral. Because incomes are typically pooled among family members to set family consumption levels, all members tend to share a common economic fortune. At the very least, poverty is definitionally sex-neutral because all family members are assigned as a group to their income class.

Over 90% of all 1940 families included a husband and wife. As a result, the margin for any sex differential in poverty rate was very small. The margin that did exist had little effect because poverty rates of families headed by men were little different from the overall family rate.[5] The higher 1940 incidence of female-headed families resulted in some black feminization of poverty. But by and large it is no surprise that the coinage of the term *feminization of poverty* is of recent origin. One reason less concern was registered historically about income disparities by gender than about racial wage differences is that the implications were quite different concerning levels of economic well-being. Unless resources were very unequally distributed within families, Table 5 indicates that in 1940 men and women shared a similar economic lot across the entire income distribution. This is no longer the case.

Although the feminization of poverty is a real phenomenon, it should not obscure the fact that poverty rates have declined substantially for men and women alike. Poverty rates of women were about one in nine in 1980, a threefold reduction across these 40 years. But with the breakup of the two-parent family, rates for women and men have increasingly diverged. A direct consequence of the growth of the single-parent family is that economic well-being became linked to the sex-specific earnings capacity of a single person.

Poverty rates among families headed by women are higher because they are disadvantaged from both sides of the computed income/needs ratios; women earn less than men, and mothers' "needs" are larger because children typically live with them. The fraction of all adult women (i.e., wives) in intact families actually changed very little between 1940 and 1960 (see Table 2). The expanding feminization of poverty during those years resulted from the increasing income divergence between intact and female-headed families. Their incomes continued to diverge during the subsequent 20 years. In addition, the fraction of women heading families increased to 14% in 1980 (from 8% in 1960), accelerating the feminization of poverty. Of adults in 1980 below the poverty cutoff, 62% were women, as compared with 52% 20 years earlier (not shown in tables). Given this direct link to the rising prevalence of female-headed households, the feminization of poverty is more acute among blacks and Puerto Ricans. Of the 1960 adults in poor black families, 58.6% were women; by 1980, 68.7% were women. Similarly, whereas poverty rates among Puerto Rican women have been rising since 1960 (from 30% to 38%), rates among Puerto Rican men fell (from 26% to 23%).

The Full Distribution of Family Income

Our exclusive concentration to this point on these broad income groups does not give us detailed information concerning the plight of the families well below

---

[5]To illustrate, assume that there was one adult of each sex in intact families and only one adult in the single-headed families. Using the numbers in Tables 2 and 3, the poverty rate for adult women would be $(876/962 \cdot .33 + .089/.962 \cdot 47) = .34$.

the poverty line or how many families might be just above it. A graphic exposition depicts the characteristics of families along the full distribution of income. Throughout the remainder of this chapter, discussion concentrates on comparisons of black and white families only.

Figure 1 measures the cumulative percentage of families that are female-headed at each point along the income distribution. To derive this percentage, all families were first ranked from bottom to top of the distribution, using as a metric their income relative to my adjusted poverty line (to take into account increases in real family income and the different "needs" of families of different

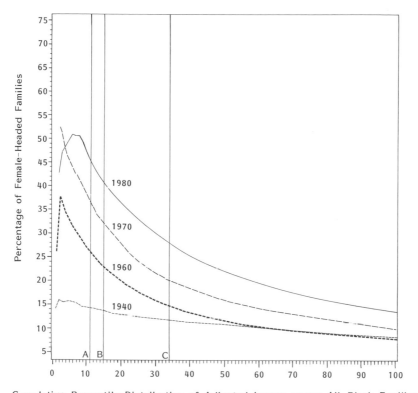

Cumulative Percentile Distribution of Adjusted Income among All Black Families

Figure 1. Cumulative percentages of female-headed families in the income distribution for all families, 1940, 1960, 1970, and 1980. Families are ranked from bottom to top of the distribution by their income relative to the author's adjusted poverty threshold. Each percentile represents the total of families at *and below* this point in the distribution. The vertical lines are the author's poverty thresholds for the indicated years; families to the left of those lines were considered poor under this measure (see Table 1). Key to vertical lines: A = poverty line, 1970 and 1980; B = poverty line, 1960; C = poverty line, 1940.

sizes). The horizontal axis represents this family income distribution. The vertical axis tells us the fraction of families headed by women among all families. The beginning of each plotted line in the graph, at its intercept on the vertical axis at the left, thus represents the fraction of female-headed households among all families with the lowest incomes; the end of each line, at its intercept with 100% of the cumulative distribution on the right, is the total proportion of female-headed families in the population. The slope of each line indexes the proportion of female-headed families at each point along the income distribution. For example, the curve for 1980 indicates that approximately 45% of the families whose income was in the bottom 11% of the income distribution were headed by women (intercept of 45% on the vertical axis, 11% on the horizontal axis), whereas female-headed families constituted less than 20% of all families (intercept of the line at 100% of the distribution, the end of the line on the right). The three solid vertical lines within the figure represent the position of the poverty lines for 1940, 1960, 1970, and 1980.[6] These lines demonstrate the proportion of all families below the poverty line in each of those years.

Figure 2 shows, rather than the cumulative percentage, the precise percentage of female-headed families at each point of the income distribution. For example, among families who were at the 11th income percentile in 1980, almost 35% were headed by women.[7] Figures 3 and 4 depict these same relationships among black families alone.

Figure 1 shows, across the decades, the increasing concentration of female-headed households among families with the lowest incomes. Poverty rates were always higher among female-headed families, even in 1940, when the fraction of female-headed families ranged from 14.3% among the poorest 10% of families to 5.9% of the families at or below the 90th percentile, and 12% of families at or below the poverty line for 1940 had women as heads. However, this 1940 relationship pales into insignificance when placed alongside the subsequent decades. By 1960, a pronounced negative relation emerged between family income position and family type: among the poorest 5%, one-third of all families were female-headed; within the poorest 10%, more than a quarter were headed by women. The concentration of poverty among these families became even more severe by 1980, when half of all families the lowest 5% did not have a husband present.

The curves shown in Figure 2 indicate that the heaviest concentration of female-headed families is the bottom-third of the income distribution. Thereafter, the fraction of families headed by women drifts slowly downward. This pronounced negative correlation of income ranking and female-headed families

[6]The poverty lines for 1980 and 1970 are identical (11%). In 1960, 15% were poor; in 1980, 34% were poor. See Table 1.
[7]These marginal curves have been smoothed.

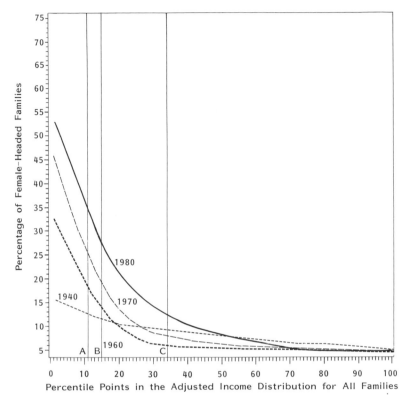

Figure 2. Percentages of female-headed families at particular points in the income distribution for all families, 1940, 1960, 1970, and 1980. Families are ranked from bottom to top of the distribution by income relative to the author's adjusted poverty threshold. Each percentile represents only the families at this point in the distribution. The vertical lines are the author's poverty thresholds for the indicated years (see Table 1). Key: A = poverty line, 1970 and 1980; B = poverty line, 1960; C = poverty line, 1940.

suggests a cautious interpretation of the composition of the poverty population (shown in the areas to the left of the solid vertical lines): as the overall poverty rate declines, the proportion of the poor who are female and members of female-headed households will almost certainly rise.

Not surprisingly, this association is sharper among black families (see Figures 3 and 4). The increasing concentration of the black poor in female-headed families reflects the greater prevalence of such families in the black population as well as a more steeply sloped association of family type with income ranking. Figure 3 shows that in 1980 close to 60% of all black families below the median black family income had women as heads, and 70% of the poorest one-fifth of

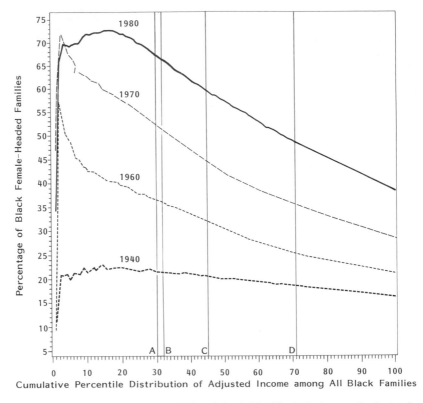

Figure 3. Cumulative percentages of black female-headed families in the income distribution for all black families, 1940, 1960, 1970, and 1980. See Figure 1 for further explanation. Key: A = poverty line, 1980; B = poverty line, 1970; C = poverty line, 1960; D = poverty line, 1940.

black families were headed by women. And Figure 4 shows that in 1980, among black families at the 90th income percentile, only 13% were headed by women. Knowing whether a black family is female-headed has become an increasingly accurate predictor of black economic status.

THE ECONOMIC IMPACT OF THE CHANGING FAMILY

The effect of the changing composition of American families on the economic welfare of its members is of central importance. Until recently, the family did not figure prominently in discussions of poverty, which focused more on labor market outcomes. The family entered mainly through concern that fertility

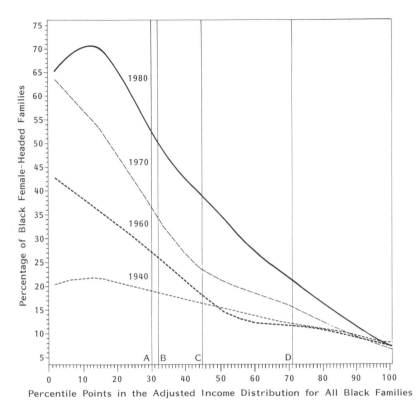

Figure 4. Percentages of black female-headed families at particular points in the income distribution for all black families, 1940, 1960, 1970, and 1980. See Figure 2 for further explanation. Key: A = poverty line, 1980; B = poverty line, 1970; C = poverty line, 1960; D = poverty line, 1940.

rates were higher among the poor, thereby expanding the relative size of a possible future underclass. Moreover, questions that were raised about the role of the family in racial terms touched raw nerves: the hostile reaction to the Moynihan (1965) report meant that the black family became an almost taboo subject for scholars and policy-makers alike.

I will concentrate exclusively on the consequences of marital instability on the distribution of economic rewards. I step aside from the difficult task of identifying the root causes of the rising incidence of families headed by women. That question remains a formidable research topic for which consensus among researchers has not yet emerged. In my view, existing research has not yet successfully isolated the main causes of the decline in the black intact family. The narrowing of differences in economic prospects between black men and

Table 6. Black Income as a Percentage of White Income
among those Aged 26–55

	Census year				
Income source	1940	1950	1960	1970	1980
Family income	41.1	48.9	56.3	61.2	62.5
Male earnings	44.0	60.7	58.1	66.9	72.2
Income of intact families	41.6	55.2	61.4	71.4	82.0

SOURCE: Computations from decennial census data.

women, the rising rates of joblessness among young black men, and the income transfer programs of the Great Society may seem to be the most promising candidates, but their effect has not yet been measured with precision.[8]

A focus on the impact of family stability on economic welfare turns attention immediately to racial differences. The much higher rate of female headship in black families has been alleged by some to be a primary determinant of current rates of black poverty as well as of the slowdown in the reductions in black poverty over time. Because of this, I organize my discussion around differences between blacks and whites.

In a recent paper, I documented the rapid long-term labor market advances made by employed black men (see Smith & Welch, 1986). In 1940, black men earned 44% as much as white men. By 1980, the typical employed black male received 72% as much as the average employed white (see Table 7 below). Including the earnings of black women would simply add to the picture of rapid improvement in the labor market status of blacks. Twenty-five years ago, the typical black woman earned half the wage of the typical white woman; today, racial wage parity prevails among women (see Smith, 1979). But have these black labor market advances led to improved levels of well-being for the typical black family?

Economic progress has indeed been less satisfactory, especially in recent years, for the black family. Table 6 compares trends in the income gap between races using family income and male income as the two metrics. Whichever income concept is used as the yardstick, the broad trends across the 40 years indicate that the income gap between races has narrowed substantially. In 1980, black family income was 63% as high as white family income, compared to 41% in 1940. There were very distinct trends within subperiods. Between 1940 and 1960, the black-family income gap closed slightly more rapidly than did the black-male income gap. But trends after 1960, and particularly during the 1970s,

[8]For an excellent discussion of these issues, see Wilson and Neckerman (1986).

were quite different. Black family income as a percentage of white family income barely increased in the 1970s (from 61.2% in 1970 to 62.5% in 1980).

The increasing disparity between the continued improvement in black labor market outcomes and stagnation in the economic welfare of the black family are best reflected in poverty statistics. Between 1940 and 1970, improvements in the economic well-being of black families moved lockstep with the substantial long-run labor market gains made by black men. The black poor shared in these labor market gains, as witnessed by the decline in the percentage of poor black families from 70% in 1940 to 32% by 1970. However, this process stopped during the 1970s, when black poverty stabilized at unacceptably high levels. In 1980, 29% of black families were poor, little different from the rate that prevailed 10 years earlier. Although black America could take little solace from the fact that poverty among white families also stagnated during the 1970s, this parallel does offer an important clue to the reasons for the slowdown.

The Black Family and Black Poverty

What are the reasons for the decline in reduction of black poverty? One frequently mentioned candidate, a cessation of the long-run improvement in black labor market skills and wages, turns out not to be plausible. It is important to remember that labor market progress in narrowing the wage gap continued during the 1970s. For example, black working men earned 73% as much as whites in 1980, as compared to 67% in 1970.

If a decline in relative labor market prospects for black workers is not a plausible explanation, what else can explain the slowdown in reduction in black family poverty? In the remainder of this section, I will argue that the continuing breakup of the black family and the absence of economic growth during the 1970s are the principal culprits.

One difficulty in assessing the role of the family, especially with the cross-sectional census data I have used thus far, is that a basic question remains unanswered. Are poor female-headed families poor because their heads are not married, or would these women remain poor even if they married? The problem arises because women heading families are unlikely to be random draws from the population, but are more likely to come from impoverished backgrounds. Compounding this problem, the selectivity of the female-headed household is likely to have changed significantly over time. Because this selectivity issue cannot be answered directly with cross-sectional data, I will rely on more indirect methods.

Analysis of the changing age distribution of female-headed families since 1940 demonstrates not only that this selectivity is real, but that it has changed a good deal over these years. Among both races, female heads of households have become much younger over time. One in every eight female-headed black families had a head under 24 years of age in 1980 compared to one in every 25 families in 1940. Parallel age trends exist for whites, where the fraction of women in the 16–24 age group who are heads of families had expanded seven-fold since 1940. Although the trend over time toward younger families is actually sharper among whites, large racial differences in the age distribution remain. In 1980, 46% of black female-headed families had a head under 35 years of age (compared to a rate of 36% among whites). The average age of the black woman heading a family remains much lower than that of her white counterpart.

To separate a possible confounding age effect, Table 7 distributes by marital status young women who reported themselves as female family heads in 1980 and 1960. The change to note across these 20 years was the spectacular rise in the proportion of unmarried female heads. Among those under 24, three-quarters of all black female heads of families were never married—more than double the proportion 20 years earlier. Most of these families consisted of unwed mothers with small children. Among whites, these younger families were approximately evenly divided between the never married and those divorced or separated, but the never-married rates among whites have more than doubled since 1960.

The changing composition of female-headed families goes a long way toward explaining the increasing divergence between the incomes of intact and female-headed families. Much more so than in the past, these families are now young unwed mothers, women with low earning capacities. But the incomes of these women are low not only because of their limited ability to earn but also because of the absence of a spouse's earnings. It is to this subject that I now turn.

Table 7. Marital Status of Female Heads of Families, 1960 and 1980 (Percentages)

	1960		1980	
Marital status	Ages 16–24	Ages 25–34	Ages 16–24	Ages 25–34
Black families				
Never married	35	15	76	39
Divorced or separated	46	64	9	54
Widowed	4	10	11	4
Married spouse absent	15	10	3	2
White families				
Never married	16	10	44	12
Divorced or separated	48	58	50	80
Widowed	6	13	2	24
Married spouse absent	29	19	4	4

SOURCE: Computations from decennial census data.

The Dynamics of Family Incomes among Female-Headed Families

Census data cannot tell us what the incomes of female heads of households would have been had these women lived in intact families. To gain some insight on that issue, I use the 14-year wave of the Panel Study of Income Dynamics (PSID). In contrast to the standard public-release tape, the version of the PSID on which my work is based includes all the families who were ever PSID members between 1967 and 1981 and who were female family heads for at least one of those years.[9]

The principal issue can be stated simply: What were the family income consequences of becoming a female head and then either marrying or remarrying? The simplicity of stating the issue is not matched, however, by ease in summarizing the complex and diverse set of ways that female-headed families form and dissolve. Tables 8–12 represent my attempt at a summary. In these tables, I have selected women (with at least one incidence of female headship) who had at a minimum an observed 7-year window in the PSID.[10] I wanted to describe the family incomes of these women during three periods: (a) before they became female heads (if observed for at least 2 years in the PSID), (b) yearly family income sequences during the years of female headship (up to 5 years), and (c) family income after the women were no longer female heads of households.

The sample in Table 8 consists of all women who became female heads by divorce or separation and who were previously observed in the PSID as married for at least 2 years. The different rows in this table index the number of years these women were divorced or separated. The final row characterizes women who were divorced or separated for at least 5 years and who were still divorced or separated during their last year in the PSID (1981 or earlier if the woman left the

---

[9]The augmented tape is described in Becketti, Lillard, and Welch (forthcoming). The "standard" PSID public release tapes for wave 14 (1968 to 1981) contain data for 19,796 individuals; the "augmented" tapes, which we used, added another 11,161 cases that had been lost owing to attrition by 1981 (for a total of 30,957 cases). Our subsample consisted of any woman who was ever coded as "head of household" on the relationship-to-head variable; there were 3,459 such women.

[10]For each woman in the sample we constructed a marital status string that indicated the woman's marital status each year; for instance the string "mmdddddddmmmmm" characterizes a woman who was in the sample for all 14 years and who was divorced in 1970 and remarried in 1977. This observation would actually be mapped into two separate 7-year windows—once as a case of divorce and once as a case of remarriage. In general, an observation will qualify for inclusion if a targeted marital status transition (divorce, remarriage, establishment of single-parent female-headed household with children, and marriage after being a single-parent female-headed household) has occurred in the third year of a string of at least 7 continuous years of data. The string "mddddddddddd.." characterizes an observation that would not fit into a 7-year window because the divorce is not preceded by 2 years of observed marriage.

Table 8. Family Income Consequences of Divorce or Separation
(1985 dollar values)

Number of years divorced	Mean income before divorce	Income during divorce years					Mean income after remarriage
		1	2	3	4	5	
1	$26,265	$19,496					$33,061
2	32,002	26,829	$17,785				40,564
3	33,042	25,356	16,216	$18,728			45,802
4	35,471	22,546	16,592	18,686	$16,710		33,010
5	42,502	25,486	17,856	20,094	21,171	$19,730	—
6	30,809	14,124	13,961	16,110	14,519	18,359	—
7	34,911	20,377	18,406	18,737	18,950	18,431	—
8	54,598	26,376	20,436	26,346	25,873	22,576	—
9	37,321	18,256	21,137	31,004	35,694	34,570	—
Divorced when last in sample	30,547	20,884	16,696	16,208	16,833	16,526	

SOURCE: Computations from data in the Panel Study of Income Dynamics.

sample). Yearly total family income for up to 5 years of divorce or separation is listed between the mean family income of women before and (if available) after this incidence of female headship.[11] The income consequences of female headship are readily apparent from Table 8. To illustrate, examine the sequence for women who remained divorced for precisely 3 years. In the 2 years before their divorce, these women lived in families with a mean total family income of $33,042 (all figures here are 1985 dollars). During the first year of divorce. family income fell by one-quarter, to $25,356, but averaged only $17,472 in the final 2 years of divorce. Following remarriage, family incomes rose to $45,802, suggesting that, for these women at least, divorce may not always have bad monetary consequences.

Women who became female heads through divorce or separation had average incomes that were half as large as when married, and only 40% of their subsequent family incomes when they remarried. Although the details are af-

[11]Family income is taken directly from the PSID and is inflated to 1985 dollars. This variable is generated by the PSID as the sum of the following variables each year: taxable income of head and wife; total transfer income of head and wife; taxable income of others (in the same household); and total transfer income of others. Because income variables in the PSID refer to the previous year, values are deflated using the consumer price index for the previous year; for example, family income in 1970 is multiplied by 0.341, the value of the consumer price index for 1969.

fected somewhat by the length of divorce or separation, the pattern just described is typical for women who became female heads through divorce. The full family income consequences of divorce are very large, cutting family incomes roughly in half.

Table 9 separates these family income dynamics by race.[12] Women of both races exhibit similar patterns; a two-step decline (in the first year, then more in subsequent years, of divorce) followed by at least a full recovery after remarriage. In one sense, black women are somewhat less affected than white women by this particular transition into female headship. The drop in their income as a result of divorce is smaller because the husbands they had married had less income than the husbands white women had married. Because black family income is so much lower than white family income, the effect on black women of divorce greatly enhances their probability of becoming poor.

Tables 10–12 show other prominent transitions into and out of female headship. Because the sample sizes for many of these specific durations are quite small, the durations are aggregated into three groups: 1–4 years, 5–9 years, and "open-ended," meaning in a particular status at least 5 years and still in the same status when last observed in the PSID sample. For the first two groups, within-duration income sequences are summarized by the mean. Table 10 includes women who were divorced or separated when first observed in the PSID but who subsequently remarried. Tables 11 and 12 deal with the other major type of female headship, women who had not married. Table 11 describes family income dynamics for women whom we observed for at least 2 years before they became single heads of families.[13] Finally, Table 12 describes women first observed as unmarried female heads and who subsequently married.

In all three of the transitions depicted in these tables, the family income consequences of entering or exiting female family headship remain large. Black women's gains from remarriage in Table 10 are much smaller than those of corresponding white women. Of particular interest for our purposes are the transitions for unmarried heads of families (Tables 11 and 12). Family incomes during years of female headship are lowest for these women. In most cases, family incomes are below $10,000 during the years of female headship, well below family incomes of the divorced women described in Table 8.

The important point to note relates, however, to black women. Not only are their incomes low during their years of female headship, but their family incomes were quite meager when they were members of a family earlier, before becoming

[12]With the exception of the initial divorce year, no strong pattern existed across other years spent divorced or separated. Because of this, in Table 9 family incomes during female headship for years 2 through *n* are summarized by the mean. This mean family income is placed under the last divorce year.

[13]The typical, but not exclusive, experience of these women was that they lived with their parents before forming their own families.

Table 9. Black and White Family Income Consequences of Divorce or Separation
(1985 dollar values)

Number of years divorced	Mean income before divorce	Income during divorce years					Mean income after remarriage
		1	2	3	4	5	
White families							
1	$27,005	$19,759					$34,591
2	32,282	26,007	$17,950				41,772
3	33,234	25,717		$17,527			46,473
4	36,033	22,811			$17,431		33,261
5	45,418	24,570				$20,874	—
6	31,779	13,763				15,422	—
7	37,527	21,317				19,630	—
8	55,138	26,753				24,163	—
9	37,321	18,256				30,601	—
Divorced when last in sample	32,508	21,875				17,652	
Black families							
1	17,168	16,265					21,430
2	30,682	30,709	17,003				34,866
3	30,605	20,774		16,781			37,277
4	14,309	12,596			13,521		25,573
5	32,772	28,466				15,838	—
6	24,669	16,412				17,736	—
7	15,066	13,244				11,052	—
8	28,659	8,297				6,769	—
9							
Divorced when last in sample	21,816	16,472				11,732	

SOURCE: Computations from data in the Panel Study of Income Dynamics.

heads. Unmarried black women who became heads of household clearly were previously members of relatively impoverished families. It is these women who represent the major new dimension of the poverty problem—women from low-income families whose incomes are depressed even further as they form their own families out of wedlock.

Table 10. Family Income Consequences of Remarriage among Divorced Women (1985 dollar values)

Number of years remarried	Mean income before remarriage	Income during remarried years					Mean income after remarriage ends
		1	2	3	4	5	
All families							
1–4	$18,800			$31,581			$21,504
5–9	17,540					$43,007	—
Open-ended[a]	19,770	$43,818	$38,562	39,524	$42,767	39,512	—
White families							
1–4	19,949			34,096			22,534
5–9	17,423					45,167	—
Open-ended[a]	19,962	45,387	39,821	40,313	44,307	40,251	—
Black families							
1–4	14,087			21,267			17,282
5–9	18,205					30,248	—
Open-ended[a]	18,080	29,997	27,480	32,574	29,202	33,000	—

[a]The open-ended category includes those women who were remarried for at least 5 years and were still remarried when last observed in the PSID sample.
SOURCE: Computations from data in the Panel Study of Income Dynamics.

Female Family Headship and Poverty

I now return to cross-sectional census data to examine the effect of changing family types on family poverty. The income consequences of transitions into and out of female headship shown by my analysis of the PSID will be used to simulate the incomes that families in the census would have if they married. A race-specific family-income multiplier was estimated for each transition.[14] Depending upon whether our census female family head was married, a different multiplier was applied.

What impact do these simulations have on observed rates of family poverty and the way these rates have changed over time? For each decade, Table 13 lists

[14]These multipliers are all expressed as mean family incomes during the female-head-of-family state divided by mean incomes during that state, no matter which transition occurred first. The multipliers are as follows: (a) *marriage to divorce*, all families = 1.75, white families = 1.76, black families = 1.54; (b) *divorce to remarriage*, all families = 1.97, white families = 2.01, black families = 1.64; (c) *to unmarried head of family*, all families = 2.20, white families = 2.28, black families = 2.04; (d) *unmarried head to married*, all families = 1.81, white families = 1.81, black families = 1.79.

Table 11. Family Income Consequences of Becoming an Unmarried Female Family Head (1985 dollar values)

Number of years as female head	Mean income before becoming single head	Income during female headship years					Mean income after single headship ends
		1	2	3	4	5	
All families							
1–4	$23,192			$10,450			$22,518
5–9	24,311					$10,253	—
Open-ended[a]	20,487	$7,427	$7,750	8,485	$8,232	9,846	—
White families							
1–4	26,724			11,706			25,015
5–9	26,741					9,318	—
Open-ended[a]	27,158	9,268	8,113	9,723	10,530	13,722	—
Black families							
1–4	15,318			7,650			16,953
5–9	17,685					13,785	—
Open-ended[a]	16,257	6,260	7,520	7,701	6,775	7,355	—

[a]The open-ended category refers to women who were unmarried heads of families for at least 5 years and during their last year in the PSID.
SOURCE: Computations from data in the Panel Study of Income Dynamics.

actual poverty rates among female-headed families in each census year and poverty rates computed by applying the simulated incomes for those families if they had married. For these calculations and those that follow, I first scaled observed family income up by using multipliers obtained from the PSID. In addition, the poverty threshold was adjusted by adding one new family member (the mythical husband).

As Table 13 shows, the effect of hypothesized marriage on poverty rates within these female-headed families was large. Instead of a rate of 35% poor among these families in 1980, only 19% would be poor if married. Almost half of all poor female-headed families would be removed from that category by marriage. The impact on poverty is strong for both racial groups. Half of black female-headed families were poor in 1980; less than a third would remain so after a hypothetical marriage. Because women and their children who are in poverty owe much of their impoverishment to rising rates of female headship, both would share more than proportionately in these poverty reductions through marriage.

Although the magnitude of poverty reduction depicted in Table 13 is large, my calculations imply that poverty rates among the hypothetically married female-headed families are still higher than those among the originally intact families. For example, 6% of white and 14% of black intact families were poor

Table 12. Family Income Consequences of Marriage after Being an Unmarried Female Family Head (1985 dollar values)

Years married	Income in last 2 years of single headship	Income during married years					Mean income after marriage ends
		1	2	3	4	5	
All families							
1–4	$11,307			$17,899			$10,925
5–9	19,598					$22,876	—
Open-ended[a]	14,823	$28,352	$29,068	29,322	$30,918	30,525	—
White families							
1–4	8,373			12,544			8,567
5–9	29,655					25,484	—
Open-ended[a]	15,097	28,153	29,944	30,065	31,831	31,410	—
Black families							
1–4	12,987			20,904			12,275
5–9	8,628					20,029	—
Open-ended[a]	13,388	29,393	24,472	25,422	26,125	25,881	—

[a]Open-ended category refers to women married at least 5 years and during their last PSID year.
SOURCE: Computations from data in the Panel Study of Income Dynamics.

Table 13. Actual and Hypothetically Adjusted[a] Poverty Rates (Percentages) among Female-Headed Families

Poverty rate	Census year			
	1940	1960	1970	1980
All families				
Actual	51	44	39	35
Adjusted[a]	33	28	23	19
White families				
Actual	44	36	32	28
Adjusted[a]	26	21	17	14
Black families				
Actual	83	68	59	51
Adjusted[a]	65	48	38	31

[a]Adjusted by computing what incomes would have been if the female family head were married, using income data from the PSID.
SOURCE: Actual poverty rates from decennial census data; adjusted rates from simulated incomes if married, computed from PSID data.

in 1980. This difference confirms that female-headed families are not randomly selected from the population but are instead families more likely to be poor in any case.

The effects of these hypothetical marriages among female-headed poor families are illustrated in Table 14, where I list the observed aggregate family-poverty rates from 1940 to 1980. Below these actual rates are listed the rate that would have prevailed if all female heads of families were married. In 1980, the aggregate poverty rate would fall by 2.2 percentage points, removing three-quarters of a million families from the poverty rolls. The size of the discrepancy between the observed and the adjusted rate has grown steadily over time as the fraction of female-headed families has risen. For example, the 1960 poverty rate would have been only 1.3 percentage points lower if we completely eliminated female headship.

The real news in Table 14 concerns racial differences. By any reasonable standard, the impact of marriage on black poverty rates is large. In 1980, black family poverty rates would be 8.2 percentage points lower than the observed rate of 29%, a one-third reduction in black poverty. Moreover, rising rates of black female headship have significantly affected time-series trends. In particular, reductions in black family poverty are much larger after 1970 in my adjusted series. The decline in black family poverty would have been twice as large after 1970 had female headship not grown.

What role, then, has the breakup of the black family played in stemming the long-term reduction in black poverty? As in many racial issues in this country, opinions have polarized. At one extreme are those who argue that if it were not for the continuing breakup of black families the problem of black poverty would

Table 14. Actual and Hypothetically Adjusted Poverty Rates among All Families[a]

Poverty rate	Census year			
	1940	1960	1970	1980
All families				
Actual	33.5	14.6	10.4	10.1
Adjusted[a]	32.1	13.3	8.7	7.9
White families				
Actual	30.1	10.8	8.3	8.4
Adjusted[a]	28.8	9.9	7.0	6.9
Black families				
Actual	70.0	43.6	31.6	29.0
Adjusted[a]	66.7	39.4	25.3	20.8

[a]Adjusted to eliminate all female-headed households.
SOURCE: Computations from the decennial censuses.

be over. Others dismiss family breakup as a cause, partly because it raises questions about the efficacy of some existing social programs.

How much of existing black poverty can legitimately be assigned to the breakup of the two-parent family? I answered this question by calculating what the poverty rate among black families would have been if the incidence of black female-headed families in 1980 was the same as that of the white population. The result of that calculation shows, not surprisingly, that the quantitative truth lies between the polar opinions. Instead of the actual rate of 29% in 1980, 23% of black families would have been poor if they had shared the same rates of female headship as white families.

To put it one way, 30% of existing racial differences in poverty are due to the instability in the black family, not an insignificant number. However, to put it another way, even if the black family issue were entirely resolved, black family poverty rates would still far exceed those of whites, and almost a quarter of black families would remain mired in poverty. Clearly other factors are also playing a central role.

One of these factors is economic growth. The sustained and rapid growth of the post-1940 American economy carried with it impressive benefits that helped blacks and whites alike. For example, inflation-adjusted incomes of white men have expanded by two and a half times since 1940. Thus the whites to whom I am comparing blacks in 1980 were far wealthier than the whites who represent our contrast group in 1940. According to my estimates for men (see Smith & Welch, 1986), 45% of the reduction in black poverty since 1940 has resulted from economic growth and the remaining 55% is due to expanded black labor market skills. Economic growth and improved black job skills, the latter principally through education, go hand in hand as the key weapons history identifies as eradicating black poverty.

Economic growth has since 1970 had its dark side. Between 1970 and 1980, real incomes grew by less than 0.7% per year, compared to an annual rate of 3.9% over the previous two decades. The virtual absence of real income growth during the 1970s carried a terrible price in limiting reductions in the ranks of the black poor. A major problem for blacks in the 1970s was not that their situation did not improve relative to whites; it was that, for the first time, the whites they were being compared to were no better off in 1980 than in 1970.

The question I now ask is what black-family poverty rates would have been in 1980 if economic growth had not slowed and if the breakup of the black family had not accelerated. If economic growth had been maintained at the rapid rate of the 20 years between 1950 and 1970, black family poverty would have been 4 percentage points lower: 25% rather than 29% of black families would have been poor. If, in addition, black female headship rates were also maintained at their 1960 levels, the black poverty rate would decline further, to 21.3%. In combination, these two factors fully account for the fact that black-family poverty rates during the 1970–1980 decade did not continue to decline at their previous rates.

To sum up, this chapter has examined the impact that the changing American family has had on the economic well-being of its members. I have argued that the rising rates of female headship have significantly altered the relationship of family type and economic status, especially among black families. The deterioration in the American family is largely responsible for the feminization of poverty, the increasing concentration of children among the poor, and the slowdown in long-term reductions in black poverty.

ACKNOWLEDGMENTS

Funds for this research were provided by a grant from the National Institute of Child Health and Human Development. The excellent programming assistance of Daniel Byrne and Judith Fischer is gratefully acknowledged. Helpful comments were provided by Walter Allen, Heidi Hartmann, Gary Sandefur, and Marta Tienda.

REFERENCES

Becketti, S., L. Lillard, & F. Welch (Forthcoming.) The panel study of income dynamics after fourteen years: An evaluation. *Journal of Labor Economics,* 6(4, October 1988), Pt. 1.

Moynihan, D. P. (1965). *The Negro family: The case for national action.* Washington, DC: U.S. Department of Labor, Office of Family Planning and Research.

Smith, J. P. (1979). The convergence to racial equality in female wages. In C. Lloyd (Ed.), *Women in the labor market.* New York: Columbia University Press.

Smith, J. P., & M. P. Ward. (1985). Time series growth in the female labor force. *Journal of Labor Economics, 3* (1), 559–590.

Smith, J. P., & F. Welch. (1986). *Closing the gap: Forty years of economic progress for blacks.* R-3330-DOL. Santa Monica, CA: RAND Corporation.

Wilson, W. J., & K. M. Neckerman. (1986). Poverty and family structure: The widening gap between evidence and public policy issues. In S. H. Danziger & D. H. Weinberg (Eds.), *Fighting poverty: What works and what doesn't.* Cambridge, MA: Harvard University Press.

7

Ethnic and Racial Patterns of Educational Attainment and School Enrollment

ROBERT D. MARE AND CHRISTOPHER WINSHIP

This chapter describes patterns of school enrollment and educational attainment among minority groups in the United States. In addition, it examines the degree to which differences among groups in educational attainment can be attributed to differences in family background.

The processes governing the causes and consequences of schooling for blacks have received considerable research attention (e.g., Featherman & Hauser, 1978; Farley, 1984), and recent work has focused on Hispanic groups (e.g., Borjas & Tienda, 1985). This chapter broadens this focus (a) to include disadvantaged groups that have received limited attention, such as American Indians; (b) to compare disadvantaged minorities and relatively successful groups, such as Asians; (c) to analyze educational stratification of blacks and Hispanics in more detail than has been done in previous work; and (d) to use uniform methods of analysis that permit precise comparisons of the educational experiences of a number of minority groups. We first provide a conceptual background through which the impact of schooling on racial and ethnic inequality can be viewed. Then we discuss our data sources, analytic methods, findings, and conclusions.

The classic sociological approach to educational attainment is to view schooling as a basic agent of social stratification. Each cohort of children enters school and experiences systematic attrition over a period of years. The timing of attrition for individuals establishes their levels of "education," credentials that

ROBERT D. MARE • Department of Sociology and Institute for Research on Poverty, University of Wisconsin-Madison, Madison, Wisconsin.   CHRISTOPHER WINSHIP • Departments of Sociology, Statistics, and Economics, Northwestern University, Evanston, Illinois.

they permanently retain. Rates and timing of dropout from school vary systematically with the socioeconomic characteristics of the families in which individuals grow up. By the time a cohort reaches adulthood, it is "stratified" by the differential amounts of schooling its members have achieved.

To some degree, this stratification mirrors differences already established among a cohort's parents; but to an important degree it also represents differentiation that is independent of the cohort's social origins. Once this stratification is established, it differentiates experiences throughout adult life. Differences among individuals in amounts of formal schooling obtained engender differences in their labor market rewards, consumption patterns, access to political power, and attitudes and values. In sum, schooling is an "intervening variable" between the life circumstances of parents and the socioeconomic achievements of their offspring (e.g., Featherman & Hauser, 1978; Hauser & Featherman, 1976; Mare, 1981b).

SCHOOLING AND RACIAL-ETHNIC STRATIFICATION

Viewing schooling as a dimension of social stratification illuminates the role of formal education in determining the socioeconomic advantages and disadvantages of racial and ethnic minorities. Minority groups differ in the average number of years that they spend in school and in the rates with which they achieve academic degrees. These differences result in part from differences in the typical family socioeconomic backgrounds of minority groups and from differences among groups in the *effects* of social background factors. Similarly, racial and ethnic minorities may differ in their rates of poverty and other indicators of economic success because they have varying amounts of schooling, or because they differ in the way that their schooling is rewarded.

One of the goals of this chapter is to describe differences in rates of school continuation and educational attainment among racial and ethnic groups in the United States and to examine the effects of family background on school continuation for these groups. A potentially important source of ethnic differences in economic hardship is differences in levels of formal educational attainment. Although a sizable literature questions the efficacy of schooling in reducing economic inequalities (e.g., Jencks *et al.*, 1972; Thurow, 1975), schooling remains a necessary—if not sufficient—means of raising socioeconomic achievement. There remains, therefore, considerable importance in understanding the processes that determine levels of schooling completed and rates of dropout from high school and college.

Racial and ethnic groups differ in the potential significance of reductions in educational inequality for socioeconomic progress. In the black population, both levels of schooling and rates of return to schooling have converged toward those of whites in recent years. This convergence has failed, however, to eliminate racial differences in the labor market. Among Hispanic groups a strikingly different picture has emerged. Hispanics substantially lag behind white non-Hispanics in educational attainment. These educational differentials, moreover, are the major source of labor market and other socioeconomic differences between Hispanics and non-Hispanics. Thus, Hispanics and blacks differ both in their educational standing and in the potential importance of schooling in reducing their respective economic hardships (Abowd & Killingsworth, 1985; Reimers, 1985). For other racial and ethnic groups, such as American Indians, little is known about the processes affecting school continuation or the potential importance of raising educational levels for increasing overall socioeconomic levels. Moreover, only recently have researchers examined the determinants and consequences of educational success among relatively *advantaged* racial and ethnic minorities, such as Asians (e.g., Chiswick, 1983).

Factors affecting education attainment and school continuation may be partitioned into family and labor market influences. Family factors include the socioeconomic characteristics of the families in which young persons live while attending schools, such as the educational attainment and income levels of parents. Additionally, they include aspects of family structure, including the size and composition of the family (such as one adult versus two adults present). Racial and ethnic groups may differ in both their levels on these factors and also in the strength of their impact on educational attainment. For some aspects of family background, such as an individual's number of siblings, the effects are weaker for blacks than for whites. For some Hispanic groups, in contrast, the effects are at least as strong as for white non-Hispanics.

School continuation decisions are also affected by the incentives faced by young persons to stay in school or to drop out. Persons differ in the economic opportunities available to them when they leave school. In addition, they differ in the quality of education available to them. Both of these factors influence the labor market return that they will receive from additional education. Persons may terminate schooling because discrimination in the labor market means that additional schooling will not provide access to a better job. Similarly, they may terminate schooling because the quality of education available to them is of such low quality as to make the expenditure of additional time in school not worthwhile.

The degree to which different factors are responsible for observed ethnic and racial differences in educational attainment is unknown. In this chapter, we examine the importance of ethnic-racial differences in family background for explaining ethnic and racial differences in educational attainment. For all groups except Asians, we find that family background explains a large proportion of the difference in educational attainment between whites and nonwhite ethnic-racial groups. In many cases, family background explains one-half to two-thirds of the difference.

A potentially important hypothesis is that groups with higher rates of return to education are also groups with higher educational attainments. In particular, groups that have been discriminated against in the labor market may receive lower returns to education, and as a result are less willing to bear the expense of staying in school. (See Hirschman, 1986, for a discussion of why in the earlier part of this century, the Chinese received high rates of return to education despite the severe discrimination they faced in this country.) This chapter, however, does not present analyses of the importance of differences in labor market experiences of ethnic-racial groups.[1]

Another argument that is not explored in this chapter is that groups differ in the number of years that they take to reach a specific level of knowledge, academic achievement, or training. Groups may differ because they have access to educational institutions of varying quality. Access to post–secondary education may be a function of the family funds which are available to support further education. In the case of secondary education, access may be more a matter of the quality of the educational program at the individual's high school. (See Lieberson, 1980, for a discussion of the effects of lack of access to high school on black educational attainment earlier in this century.) Groups may also differ in the time it takes to proceed through formal levels of schooling. For instance, it is well known that blacks are more likely to be grade-retarded than whites (e.g., Bianchi, 1984).

In this chapter, we examine differences between ethnic-racial groups in educational attainment, including their average levels of attainment as well as rates of completion of selected levels of schooling. To provide some indication of future trends in educational attainment, we also examine group differences in rates of school enrollment. In considering causes of educational differences, we limit our analysis to examining the degree to which group variation in family background can account for patterns of educational attainment.

DATA ON MINORITY SCHOOLING

Although several potentially useful data sources for the study of minority schooling are available, data remain limited for detailed comparisons among minority groups in patterns of school enrollment and educational attainment. General purpose surveys, such as the decennial censuses, the annual Current

---

[1]In analyses not reported here, we examined the relationship between levels of educational attainment and rates of economic return to schooling across ethnic-racial groups in 1980. We found no consistent pattern of relationship. (However, see Chiswick, 1983, for different results using the 1970 census.) It is beyond the scope of this chapter to analyze the sources of group differences in rates of return to schooling.

Population Survey conducted by the U.S. Bureau of the Census, and other large sets of data are potentially a basis for rigorous comparisons among racial and ethnic groups. They contain limited information, however, on individual histories and family background. Other data sets, such as the Occupational Changes in a Generation surveys, contain only small samples of individuals from the minority groups that have experienced the greatest degree of socioeconomic hardship—subgroups of the Hispanic population, American Indians, and some recent Asian foreign-born groups (as well as other groups that have enjoyed unusual socioeconomic success—notably other Asian groups).

Despite these limitations, extant data sources are useful for the analysis of educational attainment and school enrollment. In this chapter, we use two sources of data on schooling of minorities in the United States: the 1980 Census of Population and the 1973 Occupational Changes in a Generation survey (OCG), which was a supplement to the March 1973 Current Population Survey (Featherman & Hauser, 1975). These data are a good basis for a sociodemographic overview of schooling patterns of minority groups. To some degree, moreover, they have features suitable for analysis of minority schooling that have thus far not been exploited. The key features of these data for our purposes are summarized in Table 1.

Table 1. Sample Observations for Ethnic and Racial Groups Represented in 1973 Occupational Changes in a Generation and 1980 Census Data

Ethnic-racial group	1973 OCG		1980 Census	
	Respondents	Respondents plus brothers		
American Indians	282	666	47,807	(.05)[a]
Hispanics				
Cubans	166	359	33,551	(.05)
Mexicans	1,161	2,794	68,510	(.0125)
Puerto Ricans	225	535	64,029	(.05)
Asians	294	661		
Asian Indians			13,837	(.05)
Chinese			30,972	(.05)
Filipinos			24,170	(.05)
Japanese			29,213	(.05)
Koreans			12,782	(.05)
Vietnamese			7,655	(.05)
Non-Hispanic blacks	748	1,785	68,730	(.0038)
Non-Hispanic whites	1,079	2,290	69,546	(.0005)

[a]Numbers in parentheses denote sampling fraction from 1980 census.

1980 Census of Population

We use the Public Use Microdata Sample (PUMS) from the 1980 census, which is a 5% random sample of the population. Our analyses are restricted to persons aged 14 and over in 1980. The census lacks information on family socioeconomic background, but provides good data on school enrollment, educational attainment, and other characteristics of the population. From the census, we examine twelve ethnic-racial groups answering closed-ended questions on their origin or descent, race, and Hispanic ancestry. The groups are Cubans, Mexicans, Puerto Ricans, American Indians, Asian Indians, Japanese, Chinese, Filipinos, Koreans, blacks, Vietnamese, and non-Hispanic whites. Four of these groups are predominantly native born (the term used here for birth in the United States), including American Indians (97.8%), non-Hispanic whites (95.4%), non-Hispanic blacks (96.6%), and Puerto Ricans (95.9%).[2] Two of the groups are predominantly foreign born: Koreans (7.0% native) and Vietnamese (2.1%). The other six groups are more heterogeneous in nativity status: Asian Indians (17.4% native), Chinese (26.3% native), Cubans (10.6% native), Filipinos (18.6% native), Japanese (68.5% native), and Mexicans (65.4% native). For them, we subdivide the data by nativity status. As the numbers in parentheses in Table 1 show, for the largest ethnic-racial groups we further subsampled from the 5% sample in order to save computation time.

Occupational Changes in a Generation

The OCG data cover members of the male, civilian, noninstitutionalized population of the United States in March, 1973, who were aged 20 to 65. The data thus concern individuals who finished school between approximately 1923 and 1976 and exclude women, teenagers, the armed forces, and persons in institutions. They provide high-quality information on educational attainment and family socioeconomic background of respondents, such as fathers' schooling and occupational status, mothers' schooling, and the size and structure of respondents' families when they were teenagers. In this chapter, we use the OCG data to estimate the effects of the following variables on several measures of respondents' educational attainment: father's and mother's educational attainment, father's occupational status when the respondent was aged 16 measured via the Duncan Socioeconomic Index (SEI), respondent's number of siblings, a dichotomous variable that denotes whether the respondent lived with both parents or in a broken family at age 16, respondent's year of birth, and a dichotomous variable denoting whether the respondent was born in the United

---

[2]For the purpose of this study, Puerto Rico is considered part of the United States.

States. Substantial prior research has established the independent positive effects of parents' schooling and father's occupational status and the negative effects of sibship size and being raised in a broken family on the educational attainment of offspring (e.g., Featherman & Hauser, 1978; Hauser & Featherman, 1976).

A largely unexploited feature of the OCG data is its information on the schooling of respondents' brothers. Respondents were requested: "Please indicate the highest grade of school completed by the OLDEST of your brothers who lived to age 25," and, where applicable, to provide the same information for their youngest brother (Featherman & Hauser, 1978, p. 501). As discussed further below, the information on brothers' schooling facilitates our analysis of ethnic-racial patterns of schooling in two ways. The associations between brothers' characteristics are global measures of the importance of family background in determining those characteristics (e.g., Griliches, 1979). The reports of brothers' educational attainment also provide additional observations on schooling for ethnic-racial groups that appear in the OCG survey in numbers too small for reliable statistical analysis. Although the inclusion of respondents' brothers results in analyses that overrepresent men from large sibships and introduces a lack of statistical independence among observations, it permits richer analyses of educational patterns of rare groups than would otherwise be possible. Table 1 shows that samples are typically doubled by the inclusion of brothers as separate observations.

Although the OCG data identify numerous racial and ethnic groups, we focus on seven that occur in the data in sufficient numbers to permit analysis and are of social policy significance: Cubans, Puerto Ricans, Mexicans, American Indians, Asians, blacks, and non-Hispanic whites. The three Hispanic groups were identified from responses to a closed-ended question on origin: "What is _____'s origin or descent," for which "Cuban" and "Puerto Rican" are included on the list presented to the respondent. Mexicans are respondents who identified with the supplied categories "Mexican American," "Chicano," and "Mexican (Mexicano)." American Indians are persons who identified themselves as "Other" on the closed-ended question and subsequently supplied the name of an Indian tribe or a more general reference to Native American origin or descent. Asians are persons who identified themselves as "Other" on the closed-ended question and subsequently named a nation or ethnicity of origin from mainland Asia (including the Indian subcontinent), Japan, or Taiwan. Most of such persons identified with Chinese, Japanese, or Korean origins. Blacks and whites are non-Hispanics who are identified by interviewers as black or white in the March 1973 Current Population Survey.[3]

---

[3]Other sources of data are more useful for detailed investigation of the processes that determine schooling levels and differentials for large minority groups. The NCES-sponsored 1980 High School and Beyond survey and the National Longitudinal Survey of Youth, sponsored by the U.S.

Methods

The 1980 census documents basic differentials in attainment among ethnic and racial groups. Because most persons complete their schooling by their mid-twenties, by comparing age groups within the census we can ascertain trends in educational attainment within ethnic and racial groups. Analysis of enrollment data also provides insight into probable future differences in educational attainment for cohorts that have not yet finished school.

To explore some of the sources of differences in ethnic and racial educational attainment, we assess the effects of social background factors on several measures of educational attainment using the OCG data. For Asians, Indians, Cubans, and Puerto Ricans, the OCG samples are small (see Table 1), but the availability of brothers' educational attainments as distinct observations substantially enlarges our samples. Following Hauser and Featherman (1976), we estimate linear regression models of highest grade of school completed for each group and attempt to account for group differences in attainment by their differences in socioeconomic backgrounds. We further describe the effects of social background *within* ethnic-racial groups to see whether there are significant differences in the relative importance of the several dimensions of background across groups. Because many of the ethnic subsamples are small, we report standard errors of estimated regression coefficients to indicate the precision of our estimates. Because brothers have been included in the sample and because errors within families are likely to be positively correlated, the standard errors reported underestimate the true sampling variability. Group differences in the effects of social background should therefore be interpreted with caution.

The effects of social background and ethnic differences in their effects may also vary within the schooling process (see Mare, 1980, 1981a). In addition to analyses of highest year of schooling completed, we report the effects of social background on selected school transitions, including whether an individual (a) completes ninth grade (attends high school); (b) completes twelfth grade *given* that he or she completes ninth grade (graduates from high school given that he or she attends high school); and (c) completes a year beyond high school *given* that he or she completes twelfth grade (attends college given graduation from high school). These three transitions represent movement between the major divisions

---

Department of Labor, include large samples of blacks and Hispanics in their late high school and early college years. To some degree, these data have already been used to investigate some aspects of educational stratification of minorities (e.g., Fligstein & Fernandez, 1985). The limitations of these data include poor representation of small minority groups, and, to date, a focus on a restricted range of ages and grades of schooling. High School and Beyond, for example, excludes those who drop out before the tenth grade, who represent a small proportion of the total youth population but a more significant fraction of disadvantaged minorities such as blacks, Hispanics, and American Indians. The panel, moreover, is still too young to yield information about college graduation.

of the education system in the United States and are the places where attrition is most likely to occur (Duncan, 1968; Mare, 1980). We analyze the continuation probabilities associated with these transitions using logistic regression models estimated by maximum likelihood.

We obtain further information about the effects of social background on educational attainment from inspecting the correlations between the schooling of brothers, which provide global estimates of the importance of family background. We compare ethnic and racial groups in terms of the importance of within- and between-family variance in schooling, as well as the importance of the family background factors that we have *measured* relative to overall (measured and *un*measured) family effects.

EMPIRICAL RESULTS: ETHNIC AND RACIAL DIFFERENCES IN EDUCATIONAL ATTAINMENT

Table 2 reports selected measures of educational attainment for those 26 to 35 years old by ethnic-racial group and sex in 1980. This age group is old enough to have completed almost almost all of its schooling and is, with few exceptions, sufficiently homogeneous not to be affected by intercohort changes.

The first two columns in Table 2 report mean levels of educational attainment for the 18 ethnic-racial and nativity-status groups. The groups vary dramatically in their levels of educational attainment. Asian groups typically have very high mean years of schooling, often exceeding 14 or 15 years. The exceptions to this are native-born Filipinos, who average somewhat more than 13 years, and Vietnamese, who average near 12. Groups with intermediate levels of attainment include Cubans and whites, who average approximately 13 years of schooling, and American Indians, blacks, and U.S.-born Mexicans, who average approximately 12 years. Groups with the lowest levels of schooling include Puerto Ricans and foreign-born Mexicans, who average approximately 11 and 8 years, respectively.

The third and fourth columns in Table 2 show that high school attendance is the norm for most groups. The major exception is the Mexican foreign-born population, among whom nearly 60% have not attended high school. Although the majority of Puerto Ricans attend high school, a relatively large proportion have completed no high school (22.1% for men and 23.7% for women). The corresponding percentage is also relatively high for Vietnamese women (22.5%). The fifth and sixth columns show that among most groups a majority of members graduate from high school. Foreign-born Mexicans are again a dramatic exception: only 28.9% of men and 27.4% of women have graduated. Native-born Mexicans also have relatively low rates of graduation (67.9% for men and 63.5% for women). Puerto Rican rates, however, are even lower: 54.3% for men and

ROBERT D. MARE and CHRISTOPHER WINSHIP

Table 2. Selected Measures of Educational Attainment, by Ethnic-Racial Group and Sex, Persons Aged 26–35 in 1980

Group	Mean grades completed		Percentage completing less than grade 9		Percentage high school graduates		Percentage with some college	
	Men	Women	Men	Women	Men	Women	Men	Women
American Indians	12.1	11.8	9.0	8.5	74.1	71.7	36.4	29.7
Asian Indians								
Native born	15.1	13.2	3.8	6.4	90.1	79.0	70.1	51.0
Foreign born	16.8	14.7	2.7	5.3	94.0	87.0	87.1	72.6
Chinese								
Native born	15.8	15.0	21.1	2.1	97.0	96.0	86.6	81.8
Foreign born	15.0	13.6	7.3	11.5	86.8	82.6	72.5	61.6
Filipinos								
Native born	13.2	13.2	3.0	2.7	89.0	88.4	53.2	48.5
Foreign born	14.2	14.4	3.9	7.4	88.2	85.9	70.0	73.4
Japanese								
Native born	14.9	14.8	0.7	0.7	97.6	98.0	76.8	79.6
Foreign born	15.1	13.6	1.6	1.7	95.9	91.7	77.1	57.4
Koreans	14.7	12.4	2.3	12.4	94.6	78.1	67.9	43.1
Vietnamese	12.5	10.9	10.5	22.5	78.4	62.9	47.9	29.2
Cubans								
Native born	13.7	13.1	5.5	6.2	6.1	82.6	60.9	49.8
Foreign born	13.3	12.3	8.8	11.7	80.9	76.6	56.6	39.2
Mexicans								
Native born	11.6	11.2	14.7	17.0	67.9	63.5	34.0	22.3
Foreign born	7.8	7.7	57.0	59.7	28.9	27.4	13.5	11.1
Puerto Ricans	10.9	10.6	22.1	23.7	54.3	52.7	24.8	19.7
Non-Hispanic blacks	12.1	12.2	8.3	6.4	73.2	74.7	34.0	33.1
Non-Hispanic whites	13.6	13.1	4.1	3.5	87.5	87.6	53.5	43.6

SOURCE: 1980 census (see Table 1).

52.7% women. Rates for American Indians (74.1% for men and 71.7% for women) and blacks (73.2% for men and 74.7% for women) are somewhat higher than those for Mexicans native born.

The seventh and eighth columns show the proportion of each group attending college. Rates of college attendance for Asian groups are extremely high. Except for Vietnamese, rates are close to or above 50%, and in many cases are as high as 70% or 80%. Some of the highest rates are for foreign-born Asians, suggesting that many of these individuals may have come to the United States for college and graduate study and may eventually return to their countries of origin.

Table 3 shows the average levels of educational attainment by age, ethnic-racial group, and nativity status. If few individuals receive more schooling after their mid-twenties and the composition of ethnic-racial cohorts is constant with age, then differences in educational attainment across age groups provide a measure of changes in educational attainment over time. For natives, these assumptions are reasonable, particularly if we restrict our attention to differences among persons under age 65, for whom differential mortality is not an important factor. For foreign-born persons, on the other hand, differences across age groups in educational attainment may represent changes in educational attainment in the native country, as well as in the United States, or changes in the selectivity of immigration. In addition, to the degree that migration occurs at different ages, the composition of a birth cohort of foreign-born persons can change substantially with age. For foreign-born persons, therefore, differences across age groups in educational attainment may be caused by a number of factors.

The bottom row in each panel of Table 3 indicates the difference for each ethnic-racial group, by sex, between the educational attainment of those aged 26 to 35 and those aged 56 to 65. This difference represents changes in educational attainment over approximately 30 years. It contrasts persons who finished their schooling shortly after World War II and persons who had completed almost all of their schooling by 1980. Among the native born, for whom changes can be most meaningfully interpreted, all groups show substantial increases in educational attainment. The largest increase is for Mexicans: 4.55 years for men and 4.82 years for women. Average educational attainment for native-born Asian Indians, black men, and Filipino, Japanese, and Puerto Rican women all increased by more than 3.5 years. The smallest increase is for white women. Native-born Filipinos, white men, and Asian Indian women all experienced changes of less than 2.5 years. That changes for whites are among the smallest of all groups indicates a general pattern of convergence in educational attainment of other groups to the white mean. The exceptions to this pattern are several of the Asian groups, among whom the (positive) gap relative to whites has grown.

The intercohort differences in educational attainment among foreign-born age groups are, in many cases, extremely large. Foreign-born Chinese men and

Table 3. Educational Attainment by Age and Sex for Selected Ethnic-Racial and Nativity-Status Groups, 1980

Age	American Indians	Asian Indians		Blacks	Chinese		Cubans		Filipinos	
		Native born	Foreign born		Native born	Foreign born	Native born	Foreign born	Native born	Foreign born
Men										
26–35	12.13	15.05	16.77	12.12	15.78	14.95	13.74	13.30	13.22	14.21
36–45	11.30	14.43	17.09	11.25	15.08	14.38	12.55	11.64	12.68	14.84
46–55	9.75	11.81	15.99	9.96	13.79	11.31	11.48	10.59	10.66	13.76
56–65	8.93	11.40	13.37	8.26	12.45	10.05	10.87	10.49	10.87	10.34
65+	6.95	10.41	10.67	6.40	10.20	7.92	8.63	9.58	7.19	7.19
(26–35)– (56–65)[a]	3.20	3.65	3.40	3.86	3.33	4.90	2.87	2.81	2.36	3.87
Women										
26–35	11.84	13.24	14.77	12.21	15.00	13.56	13.13	12.30	13.16	14.38
36–45	10.74	12.39	14.00	11.48	13.96	10.05	12.35	10.87	12.48	14.50
46–55	9.49	11.65	11.54	10.39	12.32	8.34	11.13	10.39	10.96	12.44
56–65	9.12	11.09	8.13	8.95	11.74	7.59	10.26	9.64	9.49	9.65
65+	7.29	10.40	8.50	7.31	9.59	3.63	7.77	8.12	7.62	7.12
(26–35)– (56–65)[a]	2.72	2.16	6.64	3.26	3.27	5.97	2.87	2.66	3.67	4.73

Table 3. (Continued)

	Japanese		Koreans	Mexicans		Puerto Ricans	Vietnamese	Whites
	Native born	Foreign born		Native born	Foreign born			
Men								
26–35	14.92	15.09	14.73	11.64	7.79	10.86	12.45	13.55
36–45	14.45	15.42	15.38	10.44	6.49	9.52	12.48	12.98
46–55	13.29	14.80	14.77	8.49	5.75	8.55	11.05	12.14
56–65	11.93	13.17	12.67	7.09	5.62	7.44	9.68	11.49
65+	9.95	8.38	10.43	4.76	3.66	6.33	7.83	9.91
(26–35)–(56–65)[a]	2.99	1.92	2.06	4.55	2.17	3.41	2.77	2.06
Women								
26–35	14.82	13.55	12.35	11.12	7.65	10.59	10.89	13.05
36–45	13.97	12.37	12.17	10.83	7.56	9.10	9.90	12.46
46–55	12.68	11.77	11.42	8.11	5.34	7.83	7.86	11.84
56–65	11.05	11.46	7.95	6.30	5.47	6.50	5.37	11.88
65+	8.71	7.19	5.89	5.14	3.35	5.08	3.81	10.00
(26–35)–(56–65)[a]	3.77	2.09	4.40	4.82	2.18	4.08	5.51	1.17

[a]Denotes intercohort change between persons born 1915–1924 and 1945–1954. See text for further explanation.

Asian Indian, Chinese, Filipino, Korean, and Vietnamese women all have differences between the two age groups of more than 4.5 years. The smallest
changes are for the foreign-born Japanese (1.92 for men and 2.09 for women)
and foreign-born Mexicans (2.17 for men and 2.18 for women). As noted above,
however, these changes may result from education trends in both the nation of
origin and in the United States, as well as from the changing selectivity of
immigration.

Ethnic-Racial Differences in School Enrollment

We next describe ethnic-racial patterns of school enrollment rates in 1980
for persons aged 14 to 30. These patterns suggest the future direction of group
differences in educational attainment. Additionally, they show how ethnic-racial
groups differ in the timing of school departure and the entrance to work and other
adult roles (Mare, Winship, & Kubitschek, 1984). Figures 1–4 show the relationship between school enrollment rates and age for selected combinations of
ethnic-racial groups. Because sex differences in enrollment are generally small,
we report combined rates for men and women.

Figure 1 shows enrollment patterns for whites, blacks, American Indians,
native-born Mexicans, and native-born Chinese. Black and white enrollment
rates are similar, although they continue to differ at ages 20 and 21, when
persons typically complete their college degrees. These patterns suggest that

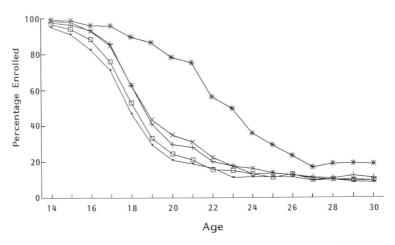

Figure 1. School enrollment rates among persons aged 14–30, 1979: Whites, Blacks, American
Indians, Native-Born Mexicans, and Native-Born Chinese. *Native-born* refers to those born in the
United States. SOURCE: 1980 Census of the Population. Key: —— = American Indians, —+— =
Blacks, —*— = Native-born Chinese, —□— = Native-born Mexicans, —×— = Whites.

black-white differences in educational attainment will continue to shrink, but will not completely disappear in cohorts completing their schooling in the early 1980s. Enrollment rates for American Indians and native-born Mexicans are similar to each other and fall below those for whites and blacks at most ages. The fiftieth percentiles for the four groups, however, are less than a year apart. If we ignore the effects of grade retardation or the return to school of persons not enrolled in 1980, these rates imply that the groups will have median completed educational attainments that differ from one another by less than 1 year. Enrollment rates for native-born Chinese are considerably higher than those for the other four groups at all ages and indicate that the large gap in educational attainment between these Chinese and the non-Asian populations as shown in Tables 2 and 3 is likely to persist, or perhaps even grow in the future. As we indicate below, this high level of enrollment is typical of many of the Asian groups.

Figure 2 shows the enrollment rates for Hispanic groups. Both native- and foreign-born Cubans have high rates of enrollment, which are more similar to those of Asian groups than to those of other Hispanics. Puerto Ricans and native-born Mexicans have very similar rates. Foreign-born Mexicans have very low rates at all ages, which is consistent with patterns of educational attainment described above. Foreign-born Mexicans have much lower rates of school enrollment and levels of educational attainment than their native counterparts.

Figure 3 shows the enrollment rates for the Asian groups, which have both

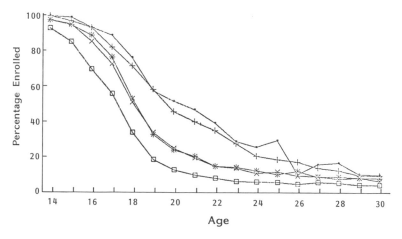

Figure 2. School enrollment rates among Hispanic persons aged 14–30, 1979. *Native-born* refers to those born in the United States. SOURCE: 1980 Census of Population. Key: —— = Native-born Cubans, —+— = Cuban immigrants, —*— = Native-born Mexicans, —□— = Mexican immigrants, —✕— = Puerto Ricans.

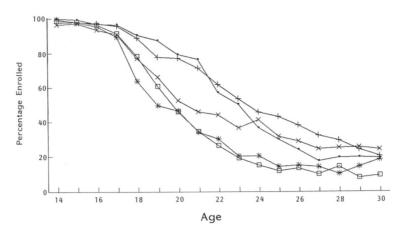

Figure 3. School enrollment rates among persons of Chinese, Filipino, and Vietnamese origin, ages 14–30, 1979. *Native-born* refers to those born in the United States. SOURCE: 1980 Census of the Population. Key: —— = Native-born Chinese, —+— = Foreign-born Chinese, —*— = Native-born Filipinos, —□— = Foreign-born Filipinos, —×— = Vietnamese.

the highest and lowest rates. Native- and foreign-born Filipinos experience the lowest rates of enrollment, though their rates exceed those for whites. Native- and foreign-born Chinese have the highest rates of all groups. The Vietnamese are an intermediate group of some interest, in that although levels of educational attainment for older Vietnamese are generally lower than for other Asian groups (see Tables 2 and 3), their enrollment rates are similar, suggesting future convergence among Asians. Figure 4 shows enrollment rates for the other Asian groups. These rates are generally between those of Filipinos and Chinese and, as such, they exceed those for other non-Asian groups.

Family Background and Ethnic-Racial Differences in Educational Attainment

In this section we examine the contribution of family socioeconomic background differences to ethnic-racial differences in levels of schooling. Table 4 reports means for selected variables for men in the OCG survey (aged 20–65 in 1973), and Table 5 indicates the effects of ethnic-racial groups and social background on several measures of schooling in the OCG sample. As noted, these men finished school between approximately 1923 and 1976. Thus their experiences may not be the same as for men completing their schooling in the 1980s. In the multivariate models summarized in Table 5, the ethnic-racial coefficients denote contrasts in grades completed or log odds of making a school transition,

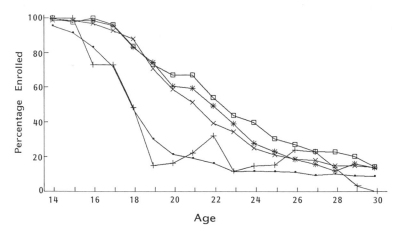

Figure 4. School enrollment rates among persons of Asian, Indian, Japanese, and Korean origin, ages 14–30, 1979. *Native-born* refers to those born in the United States. SOURCE: 1980 Census of the Population. Key: —— = Native-born Asian Indians, —+— = Foreign-born Asian Indians, —*— = Native-born Japanese, —□— = Foreign-born Japanese, —×— = Koreans.

Table 4. Means of Schooling and Social Background Variables of the Ethnic-Racial Groups, Civilian Noninstitutionalized Men, 1973

	Asians	Blacks	Cubans	American Indians	Mexicans	Puerto Ricans	Whites
Mean grades completed	13.04	10.34	11.39	10.82	8.81	8.79	12.16
Proportion completing more than 8 grades	.91	.68	.72	.71	.52	.55	.85
Proportion high school graduates	.80	.43	.61	.48	.33	.24	.68
Proportion with some college	.58	.16	.37	.19	.14	.07	.37
Age	38.87	40.44	43.52	38.65	38.26	37.50	41.05
Father's schooling (grades completed)	8.66	6.32	8.81	6.67	3.90	4.29	8.44
Mother's schooling (grades completed)	7.42	7.42	7.66	8.07	3.82	4.36	9.06
Father's occupation (SEI score)	37.03	23.23	41.07	29.11	23.66	28.81	34.45
Number of siblings	4.95	6.19	4.80	5.86	6.44	6.43	4.38
Proportion from broken family	.19	.34	.21	.25	.21	.28	.15
Proportion native born	.48	.97	.05	.99	.70	.10	.94

SOURCE: Occupational Changes in a Generation, 1973.

Table 5. Analysis of Ethnic-Racial Differences in Grades of School Completed and School Continuation Rates: Civilian Noninstitutionalized Men, 1973

	Dependent variable[a]					
				High school attendance (completes 9th grade)		
Independent variable	Highest grade completed					
Constant	14.360	11.310	10.880	3.195	1.901	1.537
Asians	.530	.991	1.374	0.127	.716	1.106
American Indians	−1.687	−.813	−.853	−0.934	−0.592	−0.655
Cubans	−0.672	−0.546	0.220	−0.849	−0.826	−0.049
Mexicans	−3.736	−1.294	−1.098	−1.910	−0.663	−0.477
Puerto Ricans	−3.794	−1.512	−0.785	−1.939	−0.832	−0.091
Blacks	−1.926	−0.730	−0.739	−1.013	−0.495	−0.525
(Whites)						
Father's schooling		0.173	0.178		0.103	0.107
Mother's schooling		0.218	0.208		0.151	0.144
Father's occupation[b]		0.086	0.095		0.036	0.424
Number of siblings		−0.138	−0.139		−0.069	−0.074
Broken family		−0.549	−0.583		−0.209	−0.243
Native born			0.891			0.901
R^2	0.21	0.35	0.35			
SEE	3.85	3.50	3.49			
−2LogL				9081	8325	8198
χ^2 (d.f.)					756 (5)	127 (1)

	High school graduation, given high school attendance			College attendance, given high school graduation		
Constant	2.616	2.082	2.180	0.823	0.107	0.614
Asians	0.602	0.844	0.779	0.486	0.730	0.430
American Indians	−0.752	−0.532	−0.521	−0.506	−0.243	−0.207
Cubans	0.648	0.634	−0.481	0.272	0.222	−0.461
Mexicans	−0.830	0.133	−0.172	−0.616	0.073	−0.057
Puerto Ricans	−1.495	−0.905	−1.042	−0.788	0.205	−0.789
Blacks	−0.768	−0.379	−0.375	−0.548	−0.061	−0.060
(Whites)						
Father's schooling		0.061	0.060		0.053	0.047
Mother's schooling		0.060	0.062		0.054	0.063
Father's occupation[b]		0.037	0.035		0.010	0.009
Number of siblings		−0.085	−0.085		−0.090	−0.093
Broken family		−0.238	−0.233		−0.337	−0.315
Native born			−0.181			−0.829
−2LogL	6533	6191	6188	6329	5911	5845
χ^2 (d.f.)		342 (5)	3 (1)		418 (5)	66 (1)

[a]Numbers for "Highest Grade Completed" are least-squares regression coefficients. Numbers for other dependent variables are logit coefficients estimated by maximum likelihood. All models include a constant and dummy variables that denote ages 20–25, 26–35, 36–45, 46–55, and 56–65, and whether an observation is a respondent, an "oldest brother," or a "youngest brother." For definitions of variables and further explanation, see text.
[b]Duncan Occupational Socioeconomic Index × 0.1.
SOURCE: Occupational Changes in Generation, 1973.

comparing each group to non-Hispanic whites. All comparisons adjust for ethnic-racial differences in age distribution (year of birth).

In Table 5, the first model (column) for each schooling measure describes age-adjusted group differences in schooling and reveals approximately the same rank ordering of the groups as was shown in Table 2. Hispanics generally have lower attainment than all other groups, although Cubans have much more schooling than Mexicans or Puerto Ricans. Mexicans lag behind Asians by about 4.3 years of schooling and lag behind whites by 3.7 years ($.530 - (-3.736) = 4.266$). Although the coefficients for the logit models for school continuation tend to decline as schooling levels increase, indicating that most ethnic differentiation in ultimate attainment occurs early in the schooling process, they roughly preserve the relative position of the ethnic groups.

The second column for each measure adjusts ethnic-racial differences for family background composition. The increase in explained variance (R^2) between the first and second regression models indicates the considerable explanatory importance of socioeconomic background. Approximately two-thirds of the difference between Mexicans and whites is attributable to differences in average family background levels of the groups (compare -3.736 to -1.294). More generally, contrasts between ethnic groups in highest grade completed are typically reduced by 33% to 75% when socioeconomic backgrounds are controlled. An exception to this pattern, however, is for the difference between whites and Asians, which *increases* when family background is controlled. The family backgrounds of Asians are disadvantageous relative to those of whites, but, as a result of other, unmeasured factors, their educational attainment more than compensates for this disadvantage. Although socioeconomic background effects on school continuation weaken as level of schooling increases, controls for background reduce ethnic differences substantially at all levels. Indeed, at the transition from high school to college, the only nontrivial ethnic difference that remains, once background is controlled, is between Asians and all other groups. That is, differences *among* Hispanics, blacks, American Indians, and whites are extremely small for this transition among men with equivalent social backgrounds. Of course, this is only a hypothetical comparison. Relatively few members of the disadvantaged minority groups both graduate from high school *and* have family background conditions equivalent to those of average high-school-graduate whites.

The final model for each measure of schooling controls for differences among ethnic groups in nativity. As a result of this control, the relative positions of American Indians, blacks, and whites—groups that are exclusively or predominantly native—tend to weaken relative to the groups with larger foreign-born populations. Nativity further accounts for the relatively low schooling levels of Hispanics, but by itself it is not as important a source of schooling differentials as family socioeconomic conditions.

In analyses not shown here, we examined the relative importance of measures of family background in determining differences in educational attainment. Nativity and differences in parents' educational attainment and father's occupation were the most important factors in explaining intergroup differences in educational attainment. Sibship size and coming from a broken family were of secondary importance.[4]

Ethnic-Racial Differences in Educational Stratification

Table 6 reports differences among ethnic-racial groups in educational inequality and in the effects of family background on highest grade of school completed. Several summary measures indicate that schooling is somewhat more unequally distributed within the Hispanic groups than the others and most equally distributed among whites and Indians. The standard deviations of schooling (SD) range from 4.7 for Mexicans down to 3.5 for whites. This pattern of dispersion is preserved when we take account of age heterogeneity in the population (SD | Age), and when both age and family background differences are taken into account (SEE). Even *within* groups that have equivalent levels on the five family background measures listed in Table 6, the standard deviation for Mexicans exceeds that for whites and American Indians by almost 1 year.

The R^2 statistics denote the proportion of variance explained by age and measured family background characteristics. These characteristics explain approximately 25% to 30% of variance in educational attainment for each ethnicracial group. This quantity can be compared to the total (both measured and unmeasured) proportion of variability in schooling that is attributable to family background. The correlation between brothers' educational attainments ("Brothers' ρ") estimates this quantity insofar as social background is defined as that which brothers share in common. As the second to last row of Table 6 indicates, this quantity is 50% to 60% for each group. The final row of the table indicates that the relative importance of measured and unmeasured sources of family background is approximately equal in every group, which means that approximately 50% of the variation in schooling is attributable to factors that brothers do not share. Such factors include specific abilities, differences in treatment by parents, differences in the life-cycle stage of the parents when the brothers were born, and different economic incentives to continue in school. Of the 50% to 60% of variation that is attributable to common family circumstances, roughly half is due to factors excluded from our models. Most important in all of this, however, is that despite differences in the overall dispersion of schooling across groups, the relative importance of nonfamily, measured family, and unmeasured family factors is similar in every ethnic-racial group.

[4]Nativity may interact within the ethnic-racial groups; in particular, it may affect Hispanics and Asians differently. Because of our limited sample size we did not attempt to estimate this effect with the OCG data.

Table 6. Regression Analysis of Socioeconomic Background Effects on Highest Grade of School Completed for Selected Ethnic-Racial Groups: Civilian Noninstitutionalized Men in 1973[a]

Social background variable	American Indians	Cubans	Mexicans	Puerto Ricans	Asians	Blacks	Whites
Father's schooling	0.032	-0.003	0.219	0.322	0.152	0.146	0.189
	(.04)	(.05)	(.02)	(.06)	(.04)	(.03)	(.02)
Mother's schooling	0.330	0.338	0.263	0.222	0.042	0.227	0.121
	(.04)	(.07)	(.03)	(.06)	(.04)	(.03)	(.03)
Father's occupation[b]	0.033	0.277	0.108	0.063	0.201	0.002	0.114
	(.04)	(.07)	(.03)	(.06)	(.06)	(.04)	(.03)
Number of siblings	-0.216	-0.269	-0.115	-0.083	0.002	-0.129	-0.223
	(.04)	(.06)	(.02)	(.05)	(.05)	(.02)	(.02)
Broken family	-0.114	-0.686	-1.055	-0.162	-0.506	0.143	-0.754
	(.32)	(.57)	(.21)	(.38)	(.36)	(.19)	(.19)
SEE	3.04	3.72	3.89	3.45	3.43	3.37	2.96
SD	Age[c]	3.52	4.26	4.45	3.97	3.67	3.76	3.36
SD	3.68	4.38	4.68	4.06	4.08	4.04	3.47
R^2	0.25	0.28	0.31	0.28	0.29	0.30	0.27
Brothers' ρ	0.53	0.53	0.63	0.59	0.52	0.51	0.49
Proportion of within-family variance explained	0.47	0.53	0.49	0.48	0.52	0.51	0.49

[a]Numbers are least-squares regression coefficients with standard errors in parentheses. All models include a constant and dummy variables that denote ages 20–25, 26–35, 36–45, 46–55, 56–65, and whether an observation is for a respondent, an "oldest brother," or a "youngest brother." Numbers of observations are presented in Table 1. For definitions of variables and further explanation, see text.

[b]Duncan Occupational Socioeconomic Index × 0.1

[c]Standard error of estimate of regression of grades of schooling on dummy variables for age groups.

Yet Table 6 also shows that groups differ in the relative importance of measured family characteristics. The patterns are complex and defy brief summary. One pattern, however, deserves comment. Among only two groups, Mexicans and whites, is being raised in a broken family a significant handicap in educational attainment. Mexicans and whites raised in broken families average approximately 1 and .75 of a grade respectively less than their counterparts from intact families. Why this pattern of effects occurs has no obvious explanation, but, from the results presented here, Mexicans and whites are also the only groups for which there are strong, independent effects of *every* family background factor included in the model. Evidently, maternal, paternal, and sibling influences are important components of family effects for these two groups, whereas for all other groups only one or two of these factors affect educational attainment. Table 6 illustrates the diverse effects of individual family background factors across ethnic-racial groups.

SUMMARY AND CONCLUSION

We have described current educational differences among ethnic-racial and nativity groups. Several Hispanic groups, including Puerto Ricans and Mexicans, have substantial educational disadvantages relative to other groups. Asians, particularly Asian Indians, Chinese, and Japanese, have substantial educational advantages. Comparisons among the cohorts represented in the 1973 OCG survey and the 1980 census suggest that the educational attainment has increased for almost all groups more than it has for whites. In particular, all U.S.-born groups have gained on whites.

Analyses of school enrollment also suggest future increases in educational attainment for all groups relative to whites. In particular, white and black enrollment rates have nearly converged, and rates for American Indians and U.S.-born Mexicans fall only slightly behind those of whites. Enrollment rates for Asian groups are high relative to those of whites and other groups, suggesting the continued advantage of these groups in educational attainment. Of particular interest among the Asian groups are the Vietnamese, who now have enrollment rates similar to other Asian groups, suggesting that although Vietnamese educational attainment now lags behind that of other Asian groups, this difference will soon disappear.

Foreign-born Mexicans experience a severe disadvantage in levels of both attained education and school enrollment. In 1980, for persons aged 26–35, this group's attainment is nearly 3.5 years below that of U.S.-born Mexicans and more than 5 years below that of whites. Intercohort comparsions also suggest that the educational attainment of recent foreign-born cohorts is only modestly higher than that of older foreign-born persons. Furthermore, the pattern of school enrollment rates suggests that the completed educational attainment of the younger foreign-born Mexican population will also substantially lag behind that of other groups.

These differences indicate that foreign-born Mexicans should be a group of considerable policy concern. In addition, it suggests that policy issues and scholarly analyses of Mexican educational attainment should distinguish between those born in the United States and foreign-born persons, a practice that is often not followed (see Orum, 1986). Although native Mexicans are clearly educationally disadvantaged relative to the majority population, the educational disadvantage of Mexican foreign-born persons is much greater.

Our analysis of the effects of family background suggests that from one-half to two-thirds of the educational difference between whites and other ethnic and racial groups can be explained by differences in family background and nativity. In particular, differences in parents' educational attainments and fathers' occupations are important sources of group differences in attainment in the offspring generation. These findings suggest that discussions of social policy should focus on the types of institutions and programs that can help compensate persons from disadvantaged backgrounds. They also imply that programs that reduce economic inequality among persons already out of school will potentially reduce educational inequalities in succeeding generations.

COMMENT: A NOTE ON THE EFFECT OF FAMILY STRUCTURE ON SCHOOL ENROLLMENT

Sara S. McLanahan and Larry Bumpass[5]

The recent growth of mother-only families in the United States and elsewhere has stimulated new interest in the role of family structure in the intergenerational transmission of poverty. This issue was first raised in the early 1960s by Daniel Patrick Moynihan, who argued that marital disruption and the growth of female-headed families were indicators of social disorganization in the black community with serious consequences for future generations of children (Moynihan, 1965). Since that time, female-headed families have become increasingly common and are intimately linked with the "feminization of poverty" and the relative decline in children's well-being across all racial and ethnic groups (Preston, 1984; Garfinkel & McLanahan, 1986).

In this research note, we examine the effect of living in a mother-only family on the high school enrollment rates of adolescents in seven racial and

[5]Sara S. McLanahan and Larry Bumpass of the Department of Sociology and the Institute for Research on Poverty, University of Wisconsin–Madison, Madison, Wisconsin.

ethnic groups: non-Hispanic whites, blacks, Mexicans, Cubans, Puerto Ricans, American Indians, and East Asians (Chinese, Korean, and Japanese). Although high school graduation represents only one of several transitions in the educational career, it is the point in the schooling process where much of the inequality among recent cohorts begins (Mare, 1981b). It is also the most critical transition in understanding the intergenerational transmission of poverty in that failure to complete high school is strongly associated with long-term economic instability and insecurity (Bane & Ellwood, 1986).

Our sample consists of 16- and 17-year-olds living in the United States in 1980. Thus, the individuals in our sample were born in 1963 or 1964, whereas individuals in the OCG sample used by Mare and Winship were born between 1908 and 1953. Our measure of school achievement is whether or not the adolescent is enrolled in school. Those who have already completed high school are included with the "enrolled" for this analysis. Enrollment is an imperfect measure of high school completion, because an additional portion of those currently enrolled will drop out before graduation, and some of those not enrolled may eventually receive high school diplomas or equivalent certification. Despite this limitation, these data have the very real advantage of providing information on family income, parents' socioeconomic status, and living arrangements while the adolescent is still living at home.

Differences in the Living Arrangements of Adolescents

Table 7 compares the living arrangements of adolescents by race and ethnic group. The statistics show that although two-parent families are the most com-

Table 7. Percentage of 16- and 17-Year-Olds Living in One- and Two-Parent Families, by Race/Ethnicity

	Both parents	Remarried parents	Mother only	Father only	Other
Whites	60.56	18.82	12.57	2.70	5.36
Blacks	28.44	17.23	38.75	3.42	12.17
Mexicans	51.49	15.81	16.23	2.86	13.61
Cubans	62.37	15.09	14.66	2.20	5.68
Puerto Ricans	33.83	14.80	37.72	2.78	10.87
American Indians	36.86	19.45	21.82	3.85	18.03
East Asians	70.25	11.09	8.94	2.02	7.70

SOURCE: Public Use Sample data tapes from the 1980 Census.

mon circumstance for adolescents, there is considerable variation across sub-groups. Furthermore, although the majority of two-parent families contain both natural parents, the proportion of offspring living with both parents as compared with a parent and stepparent also varies across groups.

East Asians, Cubans, and non-Hispanic whites are the most likely to live with both natural parents, whereas blacks, Puerto Ricans and American Indians are the least likely. Mexicans fall in between. If we ask how many adolescents live in two-parent families, including stepparents as well as biological parents, the proportions are higher but the pattern is the same.

The pattern for mother-only families is the reverse of that for two-parent families. Nearly 40% of black and Puerto Rican adolescents live with single mothers as compared with 9% of Asians and 13% of whites. Father-only families are relatively rare in all groups, between 2% and 4%. Of particular interest is the proportion of offspring living with neither parent, which is quite high for blacks, Mexicans, Puerto Ricans, and especially American Indians.

Numerous researchers have noted that in certain racial and ethnic groups single mothers are more likely to live with relatives than to live alone. Moreover, some have argued that offspring in such families are better off than those who live with only one adult. In additional tabulations, not reported here, we examined the proportion of adolescents living in mother-only families that included grandparents and/or other adults. The proportion was relatively low, ranging from 11% of Puerto Ricans and whites to 22% of Cubans. For the remaining groups, between 14% and 17% of mother-only families included other adults.

The results presented in Table 7 are interesting when compared with those reported by Mare and Winship for the OCG men in Table 4. Their estimates of exposure to a "broken family" are much lower than ours. For example, over 70% of all minority groups in the OCG data, with the exception of blacks, are categorized as living in intact families. Even among blacks the proportion is 66%. The 1980 census data show much lower proportions, especially among blacks (28%), Puerto Ricans (34%) and American Indians (37%). The difference between the two sets of estimates is due in part to differences in the way family structure is measured: the OCG asks whether respondents lived with both parents "most of the time" up until age 16, whereas the census asks whether respondents were living with both natural parents at the time of the census (i.e., ages 16, 17). The wording of the OCG question means that disruptions occurring after age 9 are not counted, as adolescents in such families would have lived with both parents "most of the time." Differences in exposure to single parenthood may also be due to real differences in the experience of cohorts. Recall that the OCG respondents were born between 1908 and 1953. Members of our sample, on the other hand, were born in the early 1960s and grew up during the time when divorce rates were accelerating.

Table 8. Percentage of 16- and 17-Year-Olds Enrolled in School, by Family
Structure and Race/Ethnicity

	Both parents	Remarried parents	Mother only	Father only	Other
Whites	95.37%	90.87%	86.80%	86.04%	73.32%
(N = 62,996)					
Blacks	93.80	93.08	89.33	88.92	80.56
(N = 60,424)					
Mexicans	88.18	83.71	82.52	73.76	56.01
(N = 18,366)					
Cubans	93.34	87.85	90.00	83.33	77.11
(N = 1,637)					
Puerto Ricans	89.34	85.00	81.67	79.17	61.61
(N = 4,324)					
American Indians	85.01	83.89	75.59	77.04	73.44
(N = 3,511)					
East Asians	97.95	96.60	95.79	93.22	91.89
(N = 2,921)					

Ethnic Differences in School Enrollment

Table 8 reports the proportion of 16- and 17-year-olds enrolled in school by family structure and race and ethnic status. Overall, enrollment levels are quite high for all groups. Recall, however, that these figures overestimate the proportion of adolescents who will graduate from high school. Some portion of those enrolled at this age are a grade or more behind and will never graduate. For example, in the October, 1979, Current Population Survey (U.S. Bureau of the Census, 1981), 17% of those aged 20–21 had not completed high school (and were not enrolled), compared to 9% of the 16–17-year-olds. Failure to graduate among those enrolled at ages 16–17 is particularly striking among blacks, for whom the above contrast was 28% to 8% for the two age groups. Thus, our measure of dropout by age 16–17 is a conservative indicator of failure to complete high school.

Table 8 shows that enrollment varies both by subgroup status and family structure. Again, whites, Asians, and Cubans are the most likely to be enrolled, whereas the more economically disadvantaged groups are least likely. Within subgroups, adolescents living with both natural parents are most likely to be in school, whereas those living with neither parent are least likely. Offspring who live with single mothers or single fathers are in between.

Table 9. Increase in the Risk of Not Being Enrolled in School Associated with Family Structure, Mothers' Education, and Family Income (Percentage increase in the odds ratio)

	Whites	Blacks	Mexicans	Puerto Ricans	Cubans	Native Americans	East Asians
Total sample							
Family structure:							
Father only	75[a]	4	52[a]	54[a]	86[a]	19	70
Mother only	122[a]	32[a]	43[a]	43[a]	44	55[a]	39
Mother's education less than high school	174[a]	80[a]	111[a]	48[a]	60[a]	101[a]	61[a]
Family income rises by $10,000[b]	−33[a]	−22[a]	−18[a]	−33[a]	−20	−22[a]	−56[a]
Men							
Mother-only family	101[a]	31[a]	42[a]	36[a]	73[a]	65[a]	14
Women							
Mother-only family	172[a]	34[a]	45[a]	48[a]	9	45[a]	72

[a]Statistically significant at the .05 percent level.
[b]Decrease in risk associated with a rise of $10,000 in family income.

Family Structure and School Enrollment

Table 9 reports estimates of the effects of living with a single parent on high school enrollment, controlling for current family income, mother's education, and sex of respondent. The multivariate model allows us to examine the association between parents' marital disruption and school enrollment net of differences in family socioeconomic status. The indicators of socioeconomic status are mother's education (measured by a set of dummy variables: less than 9 years of school, 9 to 11 years, 12 years, some college, and college degree) and family income (measured by a set of dummy variables: 0–$999, $10,000–$19,999, $20,000–$29,000, $30,000–$39,000, $40,000+).[6] The estimates reported in Table 9 were obtained from a logit model in which the log of the odds ratio of not being in school was treated as a function of family status, socioeconomic status, and sex of adolescent. The numbers represent the proportional increase in the odds ratio associated with living in a mother-only or father-only family, control-

[6]We also estimated models that treated income as a dichotomous variable—whether the family was above or below the poverty line—but these results were similar to the first set of estimates and therefore we do not report them here.

ling for socioeconomic background. The results are reported first for the total sample and then for men and women separately.

The results are striking in their consistency across race and ethnic groups. Moreover, with the exception of whites, the size of the family structure effect is surprisingly stable. Estimates for the total sample indicate that living in a mother-only family increases the odds of having dropped out of school by ages 16–17 by 122% among whites and by about 30% to 55% among the other groups. The effects are statistically significant for all groups except Cubans and Asians.

Living in a father-only family is also associated with not being in school, except among blacks. Among whites, Cubans, and Asians, living with a single father increases the odds by about 75%. Among Mexicans and Puerto Ricans, the odds are about 50% greater. The effect on American Indians is much smaller and not statistically significant.

In order to evaluate the relative importance of living arrangements, we report the increase in risk associated with mother's education and family income. The education effect represents the contrast between having a mother who attended but did not complete high school as compared with a mother who completed high school but did not attend college. The income effect represents the decrease in risk associated with a $10,000 increase in family income.

As expected, the estimates for the socioeconomic variables show that mother's education has a much stronger effect on her offspring's school behavior than whether or not she is married. The effect of education is strongest among whites, Mexicans, and American Indians, and weakest among Puerto Ricans and Cubans. Income is also associated with dropping out of school, but the association is weaker. Adolescents from families with income in the $10,000 to $20,000 range are about 20% to 30% less likely to quit school than those in the 0 to $10,000 range, and those in the $20,000 to $30,000 income category are about 40% to 60% less likely.

A comparison of the relative importance of education, income, and family structure indicates that having a mother who completed high school is significantly more important in determining school enrollment than having an additional $10,000 in income. It is also more important than family structure, especially among blacks, Mexicans, and American Indians. For the latter, having a mother who completed high school reduces the odds of dropping out of school by about 1.5 times as much as living in an intact family. The relative importance of mother's education for the educational achievement of offspring is consistent with Mare and Winship's findings with the OCG data.

Our results differ from those of Mare and Winship is one respect, and this difference is important. Whereas we find a consistent pattern of significant effects across five out of seven subgroups, Mare and Winship find significant effects for Mexicans and whites only (Table 6). Moreover, their point estimates for blacks, Americans Indians, and Puerto Ricans are virtually zero. There are several possible explanations for this discrepancy. First, as noted above, the measures of family structure are different. The OCG indicator identifies only those adolescents who did not live with both parents "most of the time" up to age 16, whereas the census indicator identifies all exposures to single parenthood up to ages 16–17. To the extent that disruptions occurring after age 8 are important, the OCG question will misclassify relevant family experiences.

Second, the outcome measures in the two analyses are different. The OCG study looks at total years of schooling, whereas we look at enrollment at ages 16–17. If family structure has a stronger effect on early school transitions as compared with later decisions (e.g., whether to attend college, whether to obtain a graduate degree), as Mare and Winship suggest, their model would yield smaller effects.

Third, the two samples represent different birth cohorts, and the OCG data exclude women. Mare and Winship note that the experience of the OCG men, "may not be the same as for men completing their schooling in the 1980s." Not only was the schooling experience of these men different from that today, but the experience of living in a single-parent family was also different in the earlier period. Notably, mother-only families were less common and a much larger proportion of single mothers were widows.

Finally, the difference in the two sets of results may be due to the fact that a much larger proportion of offspring from disadvantaged minorities are completing high school than in the past. Although the upward mobility of these subgroup members is encouraging, it increases within-group differences and highlights the disadvantage of those left behind. Our results indicate that adolescents in mother-only families are more likely to be in the latter group.

ACKNOWLEDGMENTS

Preparation of the portion of this chapter written by Robert Mare and Christopher Winship was supported by the National Institute of Aging (PO1 AG04877) and by the Graduate School of the University of Wisconsin-Madison. The portion written by Sara McLanahan and Larry Bumpass was supported by the National Institute of Child Health and Human Development (HD-19375-01). All computations were performed using facilities of the Center for Demography and Ecology at the University of Wisconsin-Madison, which are supported by the Center for Population Research of the National Institute of Child Health and Human Development (HD-5876). Mare and Winship are grateful to Meei-Shenn Tzeng and Julia Gray for research assistance.

REFERENCES

Abowd, J. M., & M. R. Killingsworth. (1985). Employment, wages, and earnings of Hispanics in the federal and nonfederal sectors: Methodological issues and their empirical consequences. In G. J. Borjas and M. Tienda (Eds.), *Hispanics in the U.S. economy.* Orlando, FL: Academic Press.

Bane, M. J., & D. T. Ellwood. (1986). Slipping into and out of poverty: The dynamics of spells. *Journal of Human Resources, 21,* 1–23.

Bianchi, S. M. (1984). Children's relative progress through school: A research note. *Sociology of Education, 57,* 184–192.

Borjas, G. J., and M. Tienda (Eds.). (1985). *Hispanics in the U.S. economy.* Orlando, FL: Academic Press.

Chiswick, B. R. (1983). An analysis of the earnings and employment of Asian-American men. *Journal of Economic Literature, 1,* 197–214.

Duncan, B. (1968). Trends in output and distribution of schooling. In E. B. Sheldon & W. E. Moore (Eds.), *Indicators of social change.* New York: Russell Sage.

Farley, R. (1984). *Blacks and whites: Narrowing the gap?.* Cambridge, MA: Harvard University Press.

Featherman, D. L., & R. M. Hauser. (1975). Design for a replicate study of social mobility in the United States. In K. C. Land & S. Spilerman (Eds.), *Social indicator models.* New York: Russell Sage.

Featherman, D. L., & R. M. Hauser. (1978). *Opportunity and change.* New York: Academic Press.

Fligstein, N., & R. Fernandez. (1985). Educational transitions of whites and Mexican-Americans. In G. Borjas and M. Tienda (Eds.), *Hispanics in the U.S. economy.* Orlando, FL: Academic Press.

Garfinkel, I., & S. S. McLanahan. (1986). *Single mothers and their children: A new American dilemma.* Washington, DC: Urban Institute Press.

Griliches, Z. (1979). Sibling models and data in economics: Beginnings of a survey. *Journal of Political Economy, 87,* S37–S64.

Hauser, R. M., & D. L. Featherman. (1976). Equality of schooling: Trends and prospects. *Sociology of Education, 49,* 99–120.

Hirschman, C. (1986). The extraordinary educational attainment of Asian-Americans: A search for historical evidence and explanations. *Social Forces, 65,* 1–27.

Jencks, C. S., M. Smith, H. Acland, M. J. Bane, D. Cohen, H. Gintis, B. Heyns, & S. Michelson. (1972). *Inequality: A reassessment of the effect of family and schooling in America.* New York: Basic Books.

Lieberson, S. (1980). *A piece of the pie: Blacks and white immigrants since 1880.* Berkeley, CA: University of California Press.

Mare, R. D. (1980). Social background and school continuation decisions. *Journal of the American Statistical Association, 75,* 295–305.

Mare, R. D. (1981a). Change and stability in educational stratification. *American Sociological Review, 46,* 72–87.

Mare, R. D. (1981b). Trends in schooling: Demography, performance, and organization. *Annals of the American Academy of Political and Social Science, 453,* 96–122.

Mare, R. D., C. Winship, & W. N. Kubitschek. (1984). The transition from youth to adult: Understanding the age pattern of employment. *American Journal of Sociology, 89,* 326–358.

Moynihan, D. P. (1965). *The Negro family: The case for national action.* Washington, DC: U.S. Department of Labor, Office of Policy Planning and Research.

Orum, L. S. (1986). *The education of Hispanics: Status and implications.* Washington, DC: National Council of La Raza.

Preston, S. H. (1984). Children and the elderly: Divergent paths for America's dependents. *Demography, 21*, 435–457.

Reimers, C. W. (1985). A comparative analysis of the wages of Hispanics, blacks, and non-Hispanic whites. In G. J. Borjas & M. Tienda (Eds.), *Hispanics in the U.S. Economy*. Orlando, FL: Academic Press.

Thurow, L. C. (1975). *Generating inequality*. New York: Basic Books.

U.S. Bureau of the Census. (1981). *School enrollment—social and economic characteristics of students: October 1979*. Current Population Reports, Series P-20, no. 360. Washington, DC: U.S. Government Printing Office.

III

Social Policy

8

The Duality in Federal Policy toward Minority Groups, 1787–1987

GARY D. SANDEFUR

The prevailing norms and values of American society prescribe a system in which all individuals are treated equally by programs and policies designed to ease or overcome social and economic disadvantages. The social welfare system emphasizes economic need as the basis for receiving transfers and services. For some purposes, however, categorization is utilized to target services, and has become an important part of the social welfare system (Gramlich, 1986). For example, Aid to Families with Dependent Children (AFDC) is generally viewed as a program targeted toward poor single mothers; the old age assistance part of the Supplemental Security Income program is designed for old poor people. The use of social criteria in determining eligibility is usually attributed to the expectation that some people (e.g., fathers, the nonelderly) should work, whereas others (e.g., mothers, the elderly) should not. As norms and values change, the use of social criteria in categorization also changes, exemplified by the growing call for programs in which poor, single mothers would be expected to work.

Although most Americans at one time viewed racial and ethnic groups as being fundamentally different, requiring different "treatment," the current view is that race and ethnicity are irrelevant to the determination of need and eligibility for social welfare programs. There are, however, two ways in which this ideal is threatened. First, members of minority groups are either over- or underrepresented among the clientele of many social programs. For example, on one hand blacks are underrepresented among recipients of social security owing to their higher rates of unemployment during their years in the labor force. On the other

GARY D. SANDEFUR • School of Social Work and Institute for Research on Poverty, University of Wisconsin-Madison, Madison, Wisconsin.

hand, blacks are overrepresented as recipients of AFDC, owing to higher rates of female headship as well as higher rates of unemployment.

Second, some programs continue to be administered on the basis of racial/ethnic criteria. The best known example is affirmative action, a policy designed to overcome the past use of racial criteria through the current use of racial criteria. A major objection to it is that race should not be used in determining eligibility for such opportunities as those involving education, new jobs, and promotions.

There are, however, other less familiar federal programs that determine eligibility through the use of racial and/or ethnic criteria. Bilingual education, initiated on a national basis in 1965, uses language—which is definitely an ethnic criterion—to determine eligibility. The most extreme case of the use of racial or ethnic criteria to determine eligibility for programs involves the set of programs available to American Indians. American Indians may participate in AFDC, social security, Medicare, Medicaid, and other programs that are available to all Americans, but they are also eligible for educational assistance, free health care regardless of economic means, and other services that are available only to them. No other group in U.S. society has access to such a comprehensive set of programs designed solely for the use of its members.

This chapter addresses three issues regarding racial and ethnic differences in the impact of the social welfare system. It first examines how race-specific programs came into existence. It next investigates the effect of group-specific programs on poverty. Perhaps the most important part of this issue is whether there are any advantages to taking racial and ethnic criteria into account in designing social welfare, especially antipoverty, policy. Third, it assesses the participation of minority groups in social insurance and public assistance programs that are available to all Americans. In doing so, it focuses on American Indians, blacks, and Hispanics.

A BRIEF POPULATION HISTORY OF MINORITY GROUPS IN THE UNITED STATES

Understanding the development of group-specific policies can be enhanced by a brief examination of the population history of American Indians, blacks, and people of Mexican, Puerto Rican, and Cuban origin. Table 1 gives the population of these groups at selected points in history, as well as the corresponding white population figures.

Although there is no way to measure with certainty the size of the American Indian population in 1492, historical demographers have estimated it as between 1 and 15 million. Thornton (1987) evaluates some of these different estimates and arrives at a figure of 5 million as the most reasonable estimate. By 1790, the

Table 1. American Indian, Black, Hispanic and White Populations,
1492–1980 (in Thousands)

Year	American Indian	Black	Mexican origin	Puerto Rican	Cuban origin	White
1492	5,000	0	0	0	0	0
1790	700	800	20	0	0	3,000
1860	400	4,400	28	0	0	27,000
1900	237	8,800	103[a]	0	11	67,000
1950	357	15,000	1,342[a]	301	33	135,000
1960	524	18,900	1,725[a]	893	125	159,000
1970	793	22,600	4,532	1,392	561	178,000
1980	1,418	26,500	8,740	2,014	803	188,000

[a]These population figures refer to individuals born in Mexico or with parents born in Mexico.
SOURCES: The American Indian population figures prior to 1970 are from Thornton (1987). The Hispanic population figures for years prior to 1970 are from Jaffe, Cullen, and Boswell (1980). The population figures for 1970 and 1980 are from the decennial censuses of the U.S. Bureau of the Census.

American Indian population had shrunk to 700,000, largely because of disease (Thornton, 1987); its size had been surpassed by that of the two populations not present in 1492: blacks and whites. In addition, it is estimated (Jaffe, Cullen, & Boswell, 1980), that in 1790 there were 20,000 individuals of Spanish and mixed Spanish-Indian descent living in what would become part of the southwestern United States.

By 1900, there were 8.8 million blacks in the United States, 103,000 individuals of Mexican origin (including the original Hispanics), and 11,000 individuals of Cuban origin (Jaffe, Cullen, & Boswell, 1980). The American Indian population continued to decline until 1900, when it reached what is generally recognized as its nadir of approximately 240,000 people. Between 1900 and 1950, the American Indian population grew to 357,000, but was surpassed by individuals of Mexican origin and was approached by a growing Puerto Rican population living on the mainland. In 1980, black Americans formed the largest minority group in the United States, followed by Mexican Americans, Puerto Ricans, American Indians, and Cuban Americans.

HISTORICAL REVIEW OF FEDERAL POLICY TOWARD THE FOCAL GROUPS

The population growth or decline of minority groups was due partly to explicit federal policies limiting or allowing growth, but also to other sorts of influences. The U.S. government was not completely responsible for the American Indian population decline between 1492 and 1900, but the fact that it did diminish worked to the advantage of the federal government, because it eased the problem of displacing Indians to open up land for settlement. The growth of the black population during the 1700s and the first half of the 1800s was due to the economic value of blacks as slaves. The growth of the Mexican-origin population prior to 1964 was partly due to problems in Mexico, but also to the demand for labor in the Southwest and to the fact that the Immigration Act of 1924 placed no restrictions on immigration from other countries in the Western Hemisphere (Estrada, Garcia, Macias, & Maldonado, 1981). The growth of the Puerto Rican population was facilitated by the fact that Puerto Ricans have been citizens of the United States since 1917 and their movement to the mainland is unrestricted. Although there was some Cuban immigration prior to the late 1950s, the growth of the Cuban population in the United States really began when Fidel Castro came to power and the United States decided to accept refugees from Cuba.

As the sizes and relative sizes of the various minority groups changed, and as their special problems became apparent, the executive, legislative and judicial arms of the federal government responded with actions directed toward specific groups. A review of these actions over time indicates that there was never a consistent "minorities" policy, nor in fact was there a consistent policy toward any of the individual groups. The principal policies and laws affecting minorities are listed in Table 2.

The Constitution recognized the special status of American Indians and assigned the federal government rather than state governments the responsibility for dealing with them. Black slaves were accorded no rights in the Constitution, and there was virtually no Hispanic population to deal with at that time. As the Constitution was being drawn up and later, during the early 1800s, the U.S. government continued to be preoccupied with Indians. At this time, the American Indian population was almost one-fourth the size of the white population and occupied land that the Federal government wanted to open to white settlement.

The solution for dealing with American Indians eventually arrived at was removal. During the 1830s, removal focused on moving as many Indian groups as possible from east of the Mississippi to west of it. The cases handled by the John Marshall Supreme Court in 1831 affirmed the principle of limited Indian sovereignty (i.e., Indian tribal governments could operate in a fashion similar to state governments). Mid-nineteenth-century removal was directed at opening up areas west of the Mississippi by confining tribes to small, isolated reservations, several of which were located in Oklahoma. At that time, Oklahoma was designated as Indian Territory.

During the 1800s, U.S. policy toward blacks underwent major changes. The lack of civil rights for black slaves was affirmed in the famous *Dred Scott* v. *Sanford* decision of 1857. The Civil War brought about the end of slavery, and the rights of blacks were institutionalized through the Thirteenth, Fourteenth, and Fifteenth Amendments to the Constitution.

In 1848, the Treaty of Guadalupe Hidalgo granted citizenship to individuals of Mexican descent who decided to remain in the new parts of the United States that were taken from Mexico.

After the Civil War, then, both blacks and Mexican Americans were granted the legal rights of citizens in principle, if not in practice. American Indians, on the other hand, could become citizens only through renouncing their status as Indians. Citizenship in a tribe was seen as incompatible with citizenship in the United States.

During the 1890s, several governmental actions altered the way in which the United States dealt with the largest minority groups. In 1891, the Court of Private Land Claims was established, mainly to deal with the claims of Hispanos (individuals of Mexican descent living in areas formerly part of Mexico) who had lost land after the 1848 Treaty. This action emphasized the rights of Hispanic citizens. The Treaty of Paris in 1898 shifted control of Puerto Rico from Spain to the United States.

The last Indian treaty was signed in 1871. During the 1890s, the U.S. government took the position that its policy of treating Indians as a distinct group was incorrect, and began to advocate the assimilation of Indians into mainstream American life. The major mechanism for doing this was to be allotment policy, established by the Dawes Act of 1887. It provided, first, that communally owned Indian land would be divided up among individual Indians; the excess land would be purchased by the federal government and opened up to white settlement. Second, Indian tribes would cease to exist, and Indians would become citizens of the United States. Allotment policy was not administered consistently. Its major impact was in Oklahoma, where all land was allotted; Oklahoma ceased to be Indian Territory. Whereas American Indians were thus being integrated into American society, blacks were being accorded a "separate but equal" status through *Plessy* v. *Ferguson.*

The first half of the twentieth century was a time of relative consistency (but not fairness) in the treatment of blacks and Puerto Ricans, and inconsistency in the treatment of American Indians and individuals of Mexican descent. "Separate but equal" guided most federal policies toward blacks. The Jones Act, which in 1917 granted citizenship to Puerto Ricans, and the commonwealth status granted to Puerto Rico in 1952 guaranteed free movement of Puerto Ricans between the island and the mainland.

The Snyder Act of 1921 authorized the federal government to provide special services to Indians. All American Indians were granted U.S. citizenship in 1924 regardless of whether they lived on tribal or privately owned land. However, in 1934 Congress passed the Indian Reorganization Act, which ceased allotments and reinstitutionalized tribal governments. Under reorganization, it

Table 2. Major Laws, Federal Policies, and Supreme Court Decisions regarding American Indians, Blacks, and Hispanics, 1787–1980

Year	American Indians	Blacks	Mexican origin	Puerto Ricans	Cuban origin
1787	U.S. Constitution				
1830	Indian Removal Act				
1831	Marshall's Supreme Court *Cherokee Nation v. Georgia*, *Worcester v. Georgia*				
1848			Treaty of Guadalupe Hidalgo		
1857		*Dred Scott v. Sanford*			
1863		Emancipation Proclamation			
1868		Fourteenth Amendment			
1871	Last treaty; legislative era begins				
1887	Dawes Act (allotment policy)				
1891			Court of Private Land Claims		
1896		*Plessy v. Ferguson*			
1898				Treaty of Paris	
1917			First Bracero program	Jones Act (citizenship)	
1921	Snyder Act				
1924	Citizenship Act		—Immigration Act (no restrictions on Western Hemisphere immigration)—		
1929–1934			"voluntary repatriation"		

Year	American Indians	Hispanics	Blacks
1934	Indian Reorganization Act; Johnson-O'Malley Act		
1942		Second Bracero program	
1952		Commonwealth status	
1953	House Concurrent Resolution 108: Termination		
1954		Operation Wetback	Brown v. Board of Education
1961		Cuban Refugee Program	
1964			Civil Rights Act
1965		Immigration Act (hemispheric restrictions)——— / Bilingual education———	Voting Rights Act
1967		Migrant Education Program	
1968			Fair Housing Act
1974	Morton v. Mancari		
1975	Indian Self-Determination and Educational Assistance Act	———Bilingual ballots———	
1978			UC v. Bakke
1979			United Steelworkers v. Weber
1980			Fullilove v. Klutznick

Note: The federal government also enacted a number of Asian-specific policies in the late nineteenth and twentieth centuries. These programs do not appear in the table, owing to the focus of this chapter on American Indians, blacks, and Hispanics.

SOURCES: Burns (1981); Estrada et al. (1981); Prucha (1984); U.S. Congress, Office of Technology Assessment (1986).

was possible to be a tribal citizen as well as a U.S. citizen. In addition, Congress enacted the Johnson-O'Malley program, which authorized the federal government to contract with state and local governments to provide services to American Indians. One of the important consequences of this program was that Indians in Oklahoma and other areas were integrated into white schools long before blacks and Hispanic Americans. This integration was facilitated by the money given to local school districts for each Indian student, and by the relatively small size of the population of Indian students in most of those districts. School districts continue to receive per capita payments for American Indian students, although the Reagan administration proposed elimination of this program.

For Mexican Americans, the early part of the twentieth century saw the first contract labor (bracero) program and the Immigration Act of 1924, which placed no restrictions on Western Hemisphere immigration. This was followed by "voluntary repatriation" during the Great Depression and a second contract labor program during the 1940s. Although "voluntary repatriation" was directed toward Mexicans rather than Mexican Americans, many of the latter were illegally forced to move to Mexico. In summary, during the first half of the twentieth century the actions of the federal government reinforced the "differences" between the focal minority groups and the white majority, although its actions toward Mexican Americans and American Indians were inconsistent.

Federal actions since 1950 have largely been designed to eliminate racial and ethnic differences in treatment, with a few exceptions and with a great deal of inconsistency. In 1953, the House of Representatives and Senate passed House Concurrent Resolution 108, which called for the termination of the special legal relationship between the federal government and tribal governments. The major principles underlying termination were that the federal government would end its special relationship with Indian tribes, and Indian tribes would give up their rights and privileges as governments. This would have ended the unique legal status of Indians and made them "just another minority group" in the United States. A number of tribes were terminated under this resolution. Another part of the termination program was relocation, which provided assistance to Indians who wished to move from isolated rural areas to urban areas that offered better opportunities for housing and jobs. The ending of their "special status" was not well received by Indian leaders.

In 1954, the U.S. Supreme Court ruled that the "special status" of blacks was unconstitutional. The decision was applauded by black leaders, since their special status was used to deny them rights and privileges, whereas the special status of Indians was used to grant them rights and privileges.

Operation Wetback, designed to apprehend and deport undocumented Mexican workers, was also initiated in 1954. Although it was directed at illegal Mexican immigrants rather than legal Mexican immigrants and Mexican Americans, the title and spirit of the actions of the Immigration and Naturalization Service offended the Mexican American community.

In 1959, Fidel Castro gained control of Cuba, and in 1961 the U.S. government began a Cuban refugee program to assist "political" refugees from Cuba at the same time that it was seeking to limit the flow of "economic" refugees from Mexico.

The 1960s brought major civil rights legislation, directed toward blacks but also applicable to American Indians and Hispanic Americans. The Civil Rights Act of 1964, the Voting Rights Act of 1965, and the Fair Housing Act of 1968 were all designed to ensure that race/ethnicity did not prevent individuals from enjoying the basic rights that were guaranteed to all people.

The Immigration Act of 1965 replaced the national-origin quota system with hemispheric limits on immigration. In the same year, bilingual education, which was directed primarily at Hispanic Americans, was initiated, and in 1967 the Migrant Education program was developed to establish and improve efforts to meet the special educational needs of the children of migrant workers. Also, the enforcement of other rights began to take race/ethnicity into account. That is, not only did the federal government commit itself to ensuring that blacks, Indians, and Hispanics would not be discriminated against in the future, it also committed itself to efforts to overcome the effects of past discrimination. This, of course, required the use of race/ethnicity to determine who had suffered from such discrimination.

In the *Morton* v. *Mancari* decision of 1974, the Supreme Court ruled that special Indian programs are not racial in nature but are based on a unique political relationship between Indian tribes and the federal government. In 1975, the federal government further institutionalized the use of race and ethnicity in programs and policies through the Indian Self-Determination and Educational Assistance Act and legislation requiring that bilingual ballots be available in areas with concentrations of bilingual or non-English speakers. Indian self-determination was designed to replace termination as official federal policy. Self-determination reaffirmed the role of tribal governments in dealing with Indian issues and problems and provided mechanisms through which programs previously administered by the federal government through the Bureau of Indian Affairs were turned over to tribal governments.

The late 1970s and 1980s have seen the Supreme Court rule in favor of the special status of American Indians and in the use of race and ethnicity in overcoming past discrimination. There were several landmark decisions during this period. In the 1978 *Bakke* case, the Supreme Court ruled that it was acceptable under certain circumstances to take race into account, but that numerical quotas of the kind used at the University of California at Davis were unconstitutional. In *United Steelworkers of America* v. *Weber*, the Court in 1979 upheld a voluntary affirmative action plan that gave blacks priority for training over white workers with more seniority. And in *Fullilove* v. *Klutznick* (1980) the Court upheld the minority set-aside program that required 10% of public construction funds go to minority contractors.

So we are at a peculiar point in American history. On the one hand, we as a society have decided that neither race nor ethnicity should be used to deny access to opportunities. On the other hand, we, or at least the three branches of the federal government, have decided that race and ethnicity must be used as criteria to overcome the effects of past discrimination. The United States still has no consistent policy for dealing with minority groups, but it is unclear whether it could or should have such a policy. One reason for this is that blacks, Hispanics, and American Indians have different needs and concerns. The major battle for black Americans has been to gain access to American society. This has resulted in a series of Supreme Court decisions and legislation designed to facilitate the full incorporation of blacks into U.S. society. This desire to participate in American society and these policies also apply to American Indians and Hispanic Americans. Another major battle for American Indians, however, has been to retain their legal status as semisovereign entities. The current policy of the U.S. government is to affirm this through support of self-determination. For Hispanic Americans, overcoming the barriers of language and the preservation of language and culture while participating in American society are important issues. The use of bilingual ballots and bilingual education is designed to facilitate the participation of Hispanic Americans in U.S. society while recognizing the distinctiveness of language and culture.

THE EFFECT OF GROUP-SPECIFIC PROGRAMS ON POVERTY

The question that is most important for the purpose of this volume is whether group-specific programs have reduced poverty among racial and ethnic minorities. Even though none of the post-1965 programs and legislation listed in Table 2 (pp. 212–213) are directed specifically at reducing poverty, several concern three important correlates of poverty: employment, education, and health.

Employment and Employment Opportunities

Although the federal government has made efforts at direct job creation and job training (exemplified in the Comprehensive Employment and Training Act of 1973), its principal minority-specific effort in the employment arena has been affirmative action. This policy has taken three major forms: (a) litigation based on Title VII provisions of the Civil Rights Act of 1964; (b) monitoring of all private firms with one hundred or more employees by the Equal Employment

Opportunity Commission (EEOC); and (c) the monitoring of all firms with federal contracts by the Office of Federal Contract Compliance (OFCC). Although the Civil Rights Act applies to all business firms, only half of the nongovernmental, noneducational work force is covered by EEOC or OFCC (Smith & Welch, 1986).

There has been a great deal of controversy over the utility of affirmative action. A number of studies have documented the failure to implement affirmative action persistently and consistently. In his review of evaluations of affirmative action by the General Accounting Office, the U.S. Commission on Civil Rights, and the House and Senate Committees on Labor and Public Welfare, Jonathan Leonard (1985) notes that those studies consistently found that affirmative action was poorly implemented. The reports were especially critical of weak enforcement and the reluctance of EEOC and OFCC to apply sanctions to employers.

Most research on the impact of affirmative action has concentrated on the federal contract sector and/or firms monitored by the EEOC. Smith and Welch (1986) report that between 1966 and 1980, the proportion of blacks who were employed in firms covered by the EEOC grew from 48% to 60%. Most of this growth took place between 1966 and 1974. Leonard (1985) reports that some increases in black employment under affirmative action have taken place in low-skilled occupations, but most are in high-skilled occupations. He also discusses evidence indicating that litigation under Title VII of the Civil Rights Act has played a significant role in increasing black employment.

Although the initial successes of affirmative action were in assisting low-skilled black workers, by the late 1970s it was beginning to increase black employment and the employment of other minority groups in skilled occupations (Leonard, 1984). The effects of affirmative action on wages were not as positive. Smith and Welch (1986) conclude that it has had no significant long-run impact on wages (it had a positive effect on the wages of younger black workers between 1967 and 1972, but in the next 5 years its effect was eroded). They attribute the initial positive effect to the efforts of employers to increase the number of black workers, and they suggest that young college-educated blacks proved the main beneficiaries of affirmative action.

Because of the special relationship between American Indians and the federal government, particular programs have been directed at Indians alone. As part of the termination efforts in the 1950s, the federal government began a voluntary relocation program that offered financial aid to American Indians who wished to leave reservations and other isolated areas and settle in urban areas where better job opportunities were supposedly available. This effort, renamed the Employment Assistance Programs, continued into the early 1980s. Although there is little evidence on the effects of this program, an early study indicated that it was beneficial to many of the Indians who participated (Sorkin, 1971).

More recent government efforts have focused on job development in Indian reservations. The Presidential Commission on Reservation Economies (1984) identified a number of barriers to the development of private enterprise on Indian reservations and suggested measures for overcoming them. One quite controversial suggestion was that tribes should give up some of their rights of limited sovereignty, which pose risks for companies that locate on Indian reservations. Developing jobs on Indian reservations will in any case be difficult because of the isolation of most reservations. Also, as only one-quarter of the Indian population currently lives on reservations, developing reservation economies will not completely resolve the Indian unemployment problem.

Health Programs and Health Status

The major group-specific effort in health care has been the Indian Health Service (IHS). A report of the Office of Technology Assessment recently described a comprehensive evaluation of it (U.S. Congress, Office of Technology Assessment, 1986), examining current Indian health conditions as well as the organization and delivery of services by IHS. Among the major conclusions of the report were that the overall health status of American Indians has improved dramatically since the Public Health Service assumed responsibility, through IHS, for Indian health programs in 1955, but the Indian population continues to be less healthy than the U.S. population in general.

The statistics provided by the Office of Technology Assessment combined with those available in annual vital statistics reports provide rough indications of the health of American Indians relative to whites and blacks. Comparable statistics for Hispanic Americans are not available, but recent research on Hispanic mortality in Texas and California allows us to make some comparisons (Markides, 1983). Table 3 contains age-adjusted, cause-specific mortality rates among American Indians in IHS service areas for the period 1980–1982 and among blacks and whites for 1981. The causes are ranked in terms of the number of American Indian deaths rather than the age-adjusted rates. The last column gives the ratio of the American Indian age-adjusted mortality rate for each cause to that for all races. The first row shows that the age-adjusted mortality rate for American Indians was 1.4 times as high as the rate for all races. This rate for Indians was slightly lower, however, than that for blacks. Evidence from Texas and California indicates that age-adjusted mortality rates among Hispanics in 1970 were closer to those of whites than to those of blacks (see Bradshaw & Fonner, 1978; Schoen & Nelson, 1981). This is a dramatic change from the 1950s, when the mortality rate of American Indians was far above that of any group.

Changes in infant mortality provide another indication of the improvement in health status of American Indians in recent years. Whereas the infant mortality rate of blacks declined from 43.9 per 1,000 live births in 1950 to 23.6 in 1977, the rate for Indians declined from 82.1 to 15.7 (Markides, 1983).

Table 3. Age-Adjusted, Cause-Specific Mortality Rates among Racial Groups, 1980–1982 (Rates per 100,000 Population in Specified Group)

Rank (among Indians)[a]	Cause	Indian (IHS areas)	White[b]	Black[b]	All races	Ratio of Indian to all races
All	All causes	778.3	544.6	803.9	568.2	1.4
1	Diseases of the heart	166.7	191.1	245.4	195.0	.9
2	Accidents/adverse effects	136.3	39.3	45.8	39.8	3.4
3	Malignant neoplasms	98.4	128.5	171.3	131.6	.7
4	Liver disease/cirrhosis	48.1	10.5	19.2	11.4	4.2
5	Cerebrovascular diseases	33.8	35.6	64.4	38.1	.9
6	Pneumonia/influenza	26.6	11.6	17.7	12.3	2.2
7	Diabetes mellitus	27.8	8.8	19.5	9.8	2.8
8	Homicide	21.2	6.6	38.9	10.4	2.0
9	Suicide	19.4	12.2	6.4	11.5	1.7
10	Perinatal conditions	9.8	7.8	17.3	9.2	1.1
11	Nephritis, etc.	12.4	3.8	11.1	4.5	2.8
12	Congenital anomalies	6.5	5.8	5.9	5.8	1.1
13	Chronic pulmonary diseases	9.6	16.7	12.6	16.3	.6
14	Septicemia	6.5	2.5	6.8	2.9	2.2
15	Tuberculosis	4.2	.4	2.6	.6	7.0
All other	All other	151.0	63.4	119.0	69.0	2.1

[a]Rank is assigned based on the raw number of deaths rather than the age-adjusted death rates.
[b]For 1981.
SOURCES: Tables 1.1 and 4.4 in U.S. Congress, Office of Technology Assessment (1986), and Table 1.7 in U.S. Center for Health Statistics (1982).

Until recently the number one cause of death among American Indians was accidents or adverse effects. Many of the accidents are assumed to be alcohol-related, though this is difficult to demonstrate conclusively. As the table shows, in the 1980–1982 period this was the number two cause of death and heart disease was number one. However, the age-adjusted mortality rate for accidents and adverse effects for American Indians was 3.4 times as high as that for the general U.S. population, and almost three times as high as that for blacks. Other causes of death that are substantially more prevalent among American Indians are liver disease, diabetes, nephritis and other kidney ailments, and tuberculosis. The age-adjusted death rate due to suicide among Indians is approximately three times as high as that among blacks, whereas the age-adjusted death rate due to homicide among blacks is almost twice as high as that among Indians. Among Hispanics, heart disease is the number one cause of death. Accidents and homicide are more significant among Hispanics than among whites, but not as significant as among blacks.

We cannot know what the health status of American Indians would be if there were no Indian Health Service. It is also difficult to know how much of the improved health of Indians is due to better housing, water, sanitation, and nutrition resulting from other federal programs. It is clear that one problem Indians traditionally faced was access to health care. The isolation of Indians on reservations and in rural areas, along with poverty, prevented them from utilizing the health care delivery system available to many non-Indians. Without the involvement of the federal government, the delivery of health care to many Indians would probably have been handled by religious and other charitable organizations, and it is unlikely that they would have had the resources necessary to develop an effective health care delivery system. Consequently, the IHS (or something like it) was needed to improve access. The evidence also suggests that tribal control of health facilities and programs, largely initiated after the Indian Self-Determination Act, further improved access to health care (U.S. Congress, Office of Technology Assessment, 1986).

It is not completely clear why there was never a Black Health Service or Mexican American Health Service. Health care is not a trust responsibility specified by treaties, but rather a service which Congress decided to provide to American Indians under the provisions of the Snyder Act of 1921. The War on Poverty, however, included designs to develop a system of community health centers that would have served a large number of poor blacks and Hispanics. In 1967, the Department of Health, Education and Welfare planned for 1,000 community health centers to serve 25 million individuals. Yet by 1977, there were only 125 centers serving approximately 1.5 million people (Starr, 1986). A review of the community health center system in 1976 by the U.S. General Accounting Office (1978) outlined a number of implementation problems and pointed out that to provide services to the estimated 45 million underserved people in 1975 would have required an additional $10 billion per year, beyond the $259 million spent in fiscal year 1975.

As was the case with affirmative action, even though process evaluations pointed to problems with the community health center system, impact evaluations indicated that they were quite successful. Starr (1986) cites evidence suggesting that community health centers had a significant effect on the health of communities at lower overall costs than for beneficiaries who received care elsewhere.

Starr suggests that community health centers never became popular with the public or politicians because of a general repudiation of the War on Poverty programs. There is also, at present, increasing pressure on the Indian Health Service to hold down costs. These pressures are largely due to two demographic factors and two economic factors. The two demographic factors are (a) population deconcentration, which meant that in 1980 only one-quarter of the Indian population lived on reservations, and (b) intermarriage and the broadening of eligibility criteria beyond the quarter-degree or more of Indian blood that was traditionally required for using IHS services. The two economic factors are (a) the rising costs of contract medical care not provided by the IHS but obtained from other health service deliverers, and (b) the rising costs of medical care in general.

The IHS system was designed to serve the reservation Indian population, most of whom have the required degree of Indian blood. In recent years, efforts have been made to serve the wider Indian population without a proportionate increase in funds. Indians who are not residents of an IHS service area or a tribal health clinic area have been allowed to return to an area with which they have some affiliation or connection to receive services. Many tribes have membership criteria that require less than one-quarter degree of Indian blood and have extended services to all tribal members. In 1980, over 50% of American Indians were married to non-Indians (Sandefur & McKinnell, 1986), and as many of such Indians are of less than half Indian blood, the proportion of the Indian population that is less than one-quarter degree will continue to increase. In addition, IHS has been pressured into providing limited services in urban areas.

The Office of Technology Assessment points out that there are three alternatives from which to choose: increase funds, cut services, or control the size of the service population by restricting eligiblity. Given the current political climate, it is unlikely that funding will be increased, and the services that are provided are the minimal ones that are needed as well as the only services available to those Indians who live far away from population centers. This leaves the third choice, controlling the size of the service population, as the method for dealing with budget problems. The IHS has proposed establishing both geographic and blood-degree requirements. The imposition of such restrictions violates the spirit of self-determination, which supposedly allows tribes to determine who is and who is not a citizen, and has led to a battle over whether the IHS or tribes should determine eligibility.

Educational Programs and Educational Status

Jencks (1986) has pointed out that our understanding of the effects of compensatory educational programs is tenuous, because there has not been enough research to allow us to come to firm conclusions about the effects of these programs. This is even more true of Indian educational programs, where our understanding is based on a handful of evaluations. A recent assessment of the Title IV-Part A program funded by the Indian Education Act indicated that (a) Indian test scores have risen significantly in 10 years in Part A districts and are now slightly below the averages of non-Indian students; there is, however, no clear evidence that this is due to compensatory education programs for Indian students; and (b) the average attendance of American Indian students in Part A programs may be at the national average; there is, however, no clear evidence that attendance levels are due to Indian educational programs (Development Associates, 1983). In other words, participants in the program are doing better than earlier cohorts of Indians, but we cannot unambiguously attribute this to the program.

The number of participants in the Title IV-Part A program in fiscal year 1983, 304,790, is dwarfed by the estimated 1,500,000 participants in state and federally funded bilingual educational programs and is little more than half the size of the 593,042 students who participated in migrant educational programs during the same period (U.S. Department of Education, Office of Planning, Budget, and Evaluation, 1984). At that time, there were over 100,000 students participating in refugee educational programs, and in the 1983–1984 school year over 240,000 students in school districts received emergency immigrant school aid (U.S. Department of Education, Office of Planning, Budget and Evaluation, 1985). A comparatively large amount of research has been conducted on bilingual education, but very little has been devoted to migrant educational programs and almost none to refugee and immigrant educational programs. The existing evidence regarding bilingual education indicates that some programs made gains, some were ineffective, and some had negative effects on achievement (Baker & de Kanter, 1983). An evaluation of migrant education showed no significant relationship between compensatory education provided through the program and the test scores of students (Research Triangle Institute, 1981).

Along with lack of evidence on their effectiveness, the programs of Indian education, bilingual education, and migrant education share three other features. First, school officials, teachers, and parents seem to perceive the programs as effective, and this has led to increased parental support for, and involvement in, education. Second, there has been much controversy over who should be eligible to participate. These separate controversies, especially the ones over Indian education and bilingual education, indicate the difficulties that arise when ethnic criteria are used in social program categorization. Concerning Indian education, arguments have occurred over the use of Indian descent—that is, demonstrated descent from an Indian ancestor—as opposed to blood quantum or tribal membership to determine eligibility for participation. After a great deal of agonizing, the Department of Education retained its use of Indian descent in defining Indians (U.S. Department of Education, Office of Budget, Planning, and Evaluation, 1984). In bilingual education, the arguments have centered on how to define Limited English Proficiency (LEP) and whether students who do not have LEP should be allowed to participate in bilingual educational programs. Currently, schools are allowed to permit a certain percentage of non-LEP students to participate in bilingual education. The controversy in migrant education has concerned how to determine whether a student's parents are actually migrant laborers during the time when the student participates in migrant educational programs. It is easy to imagine similar controversies in the future over programs for refugee and immigrant education.

A third feature shared by the programs is that the disadvantages of the target populations are clear. An obvious indication of such disadvantage is available in published census data. Table 4 contains basic descriptive statistics for several racial/ethnic groups in 1980. The first statistic refers to the median years of education for individuals 25 and older. Among the three Indian groups, reservation Indians have the lowest level of education (11 years), but theirs is slightly higher than that of Hispanics (10.8 years). The median education for all Indians lies between that of blacks and whites. Reservation Indians aged 25 and over are least likely to have graduated from high school or to have completed 4 or more years of college. It is important to remember that part of the reason for lower educational levels on reservations is the educational selectivity of migration (i.e., the likelihood of leaving reservations increases with education).

The educational attributes of individuals aged 25 and over were really not

Table 4. Educational Characteristics of Minority Groups, 1980

	All Indians	Reservation Indians	Blacks	Hispanics	Whites
Median years of education (age 25+)	12.2	11.0	12.0	10.8	12.5
Percentage completeing high school (age 25+)	55.5	43.2	51.2	44.1	68.4
Percentage with 4 or more years of college (age 25+)	7.7	3.1	8.3	7.7	17.3
Percentage enrolled in school					
Age 5–6	84.6	87.8	87.2	84.9	86.3
14–15	93.9	92.4	96.9	95.3	98.2
16–17	76.8	77.4	88.0	80.2	89.0
18–19	38.6	39.9	51.7	43.9	53.0

Note: These statistics are not directly comparable to those in Table 2 in Chapter 7; that table describes individuals aged 26–35.
SOURCES: U.S. Bureau of the Census (1983, 1986).

affected by the major educational initiatives of the 1970s. The enrollment figures for those who are expected to be in school, however, provide some indication of how effective the educational programs were, at least in retaining students. These figures show that among children aged 5–6, reservation Indians are the most likely to be in school, followed by black children and then white children. At ages 14–15, however, reservation Indians are the least likely to be enrolled in school, and Indians in general are less likely to be in school than the other groups. The remaining age groups in Table 4 are perhaps the most crucial to examine, because at these ages students are in their last years of high school or are entering college. At ages 16–17, a much smaller percentage of Hispanics and Indians are in school than are blacks and whites. At ages 18–19, the gap between Indians and other groups has widened considerably, and the gap between Hispanics on the one hand and blacks and whites on the other hand persists.

These statistics undoubtedly disguise many of the important differences across Hispanic groups, and they provide no information on tests scores or grade levels of students of the same age across racial groups. It is clear from this and other evidence (Glazer, 1986), however, that Hispanics, blacks, and Indians continue to lag behind whites in educational attainment. Unfortunately, the evidence on the effectiveness of existing programs is not compelling, and there is evidence that using ethnicity to target programs creates problems and controversies.

RACIAL AND ETHNIC DIFFERENCES IN THE EFFECTIVENESS OF ANTIPOVERTY PROGRAMS

An account of the effects of federal policies toward minority groups would not be complete without a review of the results of the direct antipoverty programs. Existing research indicates that the current cash transfer system significantly reduces poverty among members of racial and ethnic minority groups (see, for example, Chapter 2 by Tienda and Jensen in this volume). There is also evidence that the cash transfer system does not affect all groups in the same way. First, social security is the most effective transfer program in reducing poverty (Danziger & Plotnick, 1986). Groups vary in terms of their utilization of social security for three major reasons: (a) a smaller proportion of the members of minority groups are age 62 and over, (b) a smaller proportion of the members of minority groups work enough to participate in social security, and (c) among those who work long enough, wages are lower than those among whites, leading to lower benefits. The second and third reasons also explain why one would expect the use of unemployment insurance to reduce poverty less among members of minority groups than among whites. In summary, the cash social-insurance programs are less important to members of minority groups than to white non-Hispanic Americans.

AFDC, on the other hand, is more important to members of racial and ethnic minorities than to white Americans, in part because the proportion of these groups who are children is much higher than the proportion of white Americans who are children. The 1980 census, for example, showed that 27% of white persons in households were under 18, compared to 36% of black persons, and 39% of Hispanic and American Indian persons (U.S. Bureau of the Census, 1983). Further, many states do not have an AFDC-Unemployed Parent program to provide benefits to married-couple poor families with children. As Tienda and Jensen show in Chapter 2, whereas 57% of black households and 61% of Puerto Rican households in 1980 were headed by couples, 79% of Mexican households, 75% of other Hispanic households, and 80% of American Indian households were headed by married couples.

Supplemental Security Income (SSI), though a much smaller program than social security or AFDC, is quite important to disabled and elderly members of minority groups because of their limited eligibility for benefits from the social insurance programs. In December, 1985, there were a little over 4 million recipients of federally administered SSI benefits; of these, over 1 million, or approximately one-fourth, were black and 836,000, or 20%, were members of other minority groups—Hispanic, American Indian, or Asian American (*Statistical Abstract*, 1987, Table 619). There has been very little research on the importance of this program to members of racial and ethnic minorities. Root and Tropman (1984) found that among multiperson households with aged heads (65 and older), 0.4% of household income for households headed by white men came from SSI, 3.9% of household income for households headed by white women came from SSI, 6.9% of income for households headed by black men came from SSI, and 17.7% of income for households headed by black women came from SSI. This suggests that SSI is probably much more important to disabled and aged minority households than to disabled and aged white households.

There is much less information on racial and ethnic differences in the importance of in-kind transfer programs. Information from the Current Population Surveys indicates that blacks and Hispanics are more likely than whites to participate in the means-tested in-kind transfer programs such as food stamps and Medicaid, and less likely to participate in Medicare, an in-kind program that is tied to social insurance: 34% of the recipients of Food Stamps in 1983 were black and 31% of the recipients of Medicaid were black, whereas 10% of the recipients of Medicare were black (U.S. Bureau of the Census, 1984a). Further, in-kind transfers are more likely to remove poor minorities from poverty than they are to remove poor whites. If we were to value food and housing aid at their market value in 1983, for example, these in-kind transfers raised 9% of the Hispanic poor and 14% of the black poor above the poverty line, relative to only 0.1% of the white poor (U.S. Bureau of the Census, 1984b). The reason for these racial differences is primarily that the cash transfer system is more effective in reducing white poverty, both because those whites who receive transfers are more likely to receive social insurance transfers and larger social insurance transfers, and because poor whites have higher pretransfer incomes than poor nonwhites.

The major lesson to draw from these differences is that the demographic characteristics of different groups affect the extent to which they benefit from existing antipoverty programs. The age structure, extent of female headship, and previous labor force activities emerge as important determinants of group participation in the antipoverty system. The antipoverty programs are most generous toward aged individuals who were relatively successful during their working years; they are less generous to unmarried young women with children and even less generous to young couples with children. This leads to unintended differences in the effectiveness of cash and in-kind transfers across racial and ethnic groups.

SUMMARY AND CONCLUSIONS

This brief review of federal policy toward racial and ethnic minority groups indicates that the federal government has been quite inconsistent in the way that it has dealt with racial and ethnic minority groups. Part of the inconsistency is undoubtedly due to the different ways in which contact between the U.S. government and each group first took place. The first contact with Indians was as occupants of land that the U.S. government wished to control, whereas the first contact with blacks was as slaves who were essentially viewed as property. The inconsistent treatment of a specific racial and ethnic group over time is partially attributable to the changing goals of the U.S. government, and the way in which a specific group fits into these plans. Individuals of Mexican descent, for example, have been treated differently depending on the labor needs and state of the economy at different points in time. This history of changing policies has resulted in the current set of inconsistent policies, that is, a constitution and set of laws that prescribe a society blind to race and ethnicity, but programs that explicitly recognize race and ethnicity as criteria to be used in efforts to achieve this ideal.

Regardless of whether one thinks that such programs are appropriate at this point in the nation's history, the evidence on their implementation and effectiveness suggests that some have been successful in meeting their goals. Studies of the impact of affirmative action indicate that it has been effective in increasing the representation of blacks and other minority-group members in those organizations covered by the EEOC. Analyses of the Indian Health Service by the Office of Technology Assessment indicate that the IHS has been successful in improving the health of American Indians. On the other hand, for other programs the evidence is mixed or not as compelling. This is particularly true of compensatory education, including bilingual and Indian education programs. Some evidence indicates that these programs are successful; other evidence indicates certain programs have had little impact on participants. Further, evaluations of the implementation of all of these programs point to fairly consistent problems: lack of resources to implement the programs as designed, unwillingness to impose sanctions when they are called for by the program guidelines, and problems introduced by the use of racial and ethnic criteria to determine eligibility. The evidence on racial and ethnic differences in participation in and the effectiveness of antipoverty programs in the form of social insurance and public assistance indicates that blacks, American Indians, and Hispanics are underrepresented in social insurance programs and receive smaller benefits on average because of poorer work histories. On the other hand, they are overrepresented in public assistance programs. During the inflation-ridden 1970s, social security recipients received automatic cost-of-living increases. Among the cash public assistance programs, only Supplemental Security Income benefits were automatically adjusted for inflation. Consequently, the antipoverty programs that benefited minority-group members the most were the ones that were not protected from the ravages of inflation.

There is a case to be made for the usefulness of group-specific programs. Let us focus on two examples. First, one of the leading problems for blacks in the central cities is their high infant mortality rate. The success of the Indian Health Service in reducing American Indian infant mortality and the success of the community health centers suggest that federally supported and coordinated efforts at providing better health care in the central cities (which would not officially be a group-specific program) could significantly reduce black infant mortality. It is unfortunate that what Starr (1986) refers to as the general antipathy toward War on Poverty programs has undermined the development of a system of community health centers in the central cities of our nation.

Second, unemployment and underemployment continue to be serious problems for blacks, American Indians, and Hispanic Americans. The success of affirmative action in increasing employment in the federal contract sector and in firms covered by the EEOC suggests that expanded coverage and enforcement could have a significant impact on employment opportunities for members of minority groups. Instead, affirmative action has been attacked from the left as being inadequately implemented and from the right as reverse discrimination. These attacks, which ignore the limited but real success of affirmative action, may provide the basis for dismantling affirmative action. Its supporters should point to its genuine accomplishments as well as to its inadequacies.

The financial costs of setting up community health centers in central cities and increasing affirmative action efforts would be quite high. The major social cost of group-specific programs is the recognition and reinforcement of racial and ethnic boundaries. The combined economic and social costs are high enough to raise questions as to whether benefits justify expenditures. Perhaps one can argue that we have reached a point in U.S. history at which we can legitimately ignore racial and ethnic criteria in federal policy. However, the persisting economic, health, and educational problems of minority groups indicate that we have not yet reached that point. The social and economic costs of group-specific programs continue to be surpassed by the benefits of such programs in the form of the increased productivity of healthy and employed individuals.

ACKNOWLEDGMENTS

I thank Jiwon Jeon for her able research assistance and Erica Baum, Milton Morris, Eugene Smolensky, Russell Thornton, and Marta Tienda for helpful comments and suggestions.

REFERENCES

Baker, K. A., & A. A. de Kanter. (1983). An answer from research on bilingual education. *American Education, 19* (July, No. 6), 40–48.

Bradshaw, B. S., & E. Fonner, Jr. (1978). The mortality of Spanish-surnamed persons in Texas: 1969–1971. In F. D. Bean & W. P. Frisbie (Eds.), *The demography of racial and ethnic groups*. New York: Academic.

Burns, H. (1981). From Brown to Bakke and back: Race, law and social change in America. *Daedalus, 110,* 219–232.

Danziger, S., & R. Plotnick. (1986). Poverty and policy: Lessons of the last two decades. *Social Service Review, 60,* 34–51.

Development Associates. (1983). *Final report: The evaluation of the impact of the Part A Entitlement Program funded under Title IV of the Indian Education Act.* Arlington, VA.: Author.

Estrada, L. F., F. C. Garcia, R. F. Macias, & L. Maldonado. (1981). Chicanos in the United States: A history of exploitation and resistance. *Daedalus, 110,* 103–132.

Glazer, N. (1986). Education and training programs and poverty. In S. H. Danziger & D. H. Weinberg (Eds.), *Fighting poverty: What works and what doesn't.* Cambridge, MA: Harvard University Press.

Gramlich, E. M. (1986). The main themes. In S. H. Danziger & D. H. Weinberg (Eds.), *Fighting poverty: What works and what doesn't.* Cambridge, MA: Harvard University Press.

Jaffe, A. J., R. M. Cullen, & T. D. Boswell. (1980). *The changing demography of Spanish Americans.* New York: Academic.

Jencks, C. (1986). Comment on Glazer. In S. H. Danziger and D. H. Weinberg (Eds.), *Fighting poverty: What works and what doesn't.* Cambridge, MA: Harvard University Press.

Leonard, J. S. (1984). The impact of affirmative action on employment. *Journal of Labor Economics, 2,* 439–463.

Leonard, J. S. (1985). The effectiveness of equal employment law and affirmative action regulation. National Bureau of Economic Research, Working Paper no. 1745, Cambridge, MA.

Markides, K. S. (1983). Mortality among minority populations: A review of recent patterns and trends. *Public Health Reports, 98,* 252–260.

Presidential Commission on Reservation Economies. (1984). *Report and recommendations to the President of the United States.* Washington, DC: U.S. Government Printing Office.

Prucha, F. P. (1984). *The great father: The United States government and the American Indians* (2 vols.). Lincoln, NE: University of Nebraska Press.

Research Triangle Institute. (1981). *Comprehensive summary: Study of the ESEA Title I Migrant Education Program.* Research Triangle Park, NC: Author.

Root, L. S., & Tropman, J. E. (1984). Income sources of the elderly. *Social Service Review, 58,* 384–403.

Sandefur, G. D., & T. McKinnell. (1986). American Indian intermarriage. *Social Science Research, 15,* 347–371.

Schoen, R., & V. E. Nelson. (1981). Mortality by cause among Spanish-surnamed California, 1969–1971. *Social Science Quarterly, 62,* 259–274.

Smith, J. P., & F. R. Welch. (1986). *Closing the gap: Forty years of economic progress for blacks.* Santa Monica, CA: Rand Corporation.

Starr, P. (1986). Health care for the poor. In S. H. Danziger and D. H. Weinberg (Eds.), *Fighting poverty: What works and what doesn't.* Cambridge, MA: Harvard University Press.

Statistical Abstract of the United States, 1987. (1986). Washington, DC: U.S. Government Printing Office.

Thornton, R. (1987). *American Indian holocaust and survival: A population history since 1492.* Norman, OK: University of Oklahoma Press.

U.S. Bureau of the Census. (1983). *Census of the population, 1980: General social and economic characteristics of the population.* Washington, DC: U.S. Government Printing Office.

U.S. Bureau of the Census. (1984a). *Characteristics of households and persons receiving selected noncash benefits: 1983.* Washington, DC: U.S. Government Printing Office.

U.S. Bureau of the Census. (1984b). *Estimates of poverty including the value of noncash benefits: 1983.* Technical Paper 52. Washington, DC: U.S. Government Printing Office.

U.S. Bureau of the Census. (1986). *American Indians, Eskimos, and Aleuts on identified reservations and in the historic areas of Oklahoma (excluding urbanized areas).* PC80-2-1D. Washington, DC: U.S. Government Printing Office.

U.S. Center for Health Statistics. (1982). *Vital statistics, 1981: Vol. II. Mortality.* Washington, DC: U.S. Government Printing Office.

U.S. Congress, Office of Technology Assessment. (1986). *Indian health care.* Report OTA-H-290. Washington, DC: U.S. Government Printing Office.

U.S. Department of Education. Office of Planning, Budget, and Evaluation. (1984). *Annual evaluation report, fiscal year 1983.* Washington, DC: U.S. Government Printing Office.

U.S. Department of Education. Office of Planning, Budget, and Evaluation. (1985). *Annual evaluation report, fiscal year 1984.* Washington, DC: U.S. Government Printing Office.

U.S. General Accounting Office. (1978). *Are neighborhood health centers providing services efficiently and to the most needy?* Washington, DC: U.S. Government Printing Office.

9

Social Policy and Minority Groups

What Might Have Been and What Might We See in the Future?

WILLIAM JULIUS WILSON

When historians review the factors involved in the rediscovery of poverty in the early 1960s and the emergence of the Great Society programs, questions about the relative importance of race in the formulation of federal antipoverty strategies will no doubt be addressed. The issue has been a topic of discussion among social scientists for several years, but opinion has been divided. On the one hand, there is a group of writers who see the race problem as having been relatively insignificant in the initial phases of the federal government's antipoverty thrust. They have argued that although there was some discussion of the problems of black poverty, the focus of attention shortly before and immediately after the assassination of President John F. Kennedy was disproportionately on white Appalachian poverty (Levine, 1970; Moynihan, 1968; Sundquist, 1969; Yarmolinsky, 1969).

On the other hand, there are students of poverty, with rather varied political philosophies, who have argued strongly, as Nathan Glazer did over 20 years ago, that the "race problem" is "the chief reason why poverty has become a major issue in this country" (Glazer, 1965, p. 20). Glazer points out that despite the picture conveyed by the official poverty statistics, "the poorest, as defined by the public assistance rolls, are in much larger proportion Negro, Mexican American, and Puerto Rican. It is the civil rights revolution that makes poverty a great issue in America, not merely poverty" (p. 20). Likewise, Sar Levitan suggests that "the civil rights movement, which had become a potent power by 1963,

WILLIAM JULIUS WILSON • Department of Sociology, University of Chicago, Chicago, Illinois.

could have supplied the political pressure for a program in aid of the poor"
(Levitan, 1969, p. 15). Also, Rabb (1966) points out that there were discussions
with city representatives on the central involvement of racial and ethnic communities even before the Great Society's antipoverty legislation was passed in 1964.
Finally, Piven and Cloward (1971), in their controversial thesis, argue that the
creation of federal antipoverty programs was an attempt to foster the political
allegiance of inner-city minorities.

Although this issue will ultimately be settled by historians, questions about
the race factor in the emergence of the Great Society's antipoverty legislation are
not nearly as important as questions about the race factor in the implementation
of this legislation. Indeed, once the War on Poverty began, it was generally
perceived as having been created and implemented largely for racial minorities
(Wilson, 1987). I argue in this chapter that the narrow policy frameworks used
by the architects of the War on Poverty and the advocates for civil rights fed this
perception and, more important, provided fuel for the recent national shift toward a more conservative analysis of the problems of poor minorities and a more
conservative social policy agenda to address these problems. This precedes a
critical discussion of the assumptions underlying this new policy agenda toward
poor minorities, followed by a suggestion of how an alternative agenda ought to
be fashioned to more appropriately confront the fundamental problems of poverty and inequality.

THE PROBLEM OF THE WAR ON POVERTY VISION

The War on Poverty emerged paradoxically during an era of general economic prosperity and economic growth. Indeed, a budget surplus existed in the
early 1960s and economists then predicted, in a climate of widespread optimism
about economic growth, that this surplus would rise steadily throughout the latter
part of the decade. As Daniel Patrick Moynihan (1970) argued, federal revenues
were growing so rapidly that many economists (not anticipating the Vietnam War
buildup) were fearful that if new expenditures could not be generated to reduce
the growing tax surplus, it would ultimately slow economic growth. Accordingly, despite high levels of unemployment in the inner city in the early 1960s,[1] it
was not difficult for national policymakers to see minority poverty, as opposed to
poverty in general, as a problem unrelated to the national economy. As Weir,

---

[1]For example, in describing the unemployment situation in Harlem in 1960, Kenneth Clark states:
"About one out of every seven or eight adults in Harlem is unemployed. In the city as a whole, the
rate of unemployment is half that. Harlem is a young community, compared to the rest of New
York, and in 1960 twice as many young Negro men in the labor force, as compared to their white
counterparts, were without jobs. For the girls, the gap was even greater—nearly two and one-half
times the unemployment rate for white girls in the labor force" (Clark, 1965, p. 34).

Orloff, and Skocpol (1988) have argued, when the United States started to face the problems associated with the concentration of minorities in large urban ghettos, members of the Council of Economic Advisers discussed these problems not within the realm of central economic concerns but as "marginal issues of 'poverty' to be addressed by much less academically prestigious groups of labor economists and sociologists."[2]

Accordingly, increasing black joblessness was viewed as a problem of poverty and discrimination, not of American economic organization, and therefore could be addressed by antipoverty measures (such as compensatory job training, compensatory schooling, income redistribution) and antidiscrimination legislation. In the succinct words of Lawrence Mead, "the main impetus of Great Society policy, therefore, was to give the disadvantaged the income and skills they needed to function in the free market, not change the economic rules in their favor" (Mead, 1986, p. 35).

The separation of antipoverty measures from national economic policy was respected by the newly created and expanding network of "poverty researchers" who, thoughout the 1960s and 1970s, tended to ignore the effects of fundamental economic processes on the work histories of the poor while paying considerable attention to the question of individual work incentives and the association between the work efforts of the poor and income maintenance programs.[3] Walter Korpi has pointed out, in his perceptive critique of approaches to the study of poverty in this country from a European perspective, that "efforts to explain poverty and inequality in the United States . . . appear primarily to have been sought in terms of the characteristics of the poor" (Korpi, 1980). Whereas American poverty analysts have produced volumes of research on the work motivation of the poor, on problems of human capital (whereby poverty is seen as a reflection of insufficient education and occupational skills), and on the effects of income maintenance programs on the labor supply, they have largely

---

[2]Weir, Orloff, and Skocpol (1988). This is not to ignore the fact that some members of the Council of Economic Advisers did associate the problem of poverty in general with economic growth and levels of unemployment. Carl M. Brauer noted that the extent to which poverty among the general population could be alleviated by economic growth and full employment was a major concern of Walter Heller, Chairman of President Kenned's Council of Economic Advisers, as early as 1962. Brauer points out, however, that later, when the council "included a chapter on poverty in its annual report [1964], it facilely embraced culture-of-poverty theory" (Brauer, 1982, p. 106).

[3]Weir, Orloff, and Skocpol (1988). However, as Leslie Dunbar stated (private communication, 1986), there were some studies in the 1960s and early 1970s that did not focus on the faults of the poor, including the report of the Citizens Committee against Hunger and Malnutrition (Hunger, U.S.A.), and the A. Philip Randolph Institute's "Freedom Budget" for all Americans (1966). This point is well taken. Other studies that focus on the problems of employment and economic organization as a cause of poverty include Clark (1965), Rainwater (1966), and Liebow (1967). It should be noted that none of these publications represents the studies completed by the network of Great Society "poverty researchers" to which I refer.

neglected the impact of the extremely high levels of post-war unemployment on the poor. "In Europe, where unemployment has been considerably lower," states Korpi, "the concerns of politicians as well as researchers have been keyed much more strongly to the question of unemployment. It is an intellectual paradox that living in a society that has been a sea of unemployment, American poverty researchers have concentrated their research interests on the work motivation of the poor" (Korpi, 1980, p. 306).

As changes in the rate of poverty in the United States are very closely related to changes in overall economic performance, this research orientation presents a problem for those seeking a comprehensive explanation of minority poverty. Recent research by the economists Rebecca Blank and Alan Blinder of Princeton reveals that a downturn in the economy, measured in this case by a 1% increase in the base-level unemployment (unemployment rate for white men), results in an additional increase in unemployment among black men that is 2% to 2.5% greater than an additional increase in unemployment among white men (Blank & Blinder, 1986). Moreover, wage levels are closely tied to unemployment. Robert Greenstein appropriately states: "when unemployment rises and real wages fall poverty increases—and low income groups (especially black males) are affected the most" (Greenstein, 1985, p. 15).

It was only a short step to move from an analysis that segregates the economic woes of underemployed or unemployed minorities in the category of "poverty-related programs" to one that associates the crystallization of a ghetto underclass or the explosion of minority female-headed households, not with the "more inclusive economic or institutional insufficiencies in American life" (Weir, Orloff, & Skocpol, 1988), but with ghetto-specific values or family background. Thus, for example, research on the relationship between the growth of income transfers and in-kind benefits and the increase of black female-headed families has dwarfed research on the relationship between joblessness and black female-headed families in recent years (Aponte, Neckerman, & Wilson, 1985; Wilson & Neckerman, 1986).

In the final analysis, the policy agenda set by the architects of the Great Society (that is, labor economists, sociologists, and others) who fashioned the War on Poverty in the 1960s, established the vision for subsequent research on and analysis of minority poverty. Although this vision attributed the behavioral problems of the poor to adverse social conditions, the emphasis was mainly on the environments of the poor, "the disarray at the bottom of society" (Mead, 1986, p. 55), where ignorance is widespread, crime is rampant, positive role models are lacking, and apathy is endemic. Because this vision did not consider poverty as a problem of American economic organization, efforts to alter the characteristics of individuals through employment and training programs were seen as the most efficacious way to fight poverty. Lawrence Mead (1986) states:

> After 1960, poverty and disadvantage seemed rooted mostly in the limited skills of the poor themselves, yet government could do little to raise skills simply with benefits. Politically, that left unpalatable alternatives. Either equality must be achieved by a leveling of income or status without regard to the capacities of the poor, the prescription of the far left, or the poor themselves must be seen as malingerers or congenitally incompetent. Sociological analysis offered a way out. It defined a set of less obvious social barriers permitting further reformism. By providing further benefits and services, it was argued government could push back the barriers of "disadvantage" without either embracing revolutionary change or blaming the poor for their condition (pp. 55–56).

However, just as the rate of poverty is in large measure determined by the state of the economy, particularly the levels of wages and unemployment, so too does the effectiveness of training, education, and employment programs depend on a favorable economic climate. If gainful employment is problematic because of a stagnant economy, as was frequently the case with periodic recessions throughout the 1970s, participants in these programs understandably lose interest. Indeed, it would be surprising if program participants took training seriously when there is little or no chance for placement.

When the ranks of the poor were not significantly reduced by 1980, it was easy for the more conservative policy analysts to extend the logic of the War on Poverty vision by focusing on ways to force value and behavior changes, particularly among ghetto residents. Before I turn to these proposals, I would like to discuss a parallel development that compounded the problems of social policy with respect to the minority poor—namely, the limitations of race-specific policies in combating social dislocations assumed to be poverty related.

RACE-SPECIFIC POLICIES AND POOR MINORITIES

Prior to 1960, Jim Crow segregation was still widespread in parts of the nation, particularly in the Deep South. With passage of the 1964 Civil Rights Act, there was considerable optimism that racial progress would ensue and that the principle of equality of individual rights (viz., that candidates for positions stratified in terms of prestige, power, or other social criteria ought to be judged solely on individual merit and therefore should not be discriminated against on the basis of racial origin) would be upheld.

However, programs based solely on this principle are not designed to deal with the substantive inequality that exists at the time the bias is removed. In other words, centuries or even decades of racial oppression can result in a system of inequality that may persist for indefinite periods of time even after racial barriers are eliminated. This is because the most disadvantaged minority members, those who have been victimized or crippled by the cumulative effects of both racial and class subjugation (including those effects transmitted from generation to generation), are disproportionately represented among that segment of the total population that has been denied and/or lacks the resources to compete effectively in a free and open market (Fishkin, 1983).

It is important to recognize that in a modern industrial society the removal of racial barriers creates the greatest opportunities for the better trained, talented, and educated segments of the minority population—those who have been affected the least by the weight of past discrimination—because they possess the resources that allow them to compete freely with dominant group members for valued positions. As Leroy D. Clark and Judy Trent Ellis have pointed out in this connection:

> There must be a recognition that civil rights legislation can only benefit those in a position to take advantage of it. To the extent that some members of minority groups have been denied education and certain work experience, they will be able to compete for only a limited number of jobs. Certain disabilities traceable in general to racism may deprive some minority members of the qualifications for particular jobs. Title VII, however, protects only against arbitrary use of race or its equivalents as barriers to work; it does not assure one of employment or promotion if legitimate qualifications are lacking (Clark & Ellis, 1980, p. 64).

In short, the competitive resources developed by the advantaged minority members—resources that are the direct result of the family stability, schooling, and peer groups that their parents have been able to provide—results in their benefiting disproportionately from policies that promote the rights of minority individuals, policies that remove the artificial barriers and thereby enable individuals to compete freely and openly for the more desirable and prestigious positions in American society (Fishkin, 1983).

Nevertheless, since 1970 government policy has tended to focus on formal programs designed and created not only to prevent discrimination but to ensure that minorities are adequately represented in certain positions as well. This has resulted in a move from the simple formal investigation and adjudication of complaints of racial discrimination to government-mandated affirmative action programs designed to ensure minority representation in public programs, employment, and education.

However, if minority members from the most advantaged families profit disproportionately from policies built on the principle of equality of individual opportunity, they also reap disproportionate benefits from policies of preferential treatment based solely on their group membership. I say this because advantaged minority members are likely to be disproportionately represented among those of their racial group most qualified for preferred positions—such as higher paying jobs, college admissions, and promotions. Accordingly, if policies of preferential treatment for such positions are conceived not in terms of the actual disadvantages suffered by individuals, but rather in terms of racial group membership, then these policies will further enhance the opportunities of the advantaged without necessarily addressing the problems of the truly disadvantaged, such as members of the ghetto underclass.[4]

By 1980, this argument was not widely recognized or fully appreciated. Therefore, because the government not only adopted and implemented antibias legislation to promote minority individual rights, but also mandated and enforced affirmative action and related programs to enhance minority group rights, many thoughtful American citizens, including supporters of civil rights, were puzzled by social developments in the minority community, particularly the low-income areas of the inner city. Despite the passage of civil rights legislation and the creation of affirmative action programs, they sensed that conditions were deteriorating instead of improving for this segment of the minority population. This perception has emerged because of the continuous flow of pessimistic reports concerning the sharp rise in inner-city joblessness, the steady increase in the percentage of inner-city residents on the welfare rolls, and the extraordinary growth of female-headed families. The perception was strengthened by the almost uniform cry among black leaders that not only had conditions among the minority poor worsened, but that white Americans had forsaken the cause of poor minorities as well. In the face of these developments, there were noticeable signs (even before Ronald Reagan was elected president and well before his administration adopted a conspicuously laissez-faire attitude toward civil rights) that demoralization had set in among many blacks and that white liberals had come to believe that when addressing the problems of the ghetto underclass "nothing really works." This point of view was perhaps best summed up by the perceptive black columnist William Raspberry, who stated:

> There are some blacks for whom it is enough to remove the artificial barriers of race. After that, their entry into the American mainstream is virtually automatic. There are others for whom hardly anything would change if, by some magical stroke, racism disappeared from America. Everyone knows this of course. And yet hardly anyone is willing to say it. And because we don't say it, we wind up confused about how to deal with the explosive problems confronting the American society, confused about what the problem really is (Raspberry, 1980, p. A19).

However, just as architects of the War on Poverty failed to relate the problems of poverty to the broader processes of American economic organization, so too have the advocates for minority rights failed in significant numbers to

---

[4]Fishkin (1983). The term *advantaged* is meant to convey the idea that in comparison with groups such as poor minorities and poor whites, educated and trained minority members are in a superior position to compete for resources in our society not only against groups such as the black underclass, but against poor whites as well. On the other hand, the term *truly disadvantaged* is meant to suggest that the combined affliction of racial isolation and class subordination for groups such as the ghetto underclass create a special disadvantage that solidifies their position at the bottom of the socioeconomic hierarchy.

understand that many contemporary problems of race, especially those that engulfed the minority poor, emanate from the broader problems of societal organization and therefore cannot be satisfactorily addressed solely by race-specific programs to eliminate racial discrimination and eradicate racial prejudices. What is presently lacking is a comprehensive and integrated framework—in other words, a holistic approach—that shows, as we shall see below, how contemporary racial problems in America, or issues perceived to be racial problems, are often part of a more general or complex set of problems whose origin and/or development may have little or no direct or indirect connection with race (Wilson, 1987).

Thus, given the most comprehensive program of civil rights and the most comprehensive antipoverty programs in the nation's history, it becomes difficult for liberals (who approached the problems of the minority poor by either emphasizing race-specific programs or programs consistent with the vision of the War on Poverty) to explain the sharp increase in minority poverty, joblessness, female-headed families, and welfare dependency since 1970 without reference to individual or group deficiencies. By the end of the 1970s, these liberals were on the defensive. When no fresh liberal ideas emerged, a void was created which was quickly filled by two major developments: (a) the emergence of laissez-faire conservative ideas about social policy, and (b) the revival of interest in "workfare."

THE EMERGING CONSERVATIVE AGENDAS: LAISSEZ-FAIRE SOCIAL POLICY AND "WORKFARE"

Conservative scholars have traditionally stressed the importance of the interplay among cultural tradition, family biography, and individual character in explaining group differences in rates of poverty, joblessness, and other social problems. If reference is made to the larger society, it is in terms of the negative effects of various government programs on behavior and initiative. One of the basic premises of this thesis is that recent social policies exacerbate, not alleviate, ghetto-specific cultural tendencies and problems of inner-city social dislocations. Accordingly, the extraordinary rise of inner-city poverty, joblessness, and female-headed families[5] following the passage of the most sweeping antidiscrimination and antipoverty legislation in the nation's history was easily in-

---

[5]For example, in low-income black community areas in Chicago that had at least a 30% household poverty rate in 1980, the average unemployment rate increased from 9% in 1970 to 21% in 1980; the proportion of families headed by women climbed from an average of 37% in 1970 to 66% in 1980, and the average household poverty rate increased from 32% in 1970 to 43% in 1980. (Data from *Local Community Fact Book, Chicago Metropolitan Area, 1970 and 1980,* Chicago: Chicago Review Press, 1984).

terpreted by conservative analysts as proof that instead of changing the personal characteristics of the poor to facilitate social mobility, recent changes in social policy, particularly those associated with the Great Society programs, have effectively altered the rewards and penalties that govern human behavior.

However, conservatives differ on how this situation should be corrected. The extreme position is that social welfare programs, far from relieving poverty and welfare, increase them and should be eliminated so that families and individuals will once again be motivated to work for their own welfare. The modern position is that Great Society programs are ineffective in relieving poverty and welfare dependency and therefore should be replaced by programs that emphasize work obligation as a prerequisite to welfare receipt. The former view, described by Sar Levitan and Clifford Johnson as the laissez-faire philosophy of social policy (Levitan & Johnson, 1984), is most forcefully and ably represented by Charles Murray's widely read book, *Losing Ground* (1984). Murray maintains that the availability of food stamps and increases in Aid to Families with Dependent Children (AFDC) payments have had a negative effect on poor minority family formation and work incentives; that despite substantial increases in spending on social programs, the poverty rate failed to drop from 1968 to 1980; and that the failure of the poverty rate to decline cannot be attributed to the slowing of the economy because the gross national product (GNP) grew more in the 1970s than in the 1950s, when the poverty rate actually dropped. Murray therefore concludes that social welfare programs for the poor have been counterproductive and should be eliminated.

Although this argument has come under heavy, even devastating, criticism from liberal scholars,[6] it has been the focus of a great deal of national media attention, which in turn has fueled a national political debate that has liberal advocates of increased or continued social spending on the defensive. However, the political reality of this position can be questioned. As Weir, Orloff, and Skocpol (1988) argue:

> There is little prospect that wholesale dismantling of social programs could possibly occur, given the common stake of citizens, provider groups, and congressional representatives in sustaining many existing policies. In the real world of American politics, calls for sweeping policy dismantlement translate, at most, into proposals for across-the-board budget cuts; these in turn devolve into uneven cuts, differentially targeted on programs for the poor. Universal benefits are left largely intact, and welfare programs that somehow engage middle-class interests or institutional providers also fare better than benefits solely for the poor. (p. 25)

The second school of thought, requiring work obligation as prerequisite to welfare receipt, is best represented by Lawrence Mead's provocative book, *Beyond Entitlement: The Social Obligations of Citizenship*. Mead contends that:

---

[6]See, for example, Kuttner (1984), Danziger and Gottschalk (1985), Greenstein (1985), Jencks (1985), Aponte, Neckerman, and Wilson (1986), and Ellwood and Summers (1986).

> The main problem with the welfare state is not its size but its permissiveness. . . . The challenge to welfare statesmanship is not so much to change the extent of benefits as to couple them with serious work and other obligations that would encourage functioning and thus promote the integration of recipients. (1986, pp. 3–4)

He argues that the programs of the Great Society failed to overcome poverty and, in effect, increased dependency because the "behavioral problems of the poor" were ignored. Welfare clients received new services and benefits but were not told "with any authority that they ought to behave differently." Mead attributes a good deal of this to a sociological logic that attributes the responsibilities for the difficulties experienced by the disadvantaged entirely to the social environment, a logic that still "blocks government from expecting or obligating the poor to behave differently than they do" (p. 61).

Mead believes that there is a disinclination among the underclass to either accept or retain many available low-wage jobs. The problem of nonwhite unemployment, he contends, is not a lack of jobs, but a high turnover rate. Mead contends that because this kind of joblessness is not affected by changes in the overall economy, it would be difficult to place blame on the environment. Although not dismissing the role discrimination may play in the low-wage sector, Mead argues that it is more likely that the poor are impatient with the working conditions and pay of menial jobs and repeatedly quit in hopes of finding better employment. At the present time, "for most jobseekers in most areas, jobs of at least a rudimentary kind are generally available" (p. 73). For Mead, it is not the case that the poor do not want to work, but rather that they will work only under the condition that others remove the barriers that make the world of work difficult. "Since much of the burden of work consists precisely in acquiring skills, finding a job, arranging child care, and so forth," states Mead, "the effect is to drain the work obligation of much of its meaning" (p. 80).

In summary, Mead believes that the programs of the Great Society have exacerbated the situation of the underclass by not obligating the recipients of social welfare programs to behave according to mainstream norms—completing school, working, obeying the law, and so on. As virtually nothing was demanded in return for benefits, the underclass remained socially isolated and could not be accepted as equals.

If the social policy recommended by conservative analysts is to become a serious candidate for adoption as national public policy, it will more likely be based on the moderate position, that is, the kind of argument that Mead has advanced in favor of mandatory workfare. The laissez-faire social philosophy represented by Charles Murray is not only too extreme to be seriously considered by most policymakers, but also the premise upon which it is based is vulnerable to the kind of criticism raised by Sheldon Danziger and Peter Gottschalk, namely that the greatest rise in black joblessness and female-headed families occurred during the very period (1972–1980) when the real value of AFDC plus food stamps plummeted because states did not peg benefit levels to inflation (Danziger & Gottschalk, 1985).

Mead's arguments, on the other hand, are much more subtle and persuasive. If his and similar arguments in support of mandatory workfare are not adopted wholesale as national policy, aspects of his theoretical rationale on the social obligations of citizenship could, as we shall see, help to shape a policy agenda involving obligational state programs. Accordingly, as I consider the question of "what might we see in the future as far as social policy and minority groups are concerned" in the present political climate, I think immediately of a work requirement for welfare recipients ("mandatory workfare"). As Lawrence Mead has become the most articulate spokesman for this position, I should like to raise some critical questions about the assumptions that guide his policy recommendations.

Fundamental to Mead's rationale for mandatory workfare are the assumptions (a) that it is not a lack of jobs that drive the high minority unemployment rate but the high job turnover, and (b) that jobs are generally available, even rudimentary ones, in most areas. Are these assumptions supported by the best recent evidence? We shall see.

A CRITIQUE OF WORK REQUIREMENTS AS SOCIAL POLICY

There are two major developments that Mead's book fails to address, developments that have had an adverse effect on minority employment, namely, (a) decreases in real wages and increases in unemployment that accompanied the recessions of the 1970s, and (b) structural changes in the urban economy. I would like briefly to discuss the effects of these changes on minority employment.

As pointed out by Frank Levy, an economist at the University of Maryland, the 1973 OPEC oil price increase resulted in both a recession and a rise in inflation which, in turn, decreased real wages by 5% in 2 years. Levy points out that the OPEC oil increase marked the beginning of a period of a decrease in the growth of worker productivity that had been the basis of a growth in real wages of between 2.5% and 3.5% per year from the end of World War II to 1973. From 1973 to 1982, however, worker productivity grew less than 0.8% each year. Although real wages had regained their 1973 levels by 1979, the fall of the Shah of Iran and the subsequent second OPEC oil price increase repeated the cycle, resulting in a decade of wage stagnation. Levy carefully notes that it was only because the proportion of the entire population in the labor force increased from 41% to 50% between 1970 and today (owing in large measure to the increased labor force participation of women, lower birth rates, and the coming of age of the large baby boom cohorts) that "GNP per capita (i.e., per man, woman, and child) could continue to rise even though GNP per worker (wages) was not doing well" (Levy, 1986, p. 9). In a period of slow growth in worker productivity, efforts to increase money wages only produced more inflation. And policymakers allowed unemployment to rise in an attempt to reduce inflation.

Levy points out that manufacturing industries, a major source of black employment in recent years, are particularly sensitive to a slack economy and therefore have suffered many job losses, especially in the older, central-city plants in recent years. Moreover, low-wage workers and newly hired workers (disproportionately represented by blacks) are most adversely affected by a slack economy. One of the consequences of increasing unemployment, states Levy, is:

> A growing polarization in the income distribution of black men. . . . Compared to 1969, the proportions of black men with income below $5,000 and above $25,000 have both grown. Thus black men at the top of the distribution were doing progressively better while blacks at the bottom—between a fifth and a quarter of all black men ages 25–55—were doing progressively worse. (pp. 19–20)

Finally, the economic problems of low-income blacks have been reinforced by recent demographic factors resulting in a "labor surplus environment." As Levy (1986) put it:

> During the decade, women of all ages sharply increased their labor force participation and the large baby boom cohorts of the 1950's came of age. Between 1960 and 1970, the labor force (nationwide) had grown by 13 million persons. But between 1970 and 1980, the labor force grew by 24 million persons. Because of this growth, we can assume that employers could be particularly choosy about whom they hired. In 1983, the more than half of all black household heads in central city poverty areas had not finished high school, a particular disadvantage in this kind of job market. (p. 19)

This important point is the subject of a major study on the regional and urban redistribution of people and jobs in the United States.

In a paper prepared for the National Academy of Sciences, John Kasarda of the University of North Carolina points out that the transformation of major northern metropolises from centers of goods-processing to centers of information-processing has been accompanied by a major shift in the educational requirements for employment. Whereas job losses in these cities have been greatest in industries with lower educational requirements, job growth has been concentrated in industries that require higher levels of education (Kasarda, 1986).

These points are illustrated in Table 1, which presents employment change from 1970 to 1984 in industries classified by the average level of education completed by their workers. Industries are divided into those whose workers average less than 12 years of schooling (less than high school) in 1982 and those whose workers averaged more than 13 years of education (some higher education). The figures show that all the major northern cities had consistent job losses in industries where employee education averaged less than a high school degree and consistent employment growth in industries where workers on the average

Table 1. Central City Jobs in Industries, by Mean Education
of Employees, 1970 and 1984 (in Thousands)

Average level of education of industrial workers	1970	1984	Change, 1970–1984
New York			
Less than high school	1,445	953	−492
Some higher education	1,002	1,241	239
Philadelphia			
Less than high school	396	224	−172
Some higher education	205	244	39
Boston			
Less than high school	168	124	−44
Some higher education	185	252	67
Baltimore			
Less than high school	187	114	−73
Some higher education	93	105	15
St. Louis			
Less than high school	197	109	−89
Some higher education	98	96	−2
Atlanta			
Less than high school	157	148	−9
Some higher education	92	129	37
Houston			
Less than high school	280	468	188
Some higher education	144	361	217
Denver			
Less than high school	106	111	5
Some higher education	72	131	59
San Francisco			
Less than high school	132	135	3
Some higher education	135	206	71

SOURCE: Adapted from Kasarda (1986).

acquired some higher education. For example, in New York City the number of jobs in industries with the lower education requisites decreased by 492,000 from 1970 to 1984, whereas those with higher education requisites increased by 239,000. Similar losses and gains occurred in other northern cities. The city of Boston, however, actually added more jobs (67,000) in the higher-education-requisite industries than it lost (44,000) in those of lower education requisites, resulting in an overall growth of 23,000 jobs between 1970 and 1984. Whereas substantial job losses continue in manufacturing and other blue collar industries in cities in the northeastern region of the country, "their vibrant information-processing sectors are more than compensating for blue-collar job losses, reversing decades of net employment decline'' (Kasarda, 1986, p. 26).

What are the implications of this transformation of the urban economy for poor minorities? First of all, cities in the North that have experienced the greatest decline of jobs in the lower-education-requisite industries since 1970 have had, at the same time, significant increases in minority residents who are seldom employed in the high-growth industries. Indeed, despite increases in educational attainment since 1970:

> Black males (over age 16) in northern cities are still most concentrated in the education completed category where employment opportunities declined the fastest and are least represented in that category where northern central city employment has most expanded since 1970. . . [creating] a serious mismatch between the current education distribution of minority residents in large northern cities and the changing educational requirements of their rapidly transforming industrial bases. This mismatch is one major reason why both unemployment rates and labor force dropout rates among central city blacks are much higher than those of central city white residents, and why black unemployment rates have not responded well to economic recovery in many northern cities. (Kasarda, 1986, p. 30)

However, Kasarda's measure of ''lower-education-requisite'' jobs and ''higher-education-requisite'' jobs does not address the question of the actual relevance of levels of education to real job performance. Many jobs identified as ''higher education'' jobs because of the average level of education throughout the work force may not really require ''higher educational'' training. For example, a number of people have observed that the new high technology is ''user friendly'' and can be operated in most cases by people who have mastered the ''three Rs.''[7] Nonetheless, if jobs in a high growth industry depend on a mastery of the ''three Rs,'' and if employers tend to associate such skills with higher levels of formal education, then they will tend to favor those with more, not less, formal education, thereby institutionalizing ''job requirements.'' Moreover, many inner-city minorities face an additional problem when access to jobs is increasingly based on education criteria. Samuel Bowles and Herbert Gintis (1976), in a provocative study of the history of education in the United States, have argued that consignment to inner-city schools helps guarantee the future economic subordinacy of minority students. More specifically, inner-city schools train minority youth so that they feel and appear capable of performing jobs only in the low-wage sector. Citing a study of disadvantaged workers which indicated that appearance was between two and three times as important to potential employees as previous work experience, high school diplomas, or test scores, Bowles and Gintis contend that students in ghetto schools are not encouraged to develop the levels of self-esteem or the styles of presentation that em-

---

[7] I would like to thank Sar Levitan for bringing this point to my attention.

ployers perceive as evidence of capacity or ability. Second, schools adopt patterns of socialization that reflect the background and/or future social position of their students. Those schools with a high concentration of poor and minorities have radically different internal environments, methods of teaching, and attitudes toward students than predominantly white, upper-middle-class suburban schools. Bowles and Gintis (1976) state:

> Blacks and minorities are concentrated in schools whose repressive, arbitrary, generally chaotic internal order, coercive authority structures and minimal possibilities for advancement mirror the characteristics of inferior job situations. Similarly, predominantly working-class schools tend to emphasize behavioral control and rule following, while schools in well-to-do suburbs employ relatively open systems that favor greater student participation, less direct supervision, more electives and in general a value system stressing internalized standards of control. (p. 132)

If the characteristics of inferior job situations are mirrored in the internal order of ghetto schools, then the transformation of the urban economy from jobs perceived to require lower education to those perceived to require higher education, or the mastery of the "three Rs," is even more problematic for inner-city residents.

It should be noted, in this connection, that the jobless rate (unemployment and nonparticipation in the labor force) among young black men (aged 16 to 24) has increased sharply since 1969 in the large central cities of the Northeast and the Midwest. In the South and in the West, jobless rates among young central-city black men are lower. Kasarda points out that cities in these regions of the United States have either had fewer job losses or have added jobs in industries with lower education requirements. Furthermore, black men in the West not only have lower combined unemployment and labor-force nonparticipation rates than their counterparts in the rest of the nation, they also have higher levels of education. "It is not fortuitous, then, that black males residing in central cities of the West also showed the smallest rises in rates of unemployment and rates of labor force nonparticipation between 1969 and 1985" (Kasarda, 1986, p. 34).

These findings are consistent with those reported earlier by Robert Aponte, Kathryn Neckerman, and myself in a paper testing the "male-marriageable pool" hypothesis (i.e., the argument that the decline in the incidence of intact marriages among blacks is associated with the declining economic status of black men) with regional data (Aponte, Neckerman, & Wilson, 1985). We found that between 1960 and 1980 the proportion of employed black men per 100 women declined substantially in all regions of the country except the West, with the greatest declines in the Northeast and North Central regions. On the basis of these trends, it would be expected that the most rapid growth of black female household heads would also occur in the two northern regions. Our regional data firmly support this conclusion.

Finally, Kasarda points out that despite the substantial loss of lower skilled jobs in many northern urban centers in recent years, substantial increases in these jobs have occurred nationwide. In the food and drink industry, for example, over 2.1 million nonadministrative jobs were added between 1975 and 1985, which exceeds the the total number of production jobs currently available in the combined automobile, steel, and textile industries in this country. States Kasarda:

> Unfortunately, essentially all of the national growth in entry-level and other low education requisite jobs have accrued in the suburbs, exurbs, and nonmetropolitan areas far removed from growing concentrations of poorly educated urban minorities. (1986, p. 41)

Thus, whereas Mead speculates that jobs are generally available in most areas and therefore one must turn to behavioral explanations for the high jobless rate among the underclass, Kasarda, on the basis of a careful analysis of the Census Bureau's Current Population Survey's computer tapes, reveals that (a) substantial job losses have occurred in the very industries in which urban minorities are heavily concentrated and substantial employment gains have occurred in the higher education–requisite industries that have relatively few minority workers, (b) this mismatch is most severe in the northeast and midwest regions of the country (regions that also have had the sharpest increases in black joblessness and female-headed families), and (c) the current growth in entry-level jobs, particularly in the service establishments, is occurring almost exclusively outside the central cities where poor minorities are concentrated. It is obvious that these findings and Levy's general observations about the adverse effects of the recent recessions on poor urban minorities raise serious questions not only about Mead's assumptions regarding the work experience and jobs of poor minorities, but also about the appropriateness of his policy recommendations.

In raising questions about Mead's emphasis on social values as an explanation of poor minority joblessness, I am not suggesting that negative attitudes toward menial work should be totally dismissed as a contributing factor. The growing social isolation and concentration of poverty in the inner city, which have made ghetto communities increasingly vulnerable to fluctuations in the economy, undoubtedly influence attitudes, values, and aspirations (see Wilson, 1987). The issue is whether attitudes toward menial employment account in large measure for the sharp rise in inner-city joblessness and related forms of social dislocation since 1970. Despite Mead's eloquent arguments, the empirical support for his thesis is incredibly weak.[8] It is therefore difficult for me to embrace a theory that sidesteps the complex issues and consequences of changes in American economic organization with the argument that one can address the problems of the ghetto underclass by simply emphasizing the social obligation of citizenship. Nonetheless, there are clear signs that a number of policymakers are

[8]See, for example, Michael Sosin's excellent review of Mead's *Beyond Entitlement* (Sosin, 1987).

now moving in this direction, even liberal policymakers who, although viewing the problems of poor minorities from the narrow lens of the poverty and civil rights frameworks, have become disillusioned with Great Society types of programs. The emphasis is not necessarily on mandatory workfare, however. Rather, the emphasis is on what Richard Nathan has called "new-style workfare," which represents a synthesis of liberal and conservative approaches to obligational state programs (Nathan, 1986).

"NEW-STYLE WORKFARE": THE SYNTHESIS OF LIBERAL AND CONSERVATIVE PERSPECTIVES

In the 1970s, the term *workfare* was narrowly used to capture the idea that in exchange for benefits, welfare recipients should be required to work, even at "make-work" if necessary. This idea was generally rejected by liberals and those in the welfare establishment who "heaped abuse on this idea, calling it 'slavefare' " (Nathan, 1986). And no workfare program, even Governor Reagan's 1971 plan, really got off the ground. However, by 1981 President Reagan was able to get congressional approval for a provision in the 1981 budget allowing states to experiment with new employment approaches to welfare reform. These approaches represent the "new-style workfare." More specifically, whereas workfare in the 1970s was narrowly construed as "working off" one's welfare grant, the new-style workfare "takes the form of obligational state programs that involve an array of employment and training services and activities—job search, job training, education programs, and also community work experience" (Nathan, 1986, p. 18). In other words, unlike the concept of workfare in the seventies, the concept of new-style workfare not only assumes that citizens have a responsibility to move toward self-sufficiency by participating in job-related programs provided by the state, but that the state has the obligation for ensuring that opportunities for and the means to achieve self-sufficiency are available.

According to Nathan:

> We make our greatest progress on social reform in the United States when liberals and conservatives find common ground. New-style workfare embodies both the caring commitment of liberals and the themes identified with conservative writers like Charles Murray, George Gilder, and Lawrence Mead. (p. 19)

On the one hand, liberals can relate to new-style workfare because it creates short-term entry-level positions very similar to the "CETA public service jobs we thought we had abolished in 1981" (p. 20); it provides a convenient "political rationale and support for increased funding for education and training programs" (p. 19); and it targets these programs at the most disadvantaged, thereby correcting the problem of "creaming" that is associated with other employment and training programs (Nathan, 1986). On the other hand, conservatives can relate to new-style workfare because:

> It involves a strong commitment to reducing welfare dependency on the premise that dependency is bad for people, that it undermines their motivation to self-support and isolates and stigmatizes welfare recipients in a way that over a long period feeds into and accentuates the underclass mindset and condition. (Nathan, 1986, p. 21)[9]

The combining of liberal and conservative approaches does not, of course, change the fact that the new-style workfare programs hardly represent a fundamental shift from the traditional approaches to poverty in America. Once again, the focus is exclusively on individual characteristics—whether they are construed in terms of lack of training, of skills, or of education, or whether they are seen in terms of lack of motivation or other subjective traits. And, once again, the consequences of certain economic arrangements on disadvantaged populations in the United States are not considered in the formulation and implementation of social policy. Although new-style workfare is better than having no strategy at all to enhance employment experiences, it should be emphasized that the effectiveness of such programs ultimately depends upon the availability of jobs in a given area. For example, as Kasarda has noted, on the basis of an interpretation of descriptive statistics on the national work incentive (WIN) program:

> Of those who participated in WIN, only 18 percent, on average, actually entered jobs. If WIN's main function . . . is to require welfare recipients to look for jobs in the private sector, an 18 percent actual job entry success rate is not very encouraging and is suggestive of a job vacancy pool problem. (Kasarda, personal communication, 1987)

Perhaps Robert D. Reischauer, of the Brookings Institution, put it best when he stated that:

> As long as the unemployment rate remains high in many regions of the country, members of the underclass are going to have a very difficult time competing successfully for jobs that are available. No amount of remedial education, training, wage subsidy, or other embellishment will make them more attractive to prospective employers than experienced unemployed workers. (Reischauer, 1986a, p. 13)

He also appropriately points out that, given a weak economy:

> Even if the workfare program seems to be placing its clients successfully, these participants may simply be taking jobs away from others who are nearly as disadvan-

---

[9]Although Lawrence Mead is highly critical of new-style workfare (because it reinforces the sociological view of the disadvantaged by assuming that before the recipients can work, the program has to find the client a job, arrange for child care, solve the client's health problems, and so on), his elaborate theory of the social obligation of citizenship is being adopted by policymakers to buttress the more conservative side of the new workfare programs.

taged. A game of musical underclass will ensue as one group is temporarily helped while another is pushed down into the underclass (Reischauer, 1986b, p. 3)

CONCLUSION

The central arguments of this chapter are that (a) the vulnerability of poor urban minorities to changes in the economy since 1970 has resulted in sharp increases in joblessness, poverty, female-headed families, and welfare dependency despite the creation of Great Society programs, and despite antidiscrimination and affirmative action programs, (b) the War on Poverty and civil rights visions failed to relate the fate of poor minorities to the functionings of the modern American economy and therefore could not explain the worsening conditions of inner-city minorities in the post–Great Society and post–civil rights period, (c) liberals whose views embody these visions have not only been puzzled by the rise of inner-city social dislocations, they have also lacked a convincing rebuttal to the forceful arguments by conservative scholars that attribute these problems to social values of poor minorities, (d) the most persuasive conservative challenge is not the laissez-faire social policy arguments articulated by Charles Murray, but the elaborate rationale for mandatory workfare, developed by Lawrence Mead, and (e) the growing emphasis on workfare, buttressed by rationales on the social obligation of citizenship, deflects attention from the major source of the rise of social dislocations among poor minorities since 1970- –changes in the nation's economy.

I believe that to address adequately the problems of minority poverty, and the poverty of other groups in society as well, we need to recognize the dynamic interplay between economic organization and the behavior and life chances of individuals and groups and develop a program that is designed both to enhance human capital traits of poor minorities and open up the opportunity structure in the broader society and economy to facilitate social mobility. This could be accomplished by creating employment-oriented macroeconomic policies to develop a strong, inclusive economy and by building a stronger work force through, as suggested in Governor Cuomo's Task Force Report on Poverty and Welfare, "reforms in education, investments in preschool education, support for training in the private sector, compensatory training for those who lack the skills and abilities to compete in the labor market" (A New Social Contract, 1986, p. 12). New-style workfare could then be a part of, not a substitute for, this fundamental program of reform.

Before such programs can be seriously considered, however, the question of cost has to be addressed. The costs of programs to expand social and economic opportunity will be great, but they must be weighed against the economic and social costs of do-nothing policy. As Sar Levitan and Clifford Johnson have pointed out:

> The most recent recession cost the nation an estimated $300 billion in lost income and
> production, and direct outlays for unemployment compensation totaled $30 billion in a
> single year. A policy that ignores the losses associated with slack labor markets and
> forced idleness inevitably will underinvest in the nation's labor force and future
> economic growth. (Levitan & Johnson, 1984, pp. 169–170)

Furthermore, the problem of annual budget deficits of almost $200,000 billion
dollars (driven mainly by the peacetime military buildup and the Reagan administration's tax cut) and the need for restoring the federal tax base and adopting a
more balanced set of budget priorities has to be tackled before significant progress on expanding opportunities is possible (Levitan & Johnson, 1984, p. 170).

In the final analysis, the pursuit of economic and social reform ultimately
involves the question of political strategy. As the history of social provision so
clearly demonstrates, universalistic political alliances, cemented by policies that
provide benefits directly to wide segments of the population, are needed to work
successfully for major reform (see Skocpol, 1985). An important first step in this
direction would be the recognition among minority leaders, liberal researchers,
and policymakers of the need to expand the poverty and civil rights frameworks
so that issues such as changes in American economic organization that ostensibly
have little or no direct connection with poverty or race, but that nonetheless
impact heavily on the lives of poor minorities, can be meaningfully addressed.

REFERENCES

A new social contract: Rethinking the nature and purpose of public assistance. (1986). Report of the
    Task Force on Poverty and Welfare, submitted to Governor Mario M. Cuomo, State of New
    York, December.
A. Philip Randolph Institute. (1966). *A "freedom budget" for all Americans: Budgeting our re-
    sources, 1966–1975, to achieve "freedom from want".* New York.
Aponte, R., K. M. Neckerman, & W. J. Wilson. (1985). Race, family structure, and social policy.
    In *Working paper 7: race and policy.* Washington, DC: National Conference on Social Welfare.
Blank, R. M., & A. S. Blinder. (1986). Macroeconomics, income distribution, and poverty. In S.
    Danziger & D. H. Weinberg (Eds.), *Fighting poverty: What works and what doesn't.*
    Cambridge, MA: Harvard University Press.
Bowles, S. & H. Gintis. (1976). *Schooling in capitalist America: Education and the contradictions
    of economic life.* New York: Basic Books.
Brauer, C. M. (1982). Kennedy, Johnson, and the War on Poverty. *Journal of American History, 69,*
    98–119.
Clark, K. B. (1965). *Dark ghetto: Dilemmas of social power.* New York: Harper and Row.
Clark, L. D., & J. T. Ellis. (1980). Affirmative action in recessionary periods: The legal structure.
    *Adherent: A Journal of Comprehensive Employment Training and Human Resources of Devel-
    opment, 7* (64).
Danziger, S., & P. Gottschalk. (1985). The poverty of losing ground. *Challenge,* (May/June), 32–
    38.
Ellwood, D. T., & L. H. Summers. (1986). Poverty in America: Is welfare the answer or the

problem? In S. H. Danziger & D. H. Weinberg (Eds.), *Fighting poverty: What works and what doesn't.* Cambridge, MA: Harvard University Press.

Fishkin, J. S. (1983). *Justice, equal opportunity and the family.* New Haven, CT: Yale University Press.

Glazer, N. (1965). A sociologist's view of poverty. In M. S. Gordon (Ed.), *Poverty in America.* San Francisco: Chandler.

Greenstein, R. (1985). Losing faith in 'losing ground.' *New Republic, 12,* 12–17.

Jencks, C. (1985). How poor are the poor? *New York Review of Books, 32* (8).

Kasarda, J. D. (1986). *The regional and urban redistribution of people and jobs in the U.S.* Paper prepared for National Research Council, Committee on National Urban Policy, National Academy of Sciences, Washington, DC.

Korpi, W. (1980). Approaches to the study of poverty in the United States: Critical notes from a European perspective. In Vincent T. Covello (Ed.), *Poverty and public policy: An evaluation of social research.* Boston: G. K. Hall.

Kuttner, R. (1984). A flawed case for scrapping what's left of the Great Society. *Washington Post Book World,* November 25, pp. 34–35.

Levine, R. A. (1970). *The poor ye need not have with you: Lessons from the War on Poverty.* Cambridge, MA: MIT Press.

Levitan, S. A. (1969). *The Great Society's poor law: A new approach to poverty.* Baltimore, MD: Johns Hopkins University Press.

Levitan, S. A., & C. M. Johnson. (1984). *Beyond the safety net: Reviving the promising of opportunity in America.* Cambridge, MA: Ballinger.

Levy, F. (1986). Poverty and economic growth. Unpublished manuscript, School of Public Affairs, University of Maryland, College Park, MD.

Liebow, E. (1967). *Tally's corner: A study of negro streetcorner men.* Boston: Little, Brown.

Mead, L. M. (1986). *Beyond entitlement: The social obligations of citizenship.* New York: Free Press.

Moynihan, D. P. (1968). The professors and the poor. In D. P. Moynihan (Ed.), *On understanding poverty: Perspectives from the social sciences.* New York: Basic Books.

Moynihan, D. P. (1970). *Maximum feasible misunderstanding.* New York: Free Press.

Murray, C. (1984). *Losing ground: American social policy, 1950–1980.* New York: Basic Books.

Nathan, R. P. (1986). *The underclass—Will it always be with us?* Paper prepared for a Symposium at the New School for Social Research, November 14, New York, NY.

Rabb, E. (1966). A tale of three wars: What war and which poverty? *The Public Interest, 3,* 35–56.

Rainwater, L. (1966). Crucible of identity: The Negro lower-class family. *Daedalus, 96,* 176–216.

Raspberry, W. (1980). Illusion of black progress. *Washington Post,* May 28, p. A19.

Piven, F. F., & R. A. Cloward. (1971). *Regulating the poor: The functions of public welfare.* New York: Academic Press.

Reischauer, R. D. (1986a). *America's underclass: Four unanswered questions.* Paper presented at the City Club, Oregon.

Reischauer, R. D. (1986b). *Policy responses to the underclass problems.* Paper prepared for a symposium at the New School for Social Research, November 14, New York, NY.

Skocpol, T. (1985). *Brother can you spare a job? Work and welfare in the United States.* Paper presented at the Annual Meeting of the American Sociological Association, Washington, DC, August.

Sosin, M. (1987). Review of "Beyond entitlement." *Social Service Review, 61,* 156–159.

Sundquist, J. L. (1969). The origins of the War on Poverty. In J. L. Sundquist (Ed.), *On fighting poverty: Perspectives from experience.* New York: Basic Books.

Weir, M., A. S. Orloff, & T. Skocpol. (1988). The future of social policy in the United States:

Political constraints and possibilities. In Weir, Orloff, & Skocpol (Eds.), *The politics of social policy in the United States*. Princeton: Princeton University Press, 1988.

Wilson, W. J. (1987). *The truly disadvantaged: The inner city, the underclass, and public policy*. Chicago: University of Chicago Press.

Wilson, W. J., & K. M. Neckerman. (1986). Poverty and family structure: The widening gap between evidence and public policy issues. In S. H. Danziger & D. H. Weinberg (Eds.), *Fighting poverty: What works and what doesn't*. Cambridge, MA: Harvard University Press.

Yarmolinsky, A. (1969). The beginnings of OEO. In J. L. Sundquist (Ed.), *On fighting poverty: Perspectives from experience*. New York: Basic Books.

10

Social Responsibility and Minority Poverty

A Response to William Julius Wilson

LAWRENCE M. MEAD

It is perhaps no accident that Professor Wilson and I find ourselves in disagreement. He is a sociologist; I am a political scientist. Compared to economics, these disciplines have had less to say about poverty until recently. Out of ignorance, or naivete, we may be surer of our theories and readier to defend them than the practitioners of the dismal science. Perhaps in another 20 years, we will be just as doubtful about the answers to poverty as I sense economists are today.

I support the main theme of Wilson's chapter, that past policy approaches to poverty have been too narrow, too focused on racial discrimination or the limitations of the poor, too loath to consider broader questions of social organization. This tendency, however, has always been stronger in policy than in theory, more prevalent among politicians and the public than among academics and policy experts. From the early 1960s, the intellectuals who conceived the War on Poverty and later compensatory programming understood poverty in terms of social, not individual, causes. They studiously avoided "blaming the victims" for even the most personal behaviors harmful to themselves, such as illegitimacy or crime. There was, Daniel Moynihan wrote, "a near-obsessive concern to locate the 'blame' for poverty, especially Negro poverty, on forces and institutions outside the community concerned" (Moynihan, 1969, p. 31).

Also, at least among experts, there has been less neglect of economic causes of poverty than Wilson suggests. I agree that the economy was largely ignored in early antipoverty thinking. Social and cultural impediments to the poor got much more attention. But this was because the economy was too prosperous during the

---

LAWRENCE M. MEAD • Department of Politics, New York University, New York, New York.

1960s to be widely seen as a problem; as later analysis showed, blacks who worked made rapid gains relative to whites during that decade.

When chronic troubles (inflation, recession, energy, etc.) hit the economy during the 1970s, new academic theories blossomed that did connect poverty to structural economic change. One of these was the idea of a "dual labor market," the notion that the economy systematically steered whites and the better-off toward "better" jobs in government and large corporations while relegating nonwhites and the poor to low-paid, insecure jobs in the "secondary" economy (e.g., small business and service trades).[1] Another theory was the idea of a "mismatch" between the demands of an increasingly "high-tech" economy and the skills or location of inner-city jobseekers, the theory that Wilson himself and some of his sources have developed.

My analysis of the poverty problem is no more individualist than Wilson's, but we differ in the chief barriers we see. He says the main impediments facing the inner-city poor today are their social isolation from the better-off and the decline of low-skilled jobs available to them. Although admitting these forces, I think the greater problem is the permissive nature of government welfare and employment programs. Large sections of the minority poor live on these benefits, particularly in inner cities, but the programs seldom expect them to function in the ways needed for their own integration. Particularly, few adult recipients of welfare face any serious demands to work or otherwise better themselves *in return* for support. Just as Wilson traces the deterioration of inner-city opportunity to the long-term evolution of the economy (Wilson, 1980, 1985, 1987), so I find permissive programming deeply rooted in the libertarian traditions of federal politics (Mead, 1986a).

Wilson says he finds my position more persuasive than Charles Murray's, according to which welfare *per se* is demoralizing and ought to be abolished. But he questions a crucial assumption, that jobs would be available to the poor if they sought to work regularly, or were required to. Accordingly, he supports an employment strategy but opposes efforts, such as workfare, to enforce work in the existing economy. He believes government must first provide greater opportunity through new training, economic planning, and other measures.

He bases his current argument largely on recent research by Frank Levy (1986) and John D. Kasarda (1986). Both discuss adverse economic trends during the 1970s, using aggregated data. Levy shows that overall growth in incomes and productivity declined during the decade whereas labor force participation rose. Kasarda shows that low-skilled manufacturing jobs have declined in northeastern and midwestern cities since 1970, shifting either to the Sunbelt or overseas. And, whereas white residents have left the Northeast and the Midwest in droves, black and Hispanic populations there are growing. These regions have

---

[1]For an introduction, see Doeringer and Piore (1975). For a critique, see Cain (1976).

recently seen a growth in service and information-based industries, but the new jobs usually require more education than minorities have.

Both Levy and Kasarda infer that it is more difficult today for unskilled jobseekers, such as inner-city minorities, to find work. There is apparently a "mismatch" between their limited skills and urban location and the demands of an increasingly "high-tech" economy. This, the authors conclude, largely explains the catastrophic levels of unemployment now found in the inner city.

The economic trends Levy and Kasarda describe are undeniable. However, the changes would seem to have debased the quality of jobs available to Americans, not the number relative to those seeking them.[2] The nation is far from a depression. Although manufacturing jobs have declined, jobs in the service economy have boomed, raising total employment. The main adverse impact of the trends would appear to be on real wage rates, which have grown little since 1970. The income distribution in the economy is more dispersed, and inequality may be rising.[3]

It is less obvious how the trends could explain lower employment in the sense of fewer jobs or working hours, particularly in the ghetto. If pay is static or dropping relative to earlier norms, one might expect to see *more* employment rather than less, as Americans worked more jobs or hours to maintain their earlier incomes. And among working- and middle-class people since 1970, that is just what we see—wives and teenagers taking mostly low-paying jobs to maintain family income, even at the expense of other important activities such as child care or education. Only in the ghetto do hours worked in legal jobs appear to be dropping. Although that is a serious dilemma, it is hard to blame it on the overall economic trends.

Other trends suggest that the availability of jobs is actually rising. During the 1970s, job creation failed to keep pace with the entry into the labor force of the massive baby boom, the largest generation of young adults ever. Later cohorts, however, are much smaller, and in recent years new entrants to the labor force have fallen. The presence of some 5 million illegal aliens in the country testifies that there are many more menial jobs available that Americans do not seek. And the Immigration and Control Reform Act passed in 1986 is already restricting further illegal immigration. At least in low-paid jobs, the nation already faces a labor shortage.

Unemployment in the official sense, that is, those seeking work as a proportion of the labor force, has risen since 1970. But the main reason appears to be that the new jobs are commonly *less attractive* than the old, not that they are less

---

[2] I can give only a few citations on the labor market issues here. For a fuller review, see Mead (1986b).

[3] I accept here for the sake of argument that job quality really is declining, as argued by Bluestone and Harrison (1987), for example. For an opposed view, see Norwood (1987).

available. A high-unemployment rate need not mean, as it did in the 1930s, that there are literally too few jobs for those that seek them. It can also mean that some jobseekers do not find jobs they will *accept.* Today, many who can get only low-paid jobs prefer to decline them and keep looking for something better, in the meantime living off income from other family members or government benefit programs. The rise, and softening, of the unemployment rate is a long-term trend fostered by multiple-earner families and indulgent government employment policies (see Feldstein, 1973).

Kasarda is unsure why migration to the northern cities is still occurring, a sign that the job dilemma there has been exaggerated. Whereas minorities are leaving these cities, they are also still moving there, though at a reduced rate. We know they do not come primarily to go on welfare, though many end up there. There must be jobs available, perhaps because outmigration has reduced surplus labor. Or, as Kasarda suggests, there is work in the underground economy that is uncaptured by his data.

His case, moreover, is confined to the center city. He admits that low-skilled jobs are growing in adjacent areas. As the youth labor market tightens, merchants in the suburbs are already having trouble hiring help. There, even unskilled youths working at McDonald's now command well above the minimum wage. Even assuming jobs are lacking in the cities, minorities could apparently find many positions outside, if they could commute or move there. Urban unemployment may really be a problem in transportation and housing, of providing better access to existing jobs. Those difficulties are serious, but to solve them would not require the large changes in economic policy that Wilson suggests.[4]

However, suburbanization does not in fact explain most joblessness among the inner-city poor, according to studies of Chicago and Los Angeles. Blacks in these cities do commute longer distances to their jobs than whites, but this explains very little of their higher unemployment. Race and educational differences between blacks and other groups are much more important. Even when blacks live right next to whites and Hispanics, so that commuting differences are minimized, they manifest higher joblessness and a much lower proportion of adults at work (see Ellwood, 1986; Leonard, 1986).

Overall economic trends, therefore, cannot explain the very high unemployment seen in the inner city. Causes more specific to the ghetto must be operating. Kasarda emphasizes educational levels. His main evidence for a mismatch in the Northern cities is that the industries now growing there have employees with higher education on average than the manufacturing industries they replace.

His argument is based on actual educational levels in the industries; he has no information, strictly speaking, on educational requirements. And, as Wilson

[4]Kasarda (1985, pp. 55–56) discusses the transportation problem.

notes, industry averages may conceal many jobs accessible to the merely literate even within "high-tech" firms. In fact, the most numerous occupations in the "new" economy, like the old—secretaries, custodians, truckdrivers, sales-clerks—have little inherent connection to "high-tech" at all (see Samuelson, 1983).

The shift to higher education is also overstated in Kasarda's calculations. To show the changing job mix (his Table 10, which Wilson cites), he compares industries averaging less than high school education with those averaging at least one year of college. He omits industries with mean educations in between, around the high school level. But a comparison of Tables 9 and 10 shows that these industries comprised an average of 28% of all jobs in 1984 in the nine cities covered. Table 10 as it stands shows that jobs requiring higher education now outnumber those requiring less than high school in five of the nine cities. But if the excluded jobs are added to the low-skilled group, positions averaging high school education or less still outnumber the higher-skilled jobs in every city but Boston.

It is more reasonable today to define jobs requiring only a high school education as low-skilled. On that basis, the share of jobs that were low-skilled in New York City declined hardly at all, from 58% to 57%, between 1972 and 1981, according to one study. Admittedly, the nature of low-skilled work has changed. The requirement is more often for literacy, less often for manual dexterity, than in the manufacturing jobs of the past. But unless we regard literacy as an advanced skill, we cannot say that the urban labor market is very much more demanding today than it ever was.[5]

The employment problem in cities seems due not so much to the labor market as to the usual difficulty minorities have in school compared to earlier urban ethnic groups. Kasarda documents that blacks typically have less educa-tion than whites, especially in the Northeast and Midwest. In one sense, his figures overstate the difference because they do not control for the fact that blacks on average are younger, so proportionally fewer of them have completed their schooling. But in another sense he understates the gap, as unemployment is startlingly high in center cities even for black high school graduates, something he finds "troublesome and difficult to interpret" (1986, p. 29). The probable explanation is that standards have collapsed in many urban schools, to the point where even high school graduates are frequently illiterate. Employers may be raising educational requirements for employment to counteract this decline, not because the work in today's economy really demands higher skills.

---

[5]See Bailey and Waldinger (1984). Eileen Sullivan, author of the main study cited by Bailey and Waldinger, treated as "low-skilled" all jobs requiring high school education or less unless they involved at least 18 months of preemployment training.

Clearly, illiteracy is a social failure, but it is not, as Wilson suggests, a failure of *economic* organization. The failure of the schools and of inner-city family structure would seem much more to blame. The larger issue is whether we can reasonably hold the economy responsible for employing the totally unskilled. Is there no minimum of competence which society can expect every jobseeker to have? How should the responsibility for employability be shared between job-seekers and larger social structures? It is unreasonable to assign, as Wilson does, all the responsibility to society.

A more fundamental problem is that it may not be valid to reason from the aggregate trends to the character of individual labor market problems, as Wilson and Kasarda do, at least not without showing the connections more fully. The picture they draw is not consistent with other research based on individual-level data. Studies based on surveys suggest even more strongly that unemployment is often voluntary.

Analyses of the Current Population Survey (CPS) show that most unem-ployed people stay jobless only for short periods. The groups with the highest unemployment, such as women, teenagers, and nonwhites, are characterized by rapid turnover, with individuals moving into and out of jobs or the labor force rapidly, rather than by prolonged unemployment. It is true that the long-term jobless account for most of measured joblessness, but they are a minority of the unemployed, even among the most disadvantaged (Clark & Summers, 1979). This suggests that, for most of the jobless, at least low-paid jobs are readily available.

Studies based on the Panel Study of Income Dynamics (PSID) question the notion that minorities or the low-skilled are walled off from employment. Demo-graphic characteristics rarely keep people from working, though they may de-press how good a job they can get. Most poverty and dependency, like unem-ployment, is short term, and earnings are the main way poor families escape poverty, even those with female heads (Bane & Ellwood, 1986, pp. 18–21). Welfare mothers who are older, black, or unwed are just as likely to work their way off welfare as those who are younger, white, or married.[6] Although blacks do earn lower incomes than whites, their economic mobility over time is com-parable. And although black youth have very high unemployment rates, black male family heads are under, not over, represented among the long-term unem-ployed (Duncan *et al.*, 1984, Chap. 4).

When asked, poor and black people usually say they can find jobs; they complain, rather, about the quality of the jobs. According to the poverty statis-tics, only 40% of the poor who work less than full time give inability to find work as the main reason, and only 11% of those not working at all do so. These

---

[6]See Bane and Ellwood (1983). Such differences have much more effect on the chance of leaving welfare through remarriage.

figures rise to 45% and 16%, respectively, for the black poor, and 59% and 23% for poor black men, the group on whom Wilson focuses.[7] And even these figures may be inflated by response set, as inability to find work is one of the more acceptable reasons for not working. According to a separate study of inner-city black youth, a group with 40% measured unemployment, 71% said it was fairly easy to find work at the minimum wage. The main reason they were jobless is not that jobs were lacking, but that they resisted going to work at jobs paying less than white youth usually earn.[8]

In sum, explanations of urban joblessness that look only to economic changes or other social barriers are unconvincing. That is why more attention should be paid to the lack of serious work requirements in federal welfare and employment programs, an economic mainstay of ghetto communities. The experience of efforts to enforce work also provides further evidence that the labor market is a serous barrier to the poor finding employment, at least at current work levels.

The main enforcement program is the Work Incentive (WIN) program, which is supposed to put adult recipients of Aid to Families with Dependent Children (AFDC) in work or training. In several studies, I have found that WIN's performance clearly is influenced by social and economic forces. The program does place fewer clients in settings where the caseload is disadvantaged or nonwhite and unemployment is high than in locations with opposite characteristics. Such constraints help to explain why, as Wilson and Kasarda note, the share of WIN registrants entering work each year is only about a fifth.

Nevertheless, *variation* in that share across states is most strongly related, not to these conditions, but to the share of clients the programs obligates to participate in the program, usually by looking for work (Mead, 1983, 1985, 1988). *At the margin,* that is, WIN's performance depends mostly on the program's own willingness to expect clients to work, not on the labor market.[9] Studies by the Manpower Demonstration Research Corporation of newer AFDC work programs suggest the same. These programs have generated worthwhile increases in earnings and work hours by their clients. They have been con-

---

[7]Calculated from U.S. Bureau of the Census (1986, pp. 37, 46–47).

[8]See Freeman and Holzer (1985, pp. 27–30). See also Borus (1982), who finds black youth at least as willing to work as white and Hispanic youth. The difference in findings probably stems from the fact that Borus's data come from the National Longitudinal Survey of Youth Labor Market Experience, which covered all youth, whereas Freeman and Holzer's came from a special National Bureau of Economic Research survey targeted on inner-city youth.

[9]In a private communication, Kasarda objected that interpreting individual behavior from these studies, which use state-level data, was no less "ecological" than the inferences he makes from his aggregates. But the WIN aggregates are much less high-level, more reflective of the behavior of disadvantaged jobseekers. The first two studies included interviewing that clarified the meaning of the state totals for individual offices and clients. The results are also much more consistent with the picture of the urban unemployment given by other research based on individual-level data.

strained by lack of jobs mainly in rural localities, not in the urban areas stressed by Wilson (see Gueron, 1986b, p. 23). Thus. there apparently is room for higher work levels among the poor and dependent, even in today's urban job market. A general job shortage might emerge only if those levels rose considerably.

In the end, Wilson and I differ about the job situation only in degree. He does not claim there are no jobs at all for the unskilled in cities. I do not claim there would necessarily be enough if the turnover stopped and all of the unskilled tried to work steadily at once. There is no way to tell until work levels actually rise. The actual dispute is more limited—it is over whether jobs at a legal wage are ordinarily available in urban areas *at the margin,* that is, to those seeking them at a given time. Essentially, I think they are, and Wilson does not.

One reason for our difference is ignorance. The information we have about the available jobs is incomplete, though I think it favors my position. Another reason is divergent social philosophies. How easy must working be for the poor before we say jobs are truly "available"? Wilson thinks employment is tough enough so that government must first alter the labor market in favor of the poor. I think it is easy enough so that they can be expected to work in the existing labor market, as other Americans do.

The greater limitation of the labor market, again, is job quality. Jobs may be widely available to the unskilled, but they are mostly unattractive in pay and conditions compared to previous norms for the economy. This accounts for some of the alienation of inner-city job seekers from the legal labor market, even though they have opportunities to work. Professor Wilson framed the problem this way himself in an earlier publication. The difficulty, he wrote, is "not one of a declining number of available jobs but a decrease in the opportunity to obtain stable higher-paying jobs"; and, "blacks do not experience employment barriers in low-paid, menial, and casual jobs but rather in the more desirable, higher-paying jobs" (Wilson, 1980, pp. 96–109, 165–166). Thus, many refuse to take low-paid jobs, or they work only in the underground economy, where pay for the unskilled is higher.

This is the correct characterization. The real issue in work policy is whether jobs are *acceptable* in pay and conditions, not whether they *exist.* Those, like Wilson, who question the idea of work enforcement are raising an important issue, but it has to do with social standards, not economic facts. It would be truer to the evidence if opponents of workfare stopped taking measured unemployment as proof of a job shortage and instead asked what calibre of job society should view as obligatory.

Perhaps the quality of available jobs must be raised, for example by raising the minimum wage or providing universal health insurance, before we can mandate them. Job enrichment measures may have to join with enforcement in a new "social contract" before the inner-city work problem can be solved. However, any new benefits must go to all workers. To create more attractive jobs just for marginal workers would be inequitable and would not lead to integration, as our experience with government employment under the Comprehensive Employment Training Act proved.

The point of work requirements is to embody that new concordat. Wilson views "workfare" needlessly as a one-sided, individualist policy that levies all the onus of work on the clients. At the very least, enforcement programs must provide child care and other support services to welfare recipients who are training or looking for work, benefits not normally available to other jobseekers. They also commonly provide some transitional child and health care to clients after they have entered jobs. Programs that require work, not just looking for work, must also guarantee it, if necessary through government employment. In areas where jobs proved insufficient, that could require just the restructuring Wilson wants.

Yet what is most structural about workfare is precisely the work obligation. Wilson's argument that the ghetto is *socially* isolated is truer than to say it is barred from employment. For various reasons, many ghetto adults have fallen out of the pattern of steady work in available jobs that they shared with the larger society before 1960. They cannot be integrated until that pattern is restored. Experience has shown that merely to offer them new benefits, including jobs, does not achieve this. If work is only a benefit, too few of the seriously poor and dependent accept that it is also an obligation. Hence, they never come to terms with the demands made by jobs in the private sector. They need to hear more clearly that certain minimal competencies are the price of equality in this society. Just as society is obligated to help them, so they must be obligated to help themselves.[10]

To say this is not to question, or try to change, the "values" of the disadvantaged, as Wilson suggests. The long-term poor clearly want to work as strongly as other people. That is why most of the participants in welfare employment programs accept work requirements as fair and feel positively, not negatively, about their work experience (Gueron, 1986a, pp. 13–14). If they felt otherwise, to require them to work would be futile. The poor differ from the better-off mainly in how closely they live by these norms. More than for other people, work for them tends to be an *aspiration* but not an *obligation*. It is something they would like to do if government first secured them with child care or training or dealt with other barriers, but not something they feel they *must* do regardless of personal cost. If satisfying jobs are lacking, they are often willing to live on welfare rather than work (see Goodwin, 1972; Auletta, 1982).

Mandatory work programs try to change behavior, not values. They try to close the gap between norms and actual work effort. To that end, they provide a structure combining necessary support services, such as child care, health cover-

---

[10]For a review of employment policy that supports this conclusion, see Mead (1986c).

age, and training, with participation requirements. Within that structure, as experience has shown, recipients can more nearly live by the work ethic in which they already believe.

Furthermore, work programs must be mandatory to justify their generous aspects. Liberal rhetoric tends to treat lack of jobs and lack of *good* jobs as equally valid reasons for nonwork. But to the public, polls demonstrate, the two are fundamentally different. The first would justify nonwork, but the second does not. As long as the economy permits, all able-bodied family heads and single adults are supposed to work in some legal job, however menial it is, in preference to dependency or crime. There might be a constituency for raising the quality of low-paid jobs, as Wilson suggests, but only if work requirements were much more clear-cut than now. The poor must work more regularly before they can claim new economic rights (Mead, 1986a, pp. 233–240).

By emphasizing insufficient jobs, Wilson's current paper moves the debate backward. It seeks explanations for poverty only in impersonal barriers outside the poor, a search that has reached diminishing returns. His earlier position was less liberal but more radical. It raised the real issues more sharply—job quality and the work discipline of the chronically poor. How to resolve those questions hinges much more on political choices than economics. It is only by facing them—together—that we can achieve fundamental change in the inner city.

REFERENCES

Auletta, K. (1982). *The underclass.* New York: Random House.
Bailey, T., & R. Waldinger. (1984). A skills mismatch in New York's labor market? *New York Affairs, 8,* 3–18.
Bane, M. J., & D. T. Ellwood. (1983, June). *The dynamics of dependence: The routes to self-sufficiency.* Study prepared for the Department of Health and Human Services. Urban Systems Research and Engineering, Cambridge, MA.
Bane, M. J., & D. T. Ellwood. (1986). Slipping into and out of poverty: The dynamics of spells. *Journal of Human Resources, 21,* 18–21.
Bluestone, B., & B. Harrison. (1987). The grim truth about the job 'miracle': A low-wage explosion. *New York Times,* February 1, p. F3.
Borus, M. E. (1982). Willingness to work among youth. *Journal of Human Resources, 17,* 581–593.
Cain, G. G. (1976). The challenge of segmented labor market theories to orthodox theory: A survey. *Journal of Economic Literature, 14,* 1215–1257.
Clark, K. B., & L. H. Summers. (1979). Labor market dynamics and unemployment: A reconsideration. *Brookings Papers on Economic Activity,* No. 1, pp. 13–72.
Doeringer, P. B., & M. J. Piore. (1975). Unemployment and the 'dual labor market.' *The Public Interest, 38* (winter), pp. 67–79.
Duncan, G. J., R. D. Coe, M. E. Corcoran, M. S. Hill, S. D. Hoffman, & J. N. Morgan. (1984). *Years of poverty, years of plenty: The changing fortunes of American workers and families.* Ann Arbor, MI: Institute for Social Research, University of Michigan.
Ellwood, D. T. (1986). The spatial mismatch hypothesis: Are there teenage jobs missing in the

ghetto? In R. B. Freeman and H. J. Holzer (Eds.), *The black youth unemployment crisis.* Chicago: University of Chicago Press.

Feldstein, M. S. (1973). The economics of the new unemployment. *The Public Interest, 33* (fall), pp. 3–42.

Freeman, R. B., & H. J. Holzer. (1985). Young blacks and jobs—What we now know. *The Public Interest, 78* (winter), pp. 18–31.

Goodwin, L. (1972). *Do the poor want to work? A social-psychological study of work orientations.* Washington, DC: Brookings Institution.

Gueron, J. M. (1986a). *Work initiatives for welfare recipients.* New York: Manpower Research Demonstration Corporation, March.

Gueron, J. M. (1986b). *Reforming welfare with work.* New York: Manpower Demonstration Research Corporation. December.

Kasarda, J. D. (1985). Urban change and minority opportunities. In P. E. Peterson (Ed.), *The new urban reality.* Washington, DC: Brookings Institution.

Kasarda, J. D. (1986). *The regional and urban redistribution of people and jobs in the United States.* Paper prepared for the Committee on National Urban Policy, National Research Council, October.

Leonard, J. S. (1986, September). *Space, time, and unemployment: Los Angeles, 1980.* Unpublished paper, University of California, Berkeley.

Levy, F. (1986). *Poverty and economic growth.* Unpublished paper, School of Public Affairs, University of Maryland, College Park, MD.

Mead, L. M. (1983). Expectations and welfare work: WIN in New York City. *Policy Studies Review, 2,* 648–662.

Mead, L. M. (1985). Expectations and welfare work: WIN in New York State. *Polity, 18,* 224–252.

Mead, L. M. (1986a). *Beyond entitlement: The social obligations of citizenship.* New York: Free Press.

Mead, L. M. (1986b). Work and dependency, Part I: The problem and its causes. Unpublished paper, Hudson Institute, Indianapolis, IN, September.

Mead, L. M. (1986c). *Work and dependency, part II: Past policies and proposals.* Unpublished manuscript, Hudson Institute, September.

Mead, L. M. (1988). The Potential for work enforcement: A study of WIN. *Journal of Policy Analysis and Management, 7,* 264–288.

Moynihan, D. P. (1969). The professors and the poor. In D. P. Moynihan (Ed.), *On understanding poverty: Perspectives from the social sciences.* New York: Basic Books.

Norwood, J. L. (1987). The job machine has not broken down. *New York Times,* February 22, p. F3.

Samuelson, R. J. (1983). The old labor force and the new job market. *National Journal,* February 26, pp. 426–431.

U.S. Bureau of the Census. (1986). *Characteristics of the population below the poverty level: 1984.* Series P-60, No. 152. Washington, DC: U.S. Government Printing Office.

Wilson, W. J. (1980). *The declining significance of race: Blacks and changing american institutions* (2nd ed.). Chicago: University of Chicago Press.

Wilson, W. J. (1985). The urban underclass in advanced industrial society. In P. E. Peterson (Ed.), *The new urban reality.* Washington, DC: Brookings Institution.

Wilson, W. J. (1987). *The truly disadvantaged: The inner city, the underclass, and public policy.* Chicago: University of Chicago Press.

11

Epilogue

GARY D. SANDEFUR AND MARTA TIENDA

Almost 25 years have elapsed since passage of the Civil Rights Act, and it has been 20 years since the Kerner Report drew the nation's attention to deteriorating conditions in the major central cities of the United States. Both events occurred when the nation was experiencing sustained economic growth. That most minority groups improved their relative economic status during this period generated optimism about the prospects of eliminating poverty. Many social scientists concluded that continued economic growth, buttressed by governmental interventions, would further reduce poverty, if not eliminate it altogether.

The Civil Rights Act was designed to open American society to full participation by blacks and other minorities. Since then, U.S. society has in fact become more open. The number of black and Hispanic elected officials has dramatically increased, and they now include the mayors of such major cities as Atlanta, Chicago, San Antonio, Miami, and Philadelphia. William Julius Wilson and others have documented the existence and vitality of a black middle class. The idea that a black person would be a serious contender for the presidential nomination would have seemed unbelievable in the 1960s, yet is a fact of the 1980s. Nevertheless, the ideals that inspired the Civil Rights movement—a Great Society in which neither color nor national origin would influence the assignment of opportunity or material rewards—are as yet unfulfilled.

The Kerner Report (prepared by the National Advisory Commission on Civil Disorders, chaired by the Illinois governor, Otto Kerner) emphasized that even as society was becoming more hospitable toward many black Americans, circumstances in the central cities were demeaning for the blacks who were trapped there. The conditions of central cities documented in the report still exist and may have worsened in some respects; hence it is not surprising that current

GARY D. SANDEFUR • School of Social Work and Institute for Research on Poverty, University of Wisconsin–Madison, Madison, Wisconsin.   MARTA TIENDA • Department of Sociology, University of Chicago, Chicago, Illinois and Institute for Research on Poverty, University of Wisconsin–Madison, Madison, Wisconsin.

discussions of urban poverty emphasize many of the same concerns. For example, the Kerner Report attributed growing black joblessness in the central cities to changes in the urban economy, an argument reflected in current work on the problems of urban minorities. The report also pointed to the probable connection between joblessness and the prevalence of families headed by single women; current discussion focuses on this connection as a major problem for blacks and Puerto Ricans. Yet even if the Kerner Report was gloomy in its assessment of the situation at the time, it was optimistic in its view of the future and solutions to the problem.

In retrospect, we realize that it was inappropriate to rest our hopes for continued progress in the fight against poverty on economic growth. The prosperous 1960s were followed by the stagflation of the 1970s and a major recession in the early 1980s. Instead of a continued decline in poverty such as that experienced during the 1960s, the numbers of the poor rose, with the result that the general poverty rate in 1985 was higher than that in 1969. It is important to remember, however, that most of the resources committed to the fight against poverty since 1969 have gone into noncash assistance programs (such as food stamps, Medicaid, and Medicare), and the effects of such programs are not reflected in official poverty statistics that are based on cash income only. Nonetheless, even if the poverty rates are adjusted for the value of noncash benefits in the most generous way possible, the poverty rate for all persons in 1985 would be only slightly less than the poverty rate for all persons in 1969.

One conclusion from the evidence presented in this volume is that the struggle against poverty is far from over, that the greatest challenges for policy to reduce poverty lie ahead. This is particularly true for the minority groups considered in this volume. In 1985, the poverty rate for black persons was 31.3% and for Hispanic persons 29.0%, as compared to 11.4% for whites. In 1980, the poverty rate for American Indians was 27.5%. Not only are the wide differentials troubling in themselves, but so also is evidence presented in this volume showing that some minority groups improved their relative economic status (e.g., Native Americans) during this period of uneven economic growth, whereas other groups (notably Puerto Ricans) experienced a substantial deterioration in economic condition.

POVERTY POLICY ISSUES

Many of the policy issues that captured the attention of the nation in the 1960s continue to be important today. Analysts point to low labor-force participation and high unemployment rates for members of minority groups as important causes of poverty. No longer, however, is there consensus over the cause of high unemployment. Now there is controversy over whether it is primarily a lack of jobs or the availability of nonwage income that leads to the nonemployment of minority-group members. These alternative diagnoses of the problem suggest different solutions—advocates of work requirements are pitted against advocates of job programs.

The problems of the central cities remain a focus of policy debate. In fact, there is some danger that the poverty problem may become defined exclusively as a central-city problem, owing to the high concentration of the minority poor in those areas. In 1985, 61% of the black poor, 55% of the Mexican-origin poor, and 89% of the Puerto Rican poor lived in the central cities of metropolitan areas. It is tempting to focus on these populations because of their size and concentration. We should not, however, neglect the problems of the minority poor outside central cities—Indians on reservations, blacks in the rural South, and Mexican-origin workers in the nonmetropolitan Southwest. The pockets of rural poverty that were identified in the early 1960s remain in the 1980s, and the prospects for improving the economic well-being of their residents are similarly bleak.

Minority children continue to be a major concern of policy discussions, and with good reason. In 1985, 43% of black children and 40% of Hispanic children under age 18 lived in families with incomes below the poverty line. This means that a considerable proportion of black, Hispanic, and American Indian children grow up with inadequate housing, clothing, health care, and educational opportunities. Children who fail to complete high school will be seriously handicapped in the labor market of the 1990s—even more so than has been true in the past. This is because of the decline of blue-collar industrial jobs and the widening income gaps between high school and college graduates.

Finally, affirmative action continues to be the subject of debate, but of little serious study. The scant research that exists provides the basis for concluding that affirmative action has increased the employment of blacks and other minority-group members in firms where they were not previously represented. It is also clear, however, that affirmative action is not a solution to the problems of the central city, the reservation, or the rural unemployed. There appears to be growing disillusionment with affirmative action because it has spawned claims of reverse discrimination and because compliance is possible without any visible changes in outcomes.

Additional issues have been placed on the minority poverty policy agenda. One is the debate over the obligations and responsibilities of the poor. The workfare proposals discussed by Lawrence Mead and William Julius Wilson are but one example of the growing effort to require poor people who receive public assistance to contribute in return. Although the initial focus of workfare programs was on adults, especially women on AFDC, more recent proposals have raised questions about the responsibilities of children. For example, Wisconsin has initiated a "learnfare" program that reduces the benefits of families on AFDC if a family member (the head, spouse, or child) age 13–19 does not meet high school attendance and graduation requirements. Such programs will have a greater impact on members of minority groups, because they are overrepresented in the ranks of public assistance recipients and because high dropout rates are disproportionately concentrated among the poor, particularly the residents of central cities.

A second new policy issue involves the role of state, local, and federal governments in designing and implementing social welfare policy. The War on Poverty attempted to centralize many aspects of the antipoverty effort. Other proposed programs, such as a federally guaranteed annual income, or negative income tax, would have further centralized the fight against poverty. From the mid-1970s to the present, however, support for state and local control over antipoverty programs grew. A hallmark of the Reagan administration was its strong encouragement that states explore alternatives to the current social welfare system. Advocacy of state and local innovation has been accompanied by consideration of the role of other nongovernmental institutions in the fight against poverty. The Working Seminar on Family and American Social Welfare Policy (sponsored by the American Enterprise Institute) suggested that the family, churches, schools, and other community organizations take a more active role in fighting poverty.[1] Less clearly specified were guidelines about exactly how each of these institutions could participate in the fight against poverty.

Although the discussion of the responsibilities of the poor, support for state and local innovations, and the emphasis on nongovernmental institutions grows out of shifts in the ideology of how to fight poverty, a new issue—homelessness—has been forced upon us by various events identified in this volume. Although the extent and causes of homelessness are controversial issues, it is clear that homelessness is a growing problem and that minorities, by virtue of their overrepresentation among the extreme poor, are likely to be disproportionately numbered among the homeless. This issue, which has captured national attention in recent years, will remain an important research priority until the consequences and solutions are better understood.

RESEARCH ISSUES

The way in which research on minorities and poverty is conducted has changed considerably since the 1960s. A major difference has to do with the growing attention that researchers have paid to the Hispanic national-origin groups and, to a lesser extent, American Indians. This is a fruitful development, as it has increased our knowledge of Hispanics and American Indians, begun to enrich our understanding of black Americans through comparisons of their experience to that of other minority groups, and illustrated important differences in

---

[1]See Michael Novak *et al., The New Consensus on Family and Welfare: A Community of Self-Reliance* (Washington, D.C.: American Enterprise Institute; and Milwaukee, WI: Marquette University, 1987).

the poverty experiences of Mexicans, Puerto Ricans, Cubans, and American Indians.

Because of this research, we now have a good deal more information at hand regarding the social and economic conditions of the major U.S. minority groups than we had in the 1960s. There is no longer any reason for social scientists or policymakers to be ignorant of the differences in the family structure of Puerto Ricans and the Mexican-origin population or differences in the level of poverty among Indians on and off the reservation. We have, however, made less progress in explaining the differences across groups. For example, we have not explained the deteriorating situation of Puerto Ricans during the 1970s, nor the improving situation of American Indians during the same period. We have not explained persisting differences in the family structure of blacks and the Mexican-origin population, and we do not yet fully understand the reasons why racial differences in labor-force participation and unemployment have increased. Our ability to churn out new numbers and methodological advances in the empirical study of minority poverty far surpass the strengths of our theories to explain the numbers.

Another major difference in research on minorities now, as compared to the 1960s, is that we can no longer pinpoint racism as the sole cause of minority adversities. This is exemplified by research concerning central-city minority populations. The Kerner Report identified racism as a major cause of problems in the large cities. Recent work, such as that by Wilson, places less emphasis on contemporary racism and more on the structural changes in urban areas that have led to physical and social isolation of minority populations. The future will, it is hoped, produce additional work on the concentration of the poor in central cities and the consequent behavioral manifestations, and will contribute to a better understanding of individual versus structural determinants of rising poverty. Regardless of one's views concerning the existence of an "underclass," the conditions of central cities stand out as a major research area deserving attention.

We also need further research on the causes of unemployment, under-employment, and labor-force nonparticipation. Demand-side explanations emphasize the lack of jobs in the central cities, in depressed rural areas, and on Indian reservations. Supply-side explanations emphasize the availability of non-wage income from public assistance, criminal activity, and other sources. At this point, the evidence does not convincingly support *either* a demand-side or a supply-side explanation, but rather implicates both.

Finally, we need additional research on the connections between race, family structure, education, and the intergenerational transmission of poverty and disadvantage. With longitudinal data we are now in a position to investigate the effects on children of growing up poor, and the differences in these effects across racial and ethnic groups. We hope the future will see our knowledge of minority poverty expand beyond what is now available from cross-sectional studies based on Census Bureau data and the Current Population Surveys to research based on such longitudinal data bases as the Panel Study of Income Dynamics, the National Longitudinal Survey of Youth, High School and Beyond, and the Survey of Income and Program Participation, as well as research based on ethnographic studies, such as the Urban Family Life Project in Chicago, directed by William Julius Wilson. These data sets include information on Puerto Ricans, the Mexican-origin population, and American Indians, as well as blacks and whites. Our knowledge of minorities and poverty, and of the effects of family and education on poverty among minorities, should continue to grow over the next several years.

Author Index

Subject Index

DATE DUE